BRAIN GAMES
FOR
BRAIN POWER

MORE THAN 250 WORD GAMES, LOGIC PUZZLES, NUMBER CHALLENGES, AND TRIVIA QUIZZES

All-New Edition

tmb TRUSTED MEDIA BRANDS

New York / Montreal

Individual puzzles are the copyrighted property of the puzzle authors.
BrainSnack® is a registered trademark.

Copyright © 2021 Trusted Media Brands, Inc.
All rights reserved. Unauthorized reproduction, in any manner, is prohibited.
ISBN: 978-1-62145-559-2

Printed in China
10 9 8 7 6 5 4 3 2 1

Note to Readers
The consultants, writers, editors, and proofreaders have taken all reasonable measures to confirm and verify the accuracy of the information contained in this title. However, some statements of fact can be open to interpretation. Similarly, new information and research often reveal that long-held beliefs are not true. We welcome your input on any answers for which you have sound evidence may be incorrect.

STAY SHARP, STAY YOUNG

The puzzles in this book may help you improve a variety of brain skills, including your ability to remember. As the brain ages, vocabulary may remain strong, but the ability to spot meanings and search for the word you are looking for slows down.

Language puzzles exercise circuits that can help lessen forgetful moments and shorten their duration, but learning cannot become memory without concentration, and without regular maintenance, concentration shrinks with age. These puzzles provide many opportunities for improving and strengthening this important ability and many other useful brain skills:

- Pattern and pathfinding puzzles will strengthen your powers of concentration in the same way that physical exercises build aerobic stamina;
- Logic and memory puzzles will challenge your working memory because you must keep some variables in mind while you test them against others—this frontal-lobe skill is crucial to productive thinking and requires fierce concentration;
- Visual and mechanical puzzles will stretch your visual-spatial mental muscles, which you need to navigate the physical world successfully;
- Divergent-thinking puzzles will encourage your ability to think "outside the box" and see links where others see standard differences—an ability that pays off in any profession;
- Puzzles involving calculation are important to try—even if you are not a numbers person—for they light up many different parts of the brain at once.

Descriptions of the major puzzle types appear on the following pages. The games start on page 8. Good luck!

About the Puzzles

Brain Games for Brain Power is filled with a delightful mix of classic and new puzzle types. To help you get started, here are instructions, tips, and some examples.

WORD GAMES

CROSSWORD PUZZLES

Clues are the deciding factor that determine crossword-solving difficulty. Many solvers mistakenly think strange and unusual words are what make a puzzle challenging. In reality, crossword constructors generally try to avoid grid esoterica, opting for familiar words and expressions.

WORD SUDOKU

The basic sudoku puzzle is a 9 x 9 square grid, split into nine square regions, each containing nine cells. You need to complete the grid so that each row, each column, and each 3 x 3 frame contains the nine letters from the black box above the grid.

There is always a hidden nine-letter word in the diagonal from top left to bottom right.

WORD POWER

These multiple-choice quizzes test your knowledge of grammar and language and help you develop a better vocabulary. Find out where you stand on the Word Power scale by using the simple rating system included on the answer pages.

WORD SEARCHES

In a word search, the challenge is to find hidden words within a grid of letters. Words can be found in vertical columns or horizontal rows or along diagonals, with the letters of the words running either forward or backward.

NUMBER GAMES

SUDOKU

The basic sudoku puzzle is a 9 x 9 square grid, split into nine square regions, each containing nine cells. Complete the grid so that each row, each column, and each 3 x 3 frame contains every number from 1 to 9.

In addition to classic sudoku puzzles, you'll find **SUDOKU X** puzzles, where the main diagonals must include every number from 1 to 9, and **SUDOKU TWINS,** with two overlapping grids.

KAKURO

These puzzles are like crosswords with numbers. There are clues across and down, but the clues are numbers. The solution is a sum that adds up to the clue number.

Each number in a black area is the sum of the numbers that you have to enter in the next empty boxes. The empty boxes that make up the sum are called a run. The sum of the across run is written above the diagonal in the black area, while the sum of the down run is written below the diagonal.

Runs must contain only the numbers 1 through 9, and each number in a run can be used only once. The gray boxes contain only odd numbers; the white contain only even numbers.

EXAMPLE **SOLUTION**

LOGIC PUZZLES

BINAIRO

Binairo puzzles look similar to sudoku puzzles. They are just as simple and challenging, but that is where the similarity ends.

There are two versions: odd and even. The even puzzles feature a 12 x 12 grid. You need to complete the grid with zeros and ones, until there are 6 zeros and 6 ones in every row and every column. No more than two of the same number can be next to or under each other. Rows or columns with exactly the same combination are not allowed.

EXAMPLE **SOLUTION**

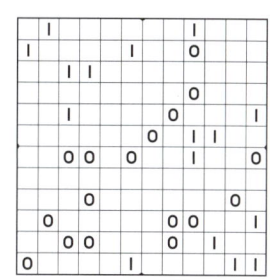

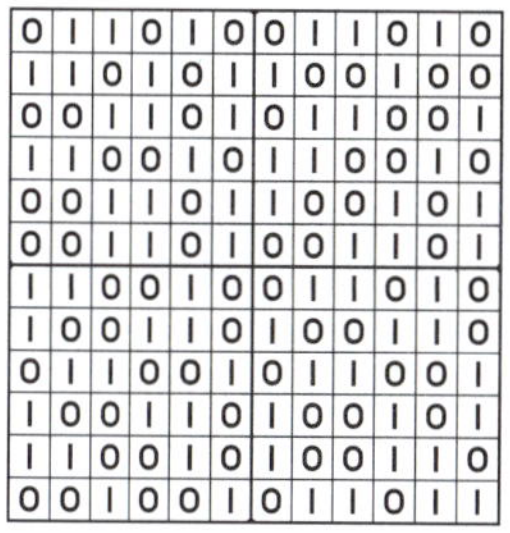

The odd puzzles feature an 11 x 11 grid. You need to complete the grid with zeros and ones until there are 5 zeros and 6 ones in every row and column.

KEEP GOING

In this puzzle, start on a blank square of your choice and connect as many blank squares as possible with one single continuous line.

You can only connect squares along vertical and horizontal lines, not along diagonals. You must continue the connecting line up until the next obstacle—i.e., the rim of the box, a black square, or a square that has already been used.

You can change direction at any obstacle you meet. Each square can be used only once. The number of blank squares left unused is marked in the upper square. There may be more than one solution, but we include only one solution in our answer key.

EXAMPLE **SOLUTION**

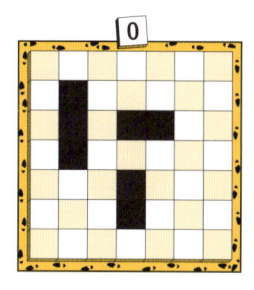

NUMBER CLUSTER

Number cluster puzzles are language-free, logical numerical problems. They consist of cubes on a 6 x 6 grid. Numbers have been placed in some of the cubes, while the rest are empty. Your challenge is to complete the grid by creating runs of the same number and length as the number supplied. So where a cube with the number 5 has been included on the grid, you need to create a run of five number 5's, including the cube already shown. The run can be horizontal, vertical, or both horizontal and vertical.

EXAMPLE   **SOLUTION**

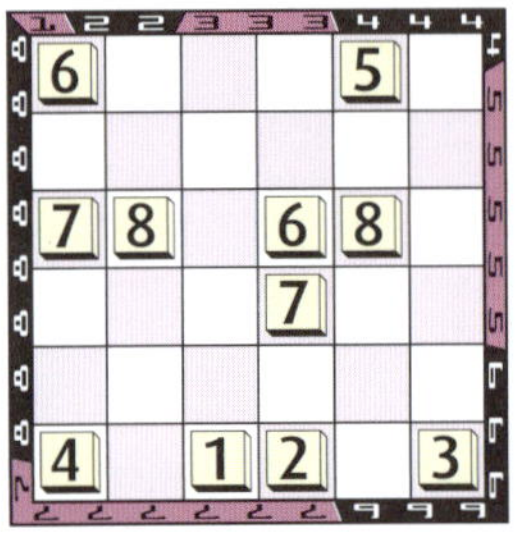

WORD PYRAMID

Each word in the pyramid has the letters of the word above it, plus a new letter.

Using the clues given, answer No.1 and then work your way to the base of the pyramid to complete the word pyramid.

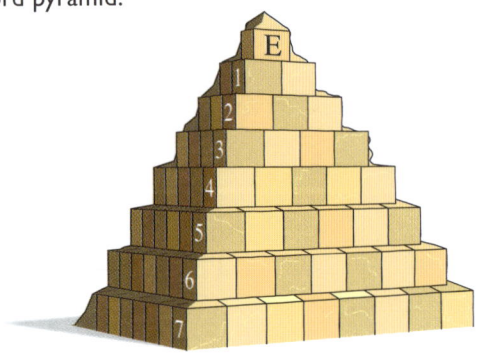

SPORT MAZE

This puzzle is presented on a 6 x 6 grid. Your starting point is indicated by a red cell with a ball and a number. Your objective is to draw the shortest route from the ball to the goal, the only square without a number. You can move only along vertical and horizontal lines, but not along diagonals. The figure on each square indicates the number of squares the ball must be moved in the same direction. You can change direction at each stop.

EXAMPLE   **SOLUTION**

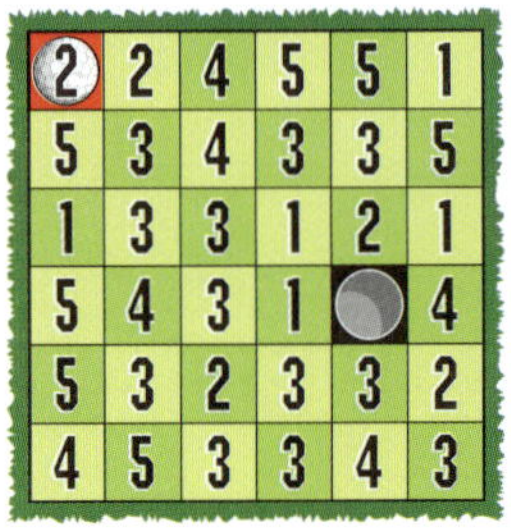

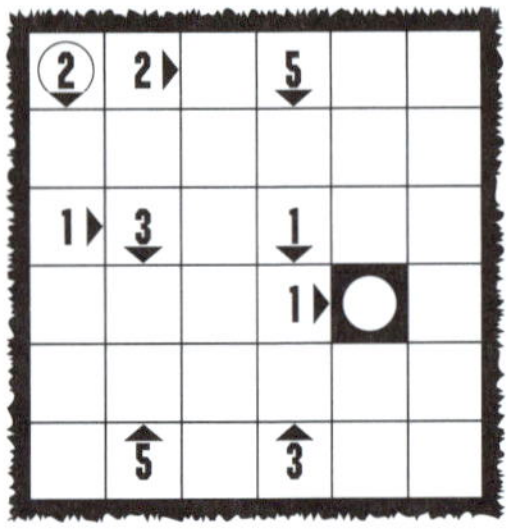

CAGE THE ANIMALS

This puzzle presents you with a zoo divided into a 16 x 16 grid. The different animals on the grid need to be separated. Draw lines that will completely divide up the grid into smaller squares, with exactly one animal per square.

EXAMPLE   **SOLUTION**

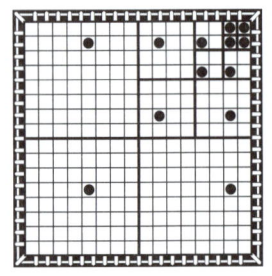

PIXEL FUN

The objective in this puzzle is to reveal a hidden image by coloring in grid squares. You have an 11 x 11 grid with numbers printed outside the grid. The numbers on the outer border, against the black or the white background, indicate the total number of black or white squares on a column or a row. The numbers on the inner border indicate the largest group of adjacent black or white squares to be found anywhere on that column or row. For instance, if there is a 6 on the outer ring and a 2 on the inner ring against a white background, then there are 6 white blocks in that row, and the biggest group or groups consist of a maximum of 2 adjacent white blocks.

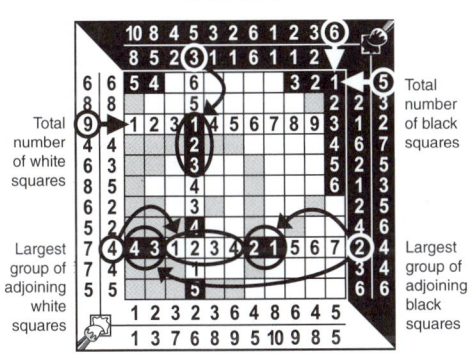

TRIVIA

TRIVIA QUIZZES & TRIVIAL PURSUITS

Trivia in a variety of formats and topics will probe the depth of your knowledge of facts. Questions and answers will tempt, tease, and tickle.

VISUAL PUZZLES

Throughout you will find unique mazes, visual conundrums, and other colorful challenges. Each comes with a new name and unique instructions. Our best advice? Patience and perseverance. Your eyes will need time to unravel the visual secrets.

BRAINSNACK® PUZZLES

To solve a BrainSnack® puzzle, you must think logically. You'll need to use one or several strategies to detect direction, differences, and/or similarities, associations, calculations, order, spatial insight, colors, quantities, and distances. A BrainSnack® ensures that all the brain's capacities are fully engaged. These are brain sports at their best!

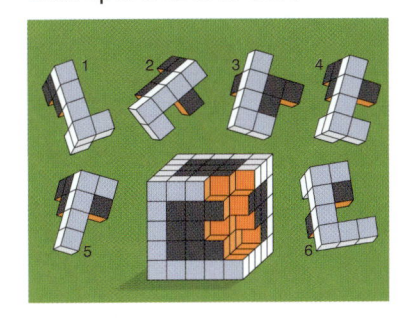

WEATHER CHARTS

We all want to know the weather forecast, and here's your chance to figure it out! Arrows are scattered on a grid. Each arrow points toward a space where a weather symbol should be, but the symbols cannot be next to each other vertically, horizontally, or diagonally. A symbol cannot be placed on top of an arrow. You must determine where the symbols should be placed.

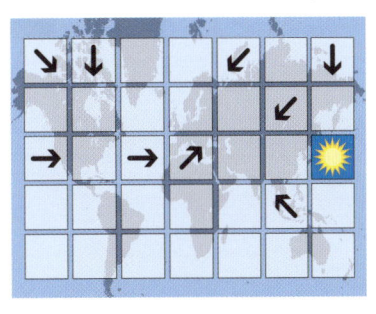

BRAINTEASERS

You'll also find short brainteasers scattered throughout these pages. These puzzles will provide some light relief from the more intense puzzles while still challenging you.

CROSSWORD: Familiar Address

ACROSS
1. Liszt's teacher
5. Blade site
10. South Beach ___
14. Curtain color
15. *The Canterbury ___*
16. Suffix for major
17. "And now, the ___ of the story"
18. Cancel a mission
19. Bash
20. Bob Dylan classic
23. Hyacinth, for one
24. ___ *the Mood for Love*
25. "Chili today, hot ___"
28. Traditional
32. French story
33. Flora and fauna
34. Craggy crest
35. *Peter Pan* dog
36. Close-knit group
37. Venetian VIP, once
38. Gold of *Entourage*
39. "Button" site
40. Twins share them
41. First Lady of 2011
43. Adjusts, as a suit
44. ___ Stanley Gardner
45. Lawrence Durrell novel
46. Billy Crystal film
53. Beam in a bridge
54. Prevaricators
55. Remini on *The King of Queens*
56. Fuzzy stuff
57. Source of the Orinoco
58. "A Dream" artist
59. Plays quizmaster
60. ___ *Revolution* (Bob Marley album)
61. Adjudge

DOWN
1. Hairy wave
2. Pacer in *Cars 2*
3. Whilom
4. Yellow turnip
5. Track building
6. "Shish" dish
7. 1990s Expo manager
8. Area
9. Approximation
10. Answer the critics of
11. *Star* topic
12. "At Last" singer James
13. Driver's ed student
21. Stubborn critter
22. Natalie's *Black Swan* role
25. Brunchtime, perhaps
26. "Donkey Kong" company
27. Frenzied
28. Edge along
29. Make amends
30. Pilot's "OK"
31. Vera Wang design
33. See 22 Down
36. Kind of phone
37. Elaborated
39. *Mary Poppins* chimney sweep
40. *For Your Eyes Only* director John
42. Bridge alternative
43. *Charmed* actress Milano
45. Copyediting mark
46. Kunis in *Black Swan*
47. Babe Ruth's 2,211
48. Made a putt
49. Dog food brand
50. *American Gigolo* actor
51. Can't stand
52. "How do you like ___ apples?"

Cage the Animals

Draw lines to completely divide up the grid into small squares, with exactly one animal per square. The squares should not overlap.

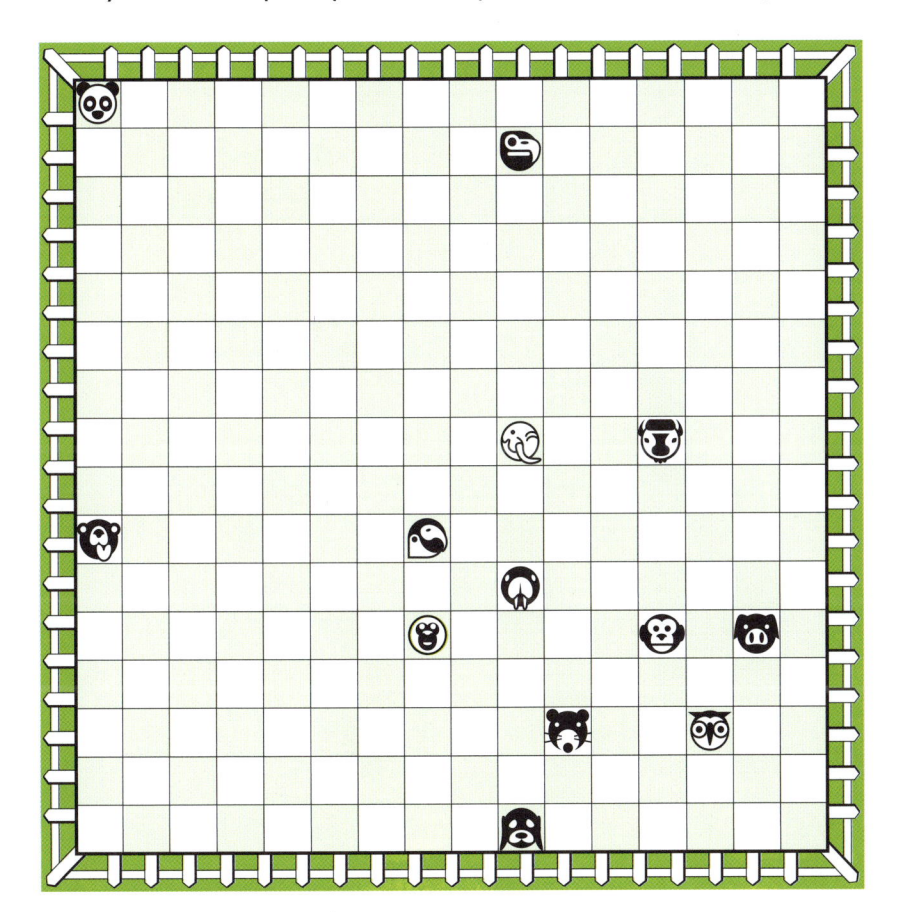

do you KNOW?

Can an ostrich fly?

DOODLE PUZZLE

A doodle puzzle is a combination of images, letters, and/or numbers that represent a word or a concept. If you cannot solve a doodle puzzle, do not look at the answer right away. Think hard—and outside the box.

D b

Word Pyramid

Each word in the pyramid has the letters of the word above it, plus a new letter.

E
(1) Second note
(2) Organ
(3) Beloved
(4) Class
(5) Risk
(6) Interpreting something that is written
(7) Imagining

do you KNOW?

How many legs does a butterfly have?

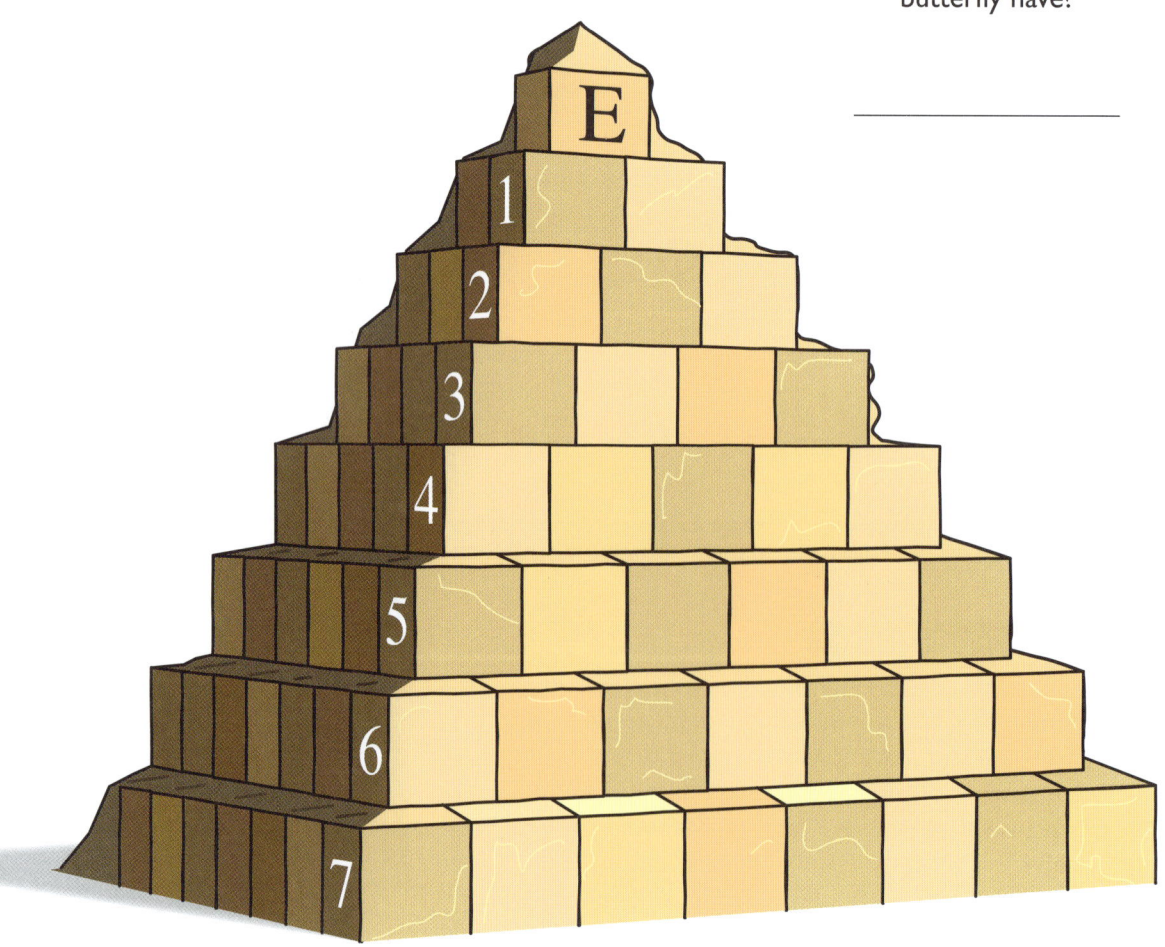

_____

WORD SEARCH: Television

All the words are hidden vertically, horizontally, or diagonally—in both directions.

```
M E D I A P A R K T E O R L E
E I N T E R L U D E I E E E R
V V I S I O N I S D R A C T U
I N T E R N E T U U E O N C T
L H N I Q O U T N E M F U O L
R S E N D I S I N E G A O T U
N R C V S S C D D S S R N A C
E C N E E I A Y I T C T N K V
I N M E G V B F M R R V A E W
O A V I E O L L N O E T G S O
G I M A G R E A E P E O S P H
C I S U M U C T A S N W O H S
N M A R K E T S H A R E D I K
L A I R E S S C E O U R N L L
T S A C D A O R B D S D O I A
A N T E N N A E V W I E R P T
S G N I T A R E E A D W I S S
T A N J O U R N A L I S T C E
```

- ANNOUNCER
- ANTENNA
- BROADCAST
- CABLE
- COMEDY
- CULTURE
- EUROVISION
- FLAT-SCREEN
- GAMES
- INTERLUDE
- INTERNET
- JOURNALIST
- LIVE
- MARKET SHARE
- MEDIA PARK
- MUSIC
- NEWS
- PHILIPS
- RATINGS
- RERUN
- SCREEN
- SERIAL
- SHOW
- SPORTS
- STUDIO
- TAKES
- TALK SHOW
- TV TOWER
- VCR
- WIDE-SCREEN

TRIVIA QUIZ # The Cold Stuff

Ice cream in various forms is a staple dessert in many cultures.
See if you can eat your way around the world in cold sweetness.

1. What do the British call an ice-cream cone with a flaky chocolate bar stuck in it?

   _____

2. What's ice cream called in India?

   _____

3. If you were in Italy, where would you go to buy a scoop of their intensely flavored ice creams?

   _____

4. From what country does the ice-cream brand Häagen-Dazs come?

   _____

5. Soft-serve ice cream was invented in Britain in the 1950s. Name one of the chemists who worked on the process before moving on to a prominent political career.

   _____

6. What is the most popular flavor of ice cream in Argentina?

   _____

7. Name the country in Europe that annually eats the most ice cream per capita.

   _____

8. Is Italian gelato lower or higher in fat than traditional ice cream?

   _____

9. If you order *matcha* ice cream in Japan, what will the flavoring be?

   _____

10. What kind of milk is the base of *dondurma*, the ice cream that is most popular in Turkey?

    _____

11. How many licks does it take to finish an ice-cream cone?

    _____

12. Name one of the most popular ice-cream brands in the United States that is made in Burlington, VT.

    _____

13. What month is National Ice Cream day celebrated?

    _____

14. What flavors are in Neopolitan ice cream?

    _____

CROSSWORD: Director's Chair

ACROSS

1. "Open" sign, often
5. Bath accessory
10. Carpet line
14. "... and to ___ good night"
15. Capital ENE of Jerusalem
16. Killer whale
17. *I Kid You Not!* author
18. "Shall we ___?"
19. Whiting and haddock
20. *The Birds* director
23. Cuban film director
24. *Garfield* canine
25. Hostage holder
28. Draw out
32. "___ a Grecian Urn"
33. Befits
34. *Ben-___* (1959)
35. Fibber
36. Binge
37. Aching
38. Comparative suffix
39. Equals
40. "F" on a quiz
41. Ethnology studies
43. Like many tours
44. Served fast and past
45. *Aqualung* group Jethro ___
46. *Schindler's List* director
53. Creep like lava
54. Molecule members
55. Norse war god
56. Vice president in 1804
57. Greyhound station
58. Disney Broadway musical
59. Eminem hit
60. Burnett and Gray
61. Dry run

DOWN

1. *Falcon Crest* valley
2. Tel Aviv carrier
3. One of Snoopy's brothers
4. Mary Alice Young, for one
5. Means of ascent
6. 1935 Kentucky Derby winner
7. 1980s Dodge model
8. Plants
9. Amusing story
10. David Beckham's sport
11. Suffix for switch
12. *Back in Black* group
13. *The Green Hornet's* wear
21. Tesla co-founder Musk
22. Sellouts
25. Baby discomfort
26. "Arrivederci!"
27. 30th anniversary gift
28. Acts contentedly
29. "Get ___ of yourself!"
30. Blaspheme
31. Out on a limb
33. Whiz kid?
36. Suitor's song
37. Sloop, for one
39. Dark purple
40. At capacity
42. Alehouse
43. Partygoers
45. *The Lion King* meerkat
46. Has a bawl
47. Tip-sheet seller
48. *The Snowy Day* author ___ Jack Keats
49. 1969 Alan Arkin film
50. *Desperate Housewives* divorcée
51. Purges
52. Airborne pest

Sudoku

Fill in the grid so that each row, each column, and each 3 x 3 frame contains every number from 1 to 9.

					1		5	
						9		
					3			7
	7		2					6
	1	4		8		2	9	
9	2			5		1	7	3
	8	3	6		5			9
				7	8		4	1
	4							

do you KNOW?

What is fear of snakes called?

BLOCK ANAGRAM

Form the word that is described in the parentheses, using the letters above the grid. One letter is already in the right place.

MASTER PET   (a diagrammatic representation of a city)

☐ ☐ ☐ ☐ ☐ ☐   ☐ **A** ☐

BRAINSNACK® Dominoes

Which domino (1–8) does not belong?

THE NUMBER IS THE QUESTION

Which number should replace the question mark?

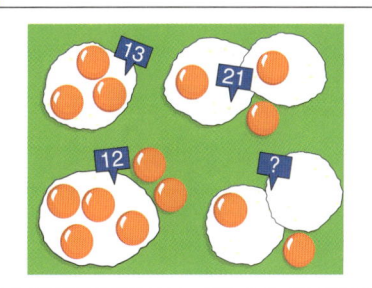

WEATHER CHART **Sunny**

Where will the sun shine? With the knowledge that each arrow points to a place where a symbol should be, can you locate the sunny spots? The symbols cannot be next to each other vertically, horizontally, or diagonally. A symbol cannot be placed on top of an arrow. We show one symbol.

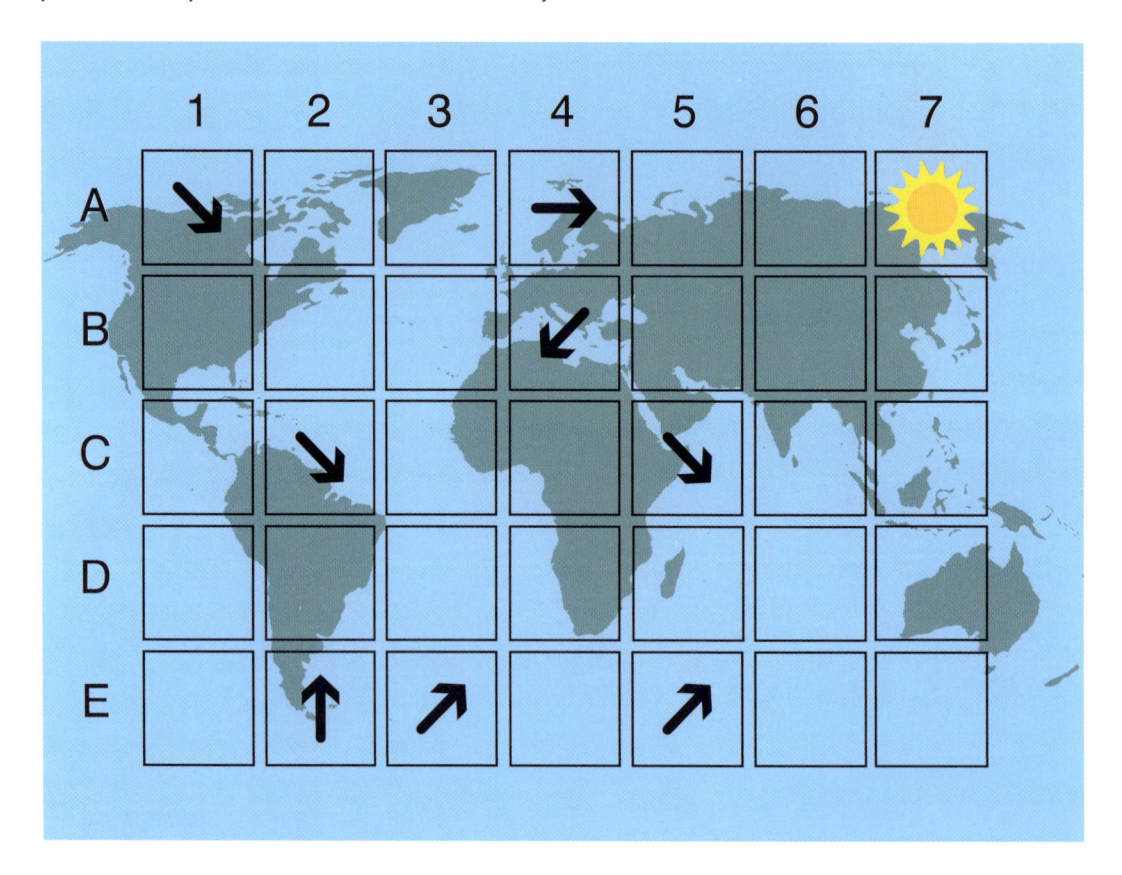

DOUBLETALK

What four-letter word is low, musically, but not eaten with a tuning fork?

CROSSWORD: Summer Pleasures

ACROSS
1 Small piece of cotton
5 Like a cellar
9 Southeast Asian country, for short
12 Faith, ___ and charity
13 British prep school
14 Commotion
15 Pitcher
16 Walking ___ on the grass is one of the pleasures of summer
18 Long-tailed rodent
20 A dance under a pole
21 ___, liquid or gas
24 With more seasoning
26 Sign of the zodiac
27 "My country ___ of thee"
28 Disco group The Bee ___
29 Meat from a pig
30 Something on a list
34 Make imperfect
35 Intense
36 Infected sore
40 Allowable by law
41 Relating to birth
42 Out of date
43 ___ dinner in the backyard is one of summer's pleasures
46 Ballerina's skirt
50 Actor Chaney
51 General Bradley
52 Greek god of love
53 School subject (abbr.)
54 Income
55 Author Frank

DOWN
1 "That's all ___ wrote"
2 Word of surprise
3 Large primate
4 Fresh-picked ___ are a summer pleasure
5 Obligation
6 Airline abbr.
7 "Neither rain ___ snow..."
8 Tolls
9 Ruth's mother-in-law
10 Southwestern bricks
11 Propulsion for a boat
17 In good shape
19 Commercials
21 Droop
22 ___ Ida potatoes
23 To bear false witness
24 Gazing at the ___ is a summer pleasure
25 Point
29 "The Eagle ___ landed"
30 A glass of ___ is a summer pleasure (2 words)
31 Pull
32 Airport abbr.
33 Singer Torme
34 Not excited
35 Totally
36 90 degrees is a right one
37 British nobleman
38 A bee's attack
39 Baseball player Ripken
42 Shrek, for one
44 "___ little teapot" (2 words)
45 Pester
47 Vase with handles
48 2,000 pounds
49 "It's no ___ crying over spilled milk"

Spot the Differences

Find the nine differences in the image on the bottom right.

do you KNOW?

What is rice paper made from?

_____

_____

trivia
- Who was mentored by Dr. Leonard Gillespie?

_____

Binairo

Complete the grid with zeros and ones until there are 6 zeros and 6 ones in every row and every column. No more than two of the same number can be next to or under each other. Rows or columns with exactly the same content are not allowed. There is only one valid solution.

	0				0						
0			1								
				0					0	0	
	0				1	1				0	
0		1							0		
					1		0	0			
			1								
			1		1					0	
						0		1	1		
		0		1			1				
			0		0						
0		0	0		1					1	

do you KNOW?

The U.S. Navy SEALs is an acronym of what?

_____

_____

LETTERBLOCKS

Move the letterblocks around so that words associated with occupations are formed on the top and bottom rows.

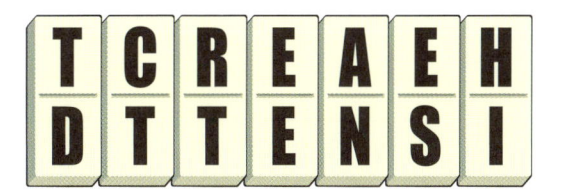

T C R E A E H
D T T E N S I

WORD POWER **A-List**

The letter A is so much more than the leader of the alphabet. It also represents a music note, blood type, Hawthorne favorite, and a mark of excellence. In its honor, here is a quiz devoted to words whose only vowel is A.

1. **banal** (buh-'nal or 'bay-nuhl) *adj.*—
   A: disallowed. B: uptight.
   C: trite.

2. **annals** ('a-nlz) *n.*—
   A: catacombs. B: chronicles.
   C: long johns.

3. **arcana** (ar-'kay-nuh) *n.*—
   A: mysterious or specialized knowledge.
   B: travel journal.
   C: rainbow.

4. **masala** (mah-'sah-la) *n.*—
   A: Chilean wine.
   B: Indian spice blend.
   C: Italian antipasto.

5. **llama** ('lah-muh) *n.*—
   A: beast of burden.
   B: heroic escape.
   C: priest or monk.

6. **bazaar** (buh-'zar) *n.*—
   A: weird event.
   B: marketplace.
   C: wailing siren.

7. **paschal** ('pas-kel) *adj.*—
   A: of computer languages.
   B: in a Gothic style.
   C: relating to Easter.

8. **amalgam** (uh-'mal-gum) *n.*—
   A: mixture. B: volcanic rock.
   C: back of the throat.

9. **plantar** ('plan-ter) *adj.*—
   A: vegetative. B: paved with asphalt.
   C: of the sole of the foot.

10. **catamaran** (ka-teh-meh-'ran) *n.*—
    A: Bengal tiger. B: black olive.
    C: boat with two hulls.

11. **balaclava** (ba-leh-'klah-vuh) *n.*—
    A: knit cap. B: Greek pastry.
    C: Russian mandolin.

12. **avatar** ('a-veh-tar) *n.*—
    A: mythological sibling.
    B: incarnation of a god.
    C: computer language.

13. **spartan** ('spar-tn) *adj.*—
    A: desertlike.
    B: marked by simplicity and lack of luxury.
    C: of classical theater.

14. **allay** (a-'lay) *v.*—
    A: refuse. B: take sides.
    C: calm.

15. **lambda** ('lam-duh) *n.*—
    A: Greek letter. B: Brazilian dance.
    C: college degree.

CROSSWORD: This and That

ACROSS
1. Recipe directive
5. Goose eggs
10. Morse clicks
14. Big fuss
15. A day's march, for troops
16. Amo, ___, amat
17. Apple of Discord thrower
18. Ryan of the Rangers
19. Mr. Gingrich
20. Waiting-room reading
22. Deems
24. Washington team, for short
25. Algonquian Indian
26. Become pale
29. Bald
33. God of the Koran
34. Think about
35. Room in a casa
36. "___ Amore"
37. *A Death in the Family* author
38. Behind with payments
40. *Damn Yankees* composer
41. Overcomes
42. 500 cars
43. Golden Rule word
44. Miss
45. Williams of *Poltergeist*
48. Hoodwinked
52. Collier's entrance
53. From the Old Sod
55. Cab passenger
56. *Dumb & Dumber* type
57. Nick in *Hotel Rwanda*
58. "O.K.!"
59. *House of Dracula* director Kenton
60. *Buffy the Vampire Slayer* role
61. "Country Slaughter"

DOWN
1. Arise (from)
2. ___ Bora, Afghanistan
3. "Cool, man!"
4. *The Aviator* star
5. Acme
6. British jackets
7. Breathing abnormality
8. German grandpa
9. Guards
10. *Harry Potter and the Deathly Hallows* star
11. Grace ender
12. Bird of prey
13. Fast fliers of yore
21. 2007 Masters winner Johnson
23. Alpert of Tijuana Brass fame
25. Dessert trays
26. Fundamental
27. Caballero's locale
28. "Sarah Jackman" singer Sherman
29. Attends, as a recital
30. Bird of prey
31. Animal in a roundup
32. Clairvoyants
34. "Cuchi-cuchi" entertainer
36. Cutting canines
39. Bullied baby, maybe
40. Alpine river
42. Assets aplenty
44. Legionnaire Beau
45. Carved gem
46. "Ewww" inducer
47. *Show Boat* tune
48. Boy in *To Kill a Mockingbird*
49. Full of oneself
50. Cubesmith Rubik
51. Poor grades
54. "Vive le ___!"

Sudoku X

Fill in the grid so that each row, each column, and each 3 x 3 frame contains every number from 1 to 9. The two main diagonals of the grid also contain every number from 1 to 9.

			4					8
3			9			5		
					1			
	9		8	5				1
5		2	1	6			8	9
6			3	1		8	2	7
		1					4	5
	5	8	7	4			1	6

do you KNOW?

Which planet is the fifth from the Sun?

_____

FIRST THINGS FIRST

Identify the well-known proverb from the first letter of each of its words.

T _ _ _   W _ _ _ _   F _ _   N _   M _ _

BRAINSNACK® Insect Out

Which insect (1–5) does not belong?

SPEAKING VOLUMES

Bibliolatry is excessive reverence for a book. A bibliophile is a collector of rare books. What do you call a seller of rare books?

_____

Legends of the Game

CROSSWORD

ACROSS
1 *Affaire d'honneur*
5 Bluenoses
10 *For Your Eyes Only* hero
14 Hence
15 Adams of *CSI: Crime Scene Investigation*
16 Jai ___
17 "Cunning hunter" in Genesis
18 Not so hot
19 Sleeveless garment
20 2004 Wimbledon winner
23 Roadside sign
24 *Heaven ___ Wait* (1978)
25 *Erin Brockovich* director Soderbergh
28 Awful
30 Foolish month: Abbr.
33 *Spartacus* costume
34 10 million equal a joule
35 On the briny
36 Swedish golf legend
39 Hawaii's "Valley Isle"
40 Level, in London
41 Windy City hub
42 Letter before omega
43 *Saturday Night Live* segment
44 Opposed
45 "Billy, Don't ___ Hero"
46 *My Name Is Asher ___*: Potok
47 2010 Wimbledon winner
55 Alan in *The Aviator*
56 County in Ireland
57 *Return of the Jedi* princess
58 *Daily Planet* reporter
59 All lit up
60 Tennyson's title
61 Simians
62 Add golds to a mine
63 "Storms in Africa" singer

DOWN
1 Adjudge
2 Polaris bear
3 Food thickener
4 "The Lion" king of France
5 House of correction
6 "If I Were a ___ Man"
7 Olympic medalist Kulik
8 Will in *The Waltons*
9 "Salt City" of New York
10 Side with eggs
11 Grieg's "___ Trygvason"
12 Valley near San Francisco
13 Fade out
21 Smart-___
22 Crony
25 2011 Tito Puente commemorative
26 Albacore and blue fin
27 Blah feeling
28 "Mending Wall" poet
29 "Fee fi fo fum" sayer
30 ___ *Is Born* (1976)
31 Seckel and Anjou
32 *Findelkind* author
34 *Caprica* actor Morales
35 Biltmore Estate city
37 "Land of Opportunity"
38 Inventive
43 Notice
44 Lets
45 Pentagon VIPs
47 Feed the pigs
48 Adams in *The Apartment*
49 Pond scum
50 Volition
51 "___ Rhythm"
52 ___ *Flux* (2005)
53 Boglike
54 *Family* actress Thompson
55 According to

Kakuro

Each number in a black area is the sum of the numbers that you have to enter in the next empty boxes. The empty boxes that make up the sum are called a run. The sum of the across run is written above the diagonal in the black area, and the sum of the down run is written below the diagonal. Runs can only contain the numbers 1 through 9, and each number in a run can only be used once. The gray boxes only contain odd numbers and the white only even numbers.

trivia

- How much did the Dutch pay for Manhattan Island?

SANDWICH

What five-letter word belongs between the word at left and the word at right, so that the first and second word, and the second and third word, each form a common compound word or phrase?

SWEET _ _ _ _ _ BREAK

Keep Going

Start on a blank square of your choice and connect as many blank squares as possible with one single continuous line. You can only connect squares along vertical and horizontal lines, not along diagonal lines. You must continue the connecting lineup until the next obstacle, i.e., the border of the box, a black square, or a square that already has been used. You can change direction at any obstacle you meet. Each square can only be used once. The number of blank squares that will be left unused is marked in the upper square. There is more than one solution. We only show one solution.

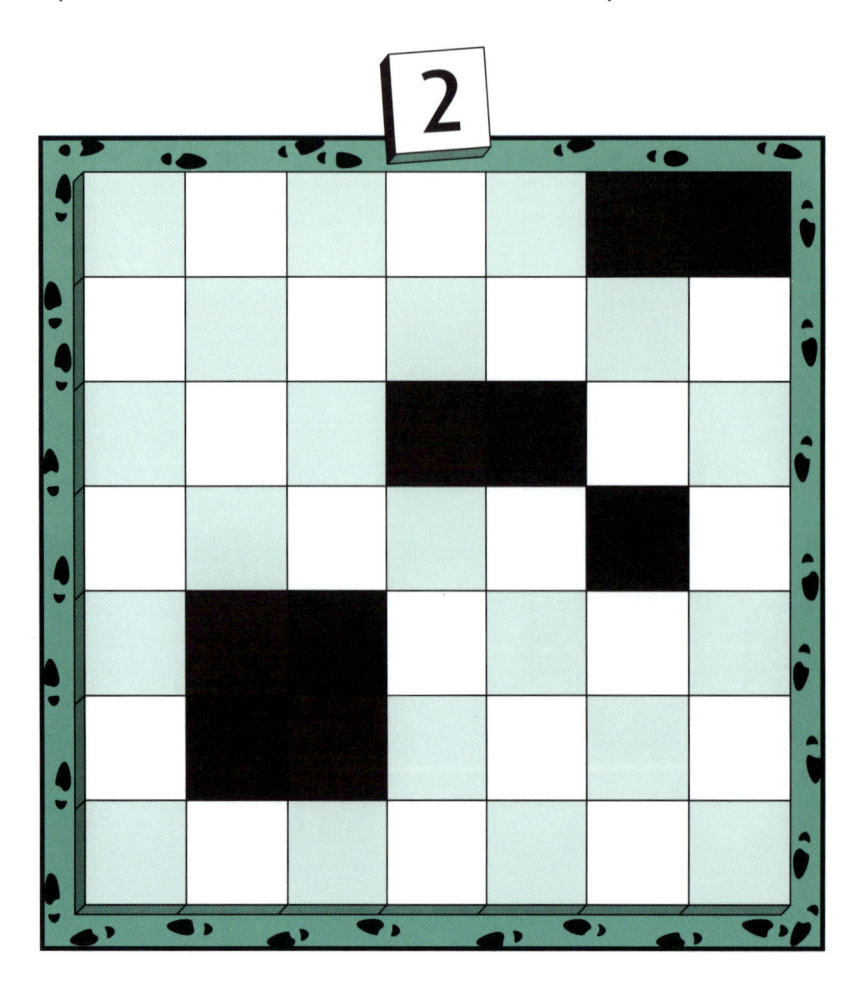

2

delete ONE

Delete one letter from
MADMANCOME ESNETTENTH
and rearrange the rest to find a set of rules.

_____

WORD SEARCH: Insects

All the words are hidden vertically, horizontally, or diagonally—in both directions.

```
H O U S E F L Y B Y L F Y A M
A G B O U T T O G G A M D S E
V I E N T Y O P D A M A G E I
M W E R B K G I T R C L Y W N
O R C I W N S E O I O A L A C
S A T O I E K W C Y C R F T H
Q E R T A C K N A L K I E E W
U M S S I L I L H F R A R R O
I E E R I A U O N E O M I M R
T S C S T T N T D S A O F I M
O O F N N E S E T R C S H T D
E M U A Y O P R E O H Q T E H
A O R B N I I O N H E U L M I
M A E L T L D T E R M I T E I
T E O N N C E L A S C T S I F
I E E D A N R I M A A O L S P
E C C I E S A S C A R A B R E
I N S E C T S Y L F T I U R F
```

- BITE
- BOOKWORM
- CENTIPEDE
- COCKROACH
- CRICKET
- DAMAGE
- DELICACY
- DISEASES
- EARWIG
- FIREFLY
- FRUIT FLY
- HONEYBEE
- HORSEFLY
- HOUSEFLY
- INCHWORM
- MAGGOT
- MALARIA
- MOSQUITO
- MAYFLY
- MOSQUITO
- MOUNTAIN CICADA
- SCARAB
- SILKWORM
- SPIDER
- STING
- TARANTULA
- TERMITE

TRIVIA QUIZ: The National Pastime

How much do you know about one of America's favorite sports?
See if you can hit a home run with this round.

1. About how large in acres is the average baseball field?

2. What is the minimum number of players on a college softball team?

3. In baseball, what do the initials NL stand for?

4. Which was the first non-American team to win the World Series in baseball?

5. With which baseball team did Babe Ruth begin his Major League career?

6. Which stadium is known as The House that Ruth Built?

7. Which baseball star was nicknamed The Yankee Clipper?

8. In baseball, what's a dinger?

9. In what year was the World Series not held because the players' strike shortened the season?

10. How many sides are on a home plate?

11. Who pitched his 2,000th strikeout to Danny Tartabull of the New York Yankees on August 11, 1993?

12. How many stitches are there on a baseball?

13. Who was the first DH (designated hitter) to receive baseball's Silver Slugger award?

14. How do you calculate slugging percentage (SLG) in professional baseball?

CROSSWORD: Comedy Teams

ACROSS

1. Knox or Dix
5. Ledger entry
10. Hugh Laurie's alma mater
14. Aunt Bee's charge
15. Age
16. Captive of Hercules
17. Nothing, in Madrid
18. Pyle of Mayberry
19. Healthy look
20. *A Night at the Opera* stars
23. Loom part
24. "Slippery when ___"
25. Washer setting
28. "As Tears Go By" singer Marianne
33. Fugard's *A Lesson From ___*
34. *Common Sense* pamphleteer
35. *Andy Capp* quaff
36. Animal abode
37. Held on
38. *True Colors* actress Merrill
39. Aliens, for short
40. Plainspoken
41. Mideast money
42. Inessential
44. Accelerate
45. Narrow shoe width
46. Carmichael and Fleming
47. *Have Rocket, Will Travel* stars
55. Groovy things
56. Bury
57. Spartan queen of myth
58. Inuit abode
59. *The Hunchback of ___ Dame*
60. Steam hole
61. Nasty
62. Epoxied
63. Historic periods

DOWN

1. Arial, e.g.
2. Moonfish
3. "Ticket to ___": Beatles
4. Trucker
5. Extent
6. Adhesive
7. Fail miserably
8. Bubbly chiller
9. Bullpen activity
10. H's position
11. Lacquered metalware
12. Swan genus
13. Intelligence
21. "When ___ said and done ..."
22. Head of France
25. Ancient Greek physician
26. Carry away, in a way
27. Bing, bang or boom
28. Goat-legged deities
29. "___ We Got Fun?"
30. Barely audible
31. Arm bones
32. Discover
34. "Besides that ..."
37. Bush-hog job
38. Break up
40. "Been there, done that" feeling
41. "Book 'em ___!"
43. Japanese car of yore
44. Odium
46. Alpine river
47. Shipshape
48. Colossal
49. "... ___ tête, Alouette!"
50. Organic compound
51. Famous last words
52. *The Waltons* actor Will
53. Krabappel of *The Simpsons*
54. Admission exams

Sudoku

Fill in the grid so that each row, each column, and each 3 x 3 frame contains every number from 1 to 9.

1			9	5		4	2		7
				2		8		9	
	4				9	7			
8	7						6	4
9		6	4		3			
			6	7	5		1	8
4			1		6			3
3			8			1		

do you KNOW?

What did the Romans call Ireland?

BLOCK ANAGRAM

Form the word that is described in the parentheses, using the letters above the grid. One letter is already in the right place.

COME OVER SIR   (delivers food and drink to guests)

☐ ☐ ☐ ☐ **M** ☐ ☐ ☐ ☐ ☐ ☐

BRAINSNACK® **Tulip Teaser**

Which tulip (1–7) is shown incorrectly?

DIARY NOTE

In a year, some months have 31 days, while some have 30. Which month has 28 days?

CROSSWORD: Divas

ACROSS

1. An egg in Caesar's salad
5. Campground lights
10. Sandler in *The Wedding Singer*
14. Italian tower city
15. "Le Roi d'Yvetot" composer
16. Singer Simone
17. State with assurance
18. Bengal cat
19. "Dinner's ready" sound
20. "Poker Face" singer
22. Circus rings
24. Painter van Eyck
25. Birth-related
27. *Calvin and Hobbes* babysitter
31. "If I Were a Boy" singer
35. Greenhouse gas
36. Missouri tribe
38. Catch the flu
39. Asthmatic sound
40. Caulking material
41. Golden vein
42. Ovine parent
43. Smooth change
44. Japanese noodles
45. "Material Girl" singer
47. "Hips Don't Lie" singer
49. Coffeehouse readers
51. 1989 Metallica hit
52. Chicken scratch
55. "Beautiful" singer Christina
60. Baghdad locale
61. Cantina cookware
63. Unit of matter
64. Café card
65. "Pet" annoyance
66. In the altogether
67. NBA great Maravich
68. Chair designer
69. Fizzles out

DOWN

1. "Fire" gem
2. ___ *Las Vegas* (1964)
3. Pre-owned
4. "Family Affair" singer Blige
5. Ceremonial prayer
6. "... nine, ten, ___ fat hen"
7. Fox in *Transformers*
8. Cellist Jacqueline du ___
9. Plan of attack
10. Ali's trainer Dundee
11. "Us" singer Celine
12. *The King and I* heroine
13. Shiny wheels
21. *The Life of David* ___ (2003)
23. "Love, Me" singer Collin
26. Eases up
27. "Air Music" composer
28. Conductor Seiji
29. Did a shoe repair
30. 3 Musketeers filling
32. Wynonna Judd's mom
33. Halloween drink
34. *The Mask of Zorro* heroine
37. *The Hangover* dentist
40. Cruz in *Nine*
41. City between Tampa and Orlando
43. Winter fall
44. *Doctor Who* villainess
46. Cloudy
48. Some ranches
50. Witch Sabrina's cat
52. Airhead
53. Montana tribe
54. Go postal
56. Donated
57. Notions case
58. Was a passenger
59. Iowa State U. city
62. Michele of *Glee*

Number Cluster

Cubes showing numbers have been placed on the grid below, with some spaces left empty. Can you complete the grid by creating runs of the same number and of the same length as the number? So, where a cube with number 5 has been included on the grid, you need to create a run of five number 5's, including the cube already shown. The run can be horizontal, vertical, or both horizontal and vertical.

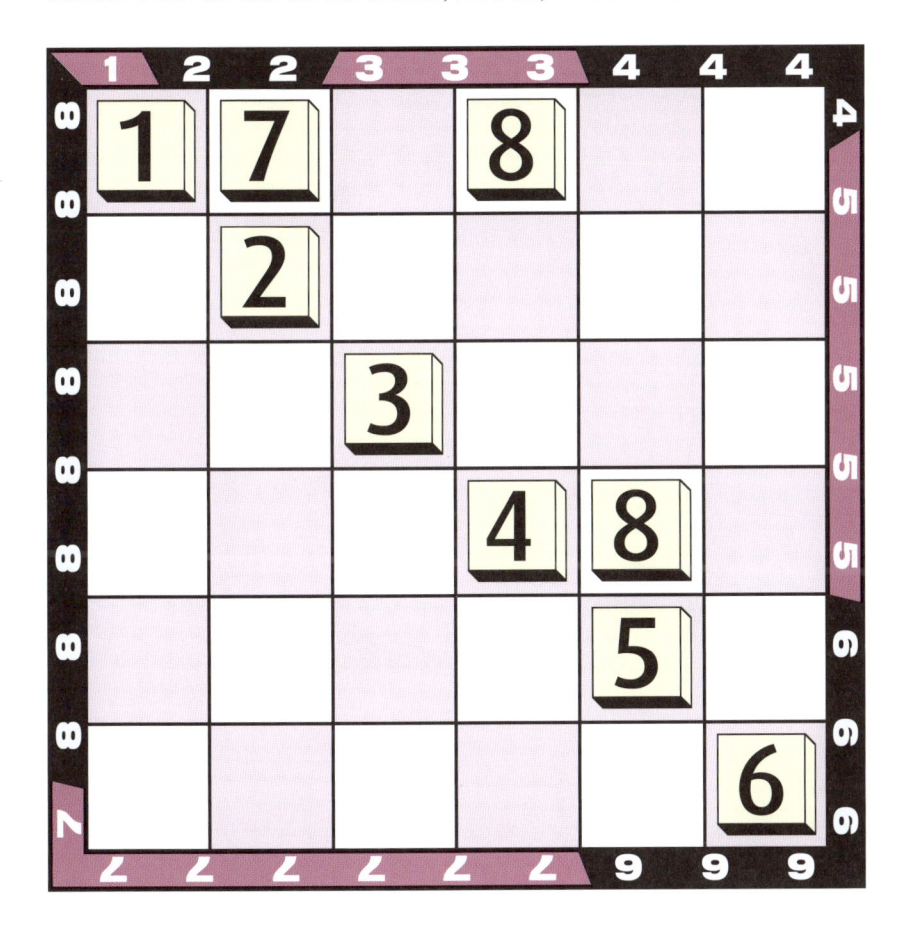

trivia

- How much does the Liberty Bell weigh?

FRIENDS
What do the following words have in common? **GROWTH CHARGE SIGNED PASSES SCORED HAND STAND**

CONCENTRATION **Match Game**

This shading exercise demands attention to detail and will help strengthen your visual memory. Shade these identical images to match each other.

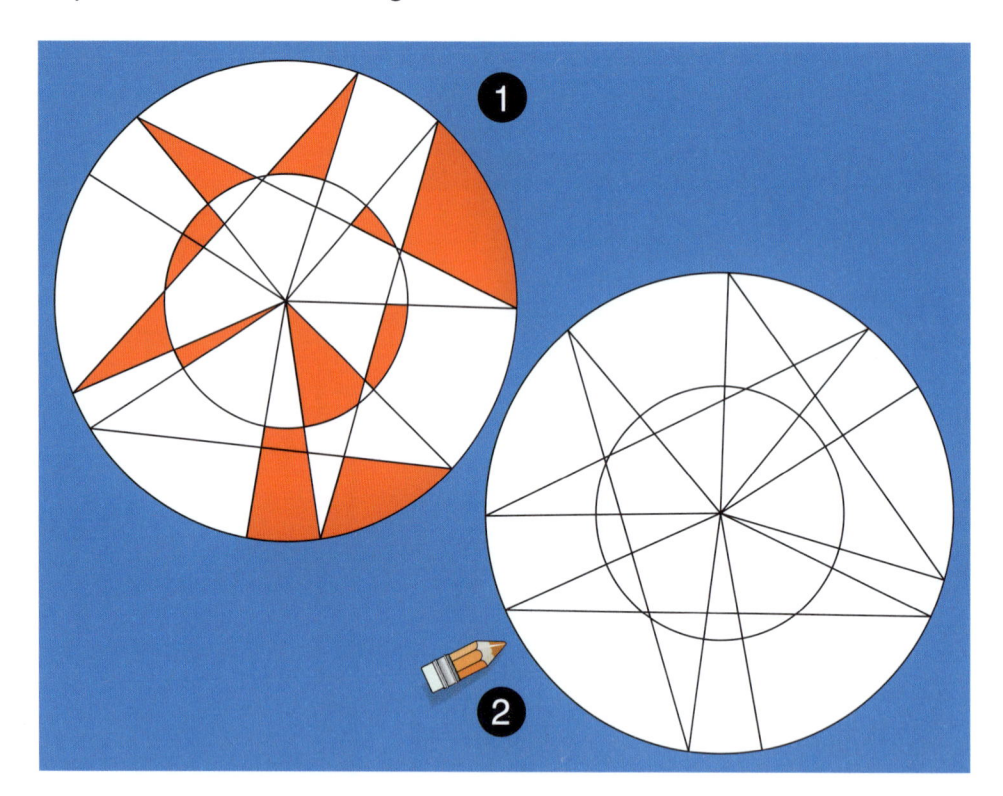

LETTER LINE

Put a letter in each of the squares below to make a word that means "a breed of dog." The number clues refer to other words that can be made from the whole.

5 8 7 PAIR • 1 3 9 5 SEAL
6 3 7 5 COVER • 8 9 5 4 UNTIE

1	2	3	4	5	6	7	8	9	10

Binairo

Complete the grid with zeros and ones until there are 6 zeros and 6 ones in every row and every column. No more than two of the same number can be next to or under each other. Rows or columns with exactly the same content are not allowed. There is only one valid solution.

		0	I	0							
			0								
		I					I		0		
	I		I	0		I					
		I	I								
I			0	0				0	0		
		I			I						
I				0		0					
				0				I			
	0	0					I	I			
	0				I		I				
		I	I		I			0			

do you KNOW?
Which two oceans does the Panama Canal link?

_____

LETTERBLOCKS

Move the letterblocks around so that words associated with marriage are formed on the top and bottom rows. In some blocks the letter from the top row has been switched with the letter from the bottom row.

```
R R A B E T O
D U H H N B S
```

TRIVIA QUIZ **Pick the Biggest**

Out of each list, from continents to counties, which is the largest?

1. Continents
   a. Africa
   b. Asia
   c. Australia
   d. Europe

2. Islands
   a. Sardinia
   b. Ibiza
   c. Minorca
   d. Corfu

3. World oceans
   a. Arctic Ocean
   b. Indian Ocean
   c. Pacific Ocean
   d. Atlantic Ocean

4. Former Soviet states
   a. Belarus
   b. Turkmenistan
   c. Ukraine
   d. Uzbekistan

5. African countries
   a. Nigeria
   b. Lesotho
   c. Rawanda
   d. Burundi

6. Cities
   a. London
   b. New York
   c. Paris
   d. Tokyo

7. Lakes
   a. Lake Toba
   b. Lake Garda
   c. Lake Windermere
   d. Lake Victoria

8. Eastern Europe
   a. Estonia
   b. Lithuania
   c. Latvia
   d. Poland

9. English counties
   a. Cumbria
   b. County Durham
   c. Lancashire
   d. Northumberland

10. United States
    a. Montana
    b. California
    c. Alaska
    d. Texas

trivia

- The largest animal in the world weighs up to 400,000 pounds. What is it?

CROSSWORD
Gray-Scale Extremes

ACROSS
1 Ally Financial, formerly
5 Basketball
10 ___ Enchanted (2004)
14 Reckless
15 Pond buildup
16 What proofers do
17 Shell competitor
18 Most-quoted Yankee
19 2009 Daniel Day-Lewis film
20 Preakness winner's blanket
23 "Ma'am," in Mexico
24 Derby Day wear
25 ___ Alamos
26 Drop anchor
28 Naughty
31 Gannet
34 Witching ___
35 Menu fish
36 All the president's men
39 Lieutenant
40 "___ It Romantic?"
41 Orderly grouping
42 Negatives
43 90° from north
44 Billiards stick
45 Ply the needle
46 Black Sea port
50 *I Love Lucy* was watched on one
56 Continental coin
57 "___ in Paradise": Poe
58 Early Manitoban
59 "In ___ of flowers …"
60 Hang like a hummingbird
61 Allege as a fact
62 Studio head
63 Glacial spur
64 Flat fee?

DOWN
1 Snatches
2 *That Girl* girl
3 Happy ___ be
4 Willy Wonka product
5 ___ corpus
6 Composer Speaks
7 "Fee, fi, fo, fum" sayer
8 Western sidekick
9 Where "she sells shells"
10 Blofeld in *Thunderball*
11 *Return of the Jedi* princess
12 *Death in Venice* author
13 Pindar poems
21 Copenhagen coin
22 Old Egypt
26 Horse
27 Banish
28 Piglet's pa
29 "A" in code
30 Overcome gravity
31 Ugly Duckling, actually
32 Columbus locale
33 Can covers
34 *Bonanza* brother
35 Vehicle for Blanche DuBois
37 Minnehaha's mate
38 Riyadh resident
43 "A mouse!"
44 Stick
45 Scrub the tub
47 Start a match
48 "Card Players Quarreling" artist
49 Prevent
50 Judo sash
51 *Los Olvidados* director Buñuel
52 Vicinity
53 Former Jordanian queen
54 Peace symbol
55 NYC PBS station

Word Sudoku

Complete the grid so that each row, each column, and each 3 x 3 frame contains the nine letters from the black box below. The hidden nine-letter word is in the diagonal from top left to bottom right.

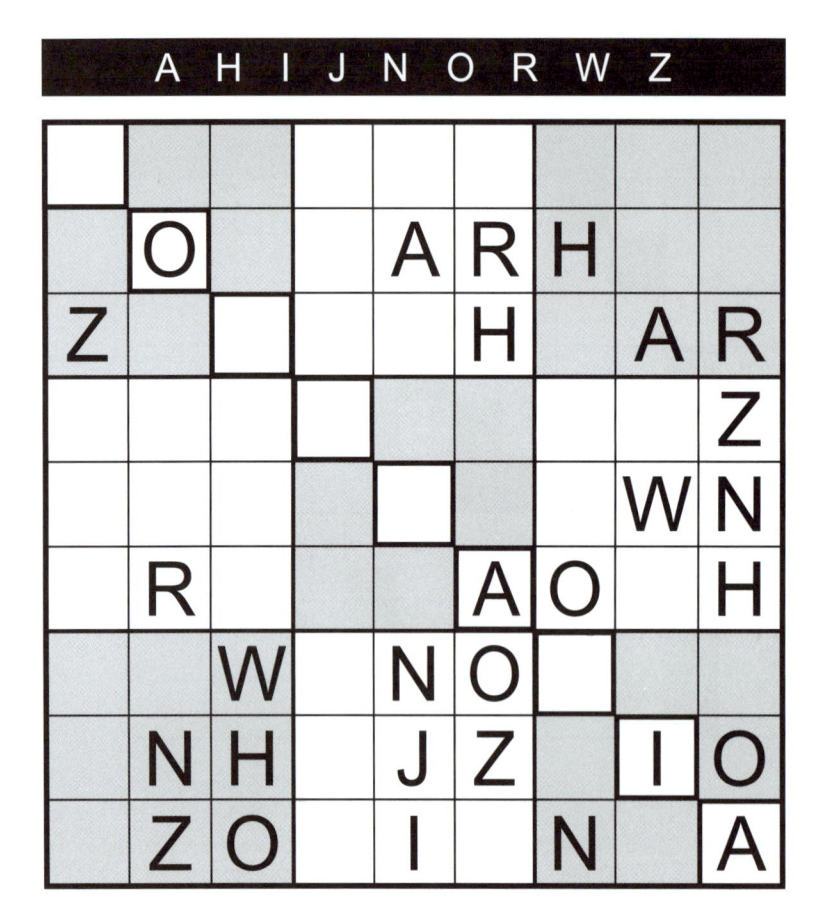

A H I J N O R W Z

	O			A	R	H		
Z				H		A	R	
							Z	
						W	N	
	R			A	O		H	
	W		N	O				
	N	H		J	Z		I	O
	Z	O		I		N		A

do you KNOW?

In which war did jets first fight each other?

UNCANNY TURN

Rearrange the letters of the phrase below to form a cognate anagram, one that is related or connected in meaning to the original phrase. The answer can be one or more words.

NICE LOVE

38

NAME THAT CAR

A Texas Native

Built in Arlington, Texas, this car has power seats, windows, brakes, and steering, along with a power antenna and a Wonder Bar radio. Under the hood is a big 401-cubic-inch V-8 and automatic transmission. The model year was the last year of the big fins. Car buffs call this four-door hardtop style a flattop.

tips

1. The brand's founder, a Scot, invented a method for enameling cast-iron bathtubs.
2. The Wildcat engine was labeled a 445 for its peak torque.
3. This was the first year the model, the brand's top of the line, was offered.
4. The model and a Lockheed plane share a name with a Texas heiress.
5. A numerical suffix refers to the car's length in inches.

CHANGELINGS

Each of the three lines of letters below spell the name of a city, but some of the letters have been mixed up. Four letters from the first name are now in the third line, four letters from the third name are in the second line, and four letters from the second name are in the first line. The remaining letters are in their original places. What are the cities?

```
C  A  S  H  I  N  A  T  O  G
L  O  P  E  N  X  R  A  E  N
A  W  E  H  A  N  D  G  N  I
```

CROSSWORD: Traffic Light

ACROSS
1 President #41 or #43
5 Shatter
10 Homophone of Lou
14 "Deal me in" indicator
15 Advantageous
16 "He was," in Caesar's time
17 Brook
18 Nureyev, for one
19 Safeguard
20 Holds for a news flash
23 *On Golden Pond* bird
24 Pigged out
25 Abaft
28 Coffeehouse order
33 "___ Were the Days"
34 *The Nanny Diaries* nanny
35 *Car Talk* network
36 Body art, slangily
37 Spotless
38 Disdainful grimace
39 "Apple cider" gal
40 Goodyear airship
41 Fate
42 Haste
44 "Friendly Skies" flier
45 "Keep a stiff upper ___"
46 Golf tourney
47 "Beat it!"
55 All fired up
56 Love poetry Muse
57 "Ah! Perfido!" is one
58 Sultan of Swat
59 "Alborada del Gracioso" composer
60 Mr. Gingrich
61 *The Call of the Wild* vehicle
62 Dummy Mortimer
63 Place for a speaker

DOWN
1 Jungle-gym features
2 Squad
3 1944 battle site
4 Dependent
5 Frosty's nose
6 Beehive State native
7 Diet ___ Cola
8 "Fresh!" follow-up
9 Aquatic turtle
10 Apartment dweller
11 Cleopatra's maid
12 Roof projection
13 SUVs
21 Piqued
22 Raison d'___
25 Loft
26 "A Whiter ___ of Pale"
27 Kind of eclipse
28 Adversary
29 Gingery cookie
30 Paddock sound
31 Bubble up
32 Attendant on Artemis
34 Dismounted
37 Oster grooming product
38 The Lower 48, to Hawaiians
40 A Stetson has a broad one
41 "... with a banjo on my ___"
43 Avoided
44 Defend against criticism
46 *Animal House* brother
47 Acts the magpie
48 Shape of "the Big A"
49 Agree
50 Persian Gulf land
51 Approach to the altar
52 Belt
53 New Zealander
54 Puts on the feed bag

Cage the Animals

Draw lines to completely divide up the grid into small squares, with exactly one animal per square. The squares should not overlap.

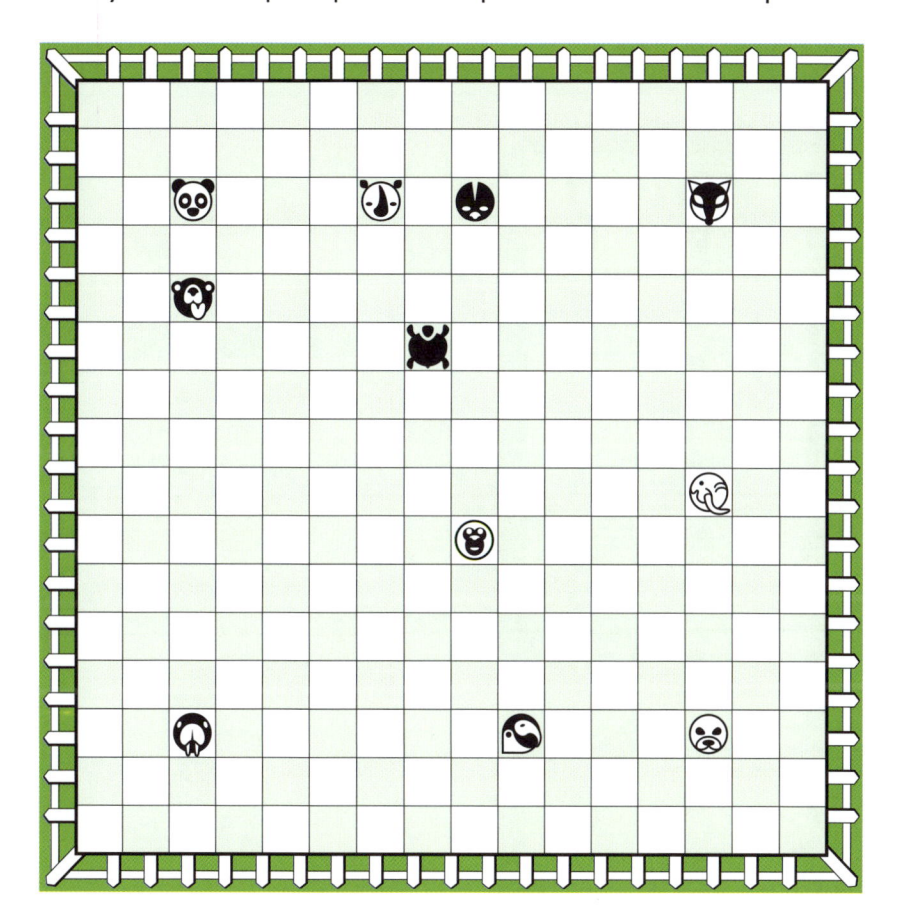

trivia
- What are the plastic ends of shoelaces called?

DOODLE PUZZLE

A doodle puzzle is a combination of images, letters, and/or numbers that represent a word or a concept. If you cannot solve a doodle puzzle, do not look at the answer right away. Think hard—and outside the box.

Sport Maze

Draw the shortest way from the ball to the goal. You can only move along vertical and horizontal lines, not along diagonal lines. The figure on each square indicates the number of squares the ball must move in the same direction. You can change direction at each stop.

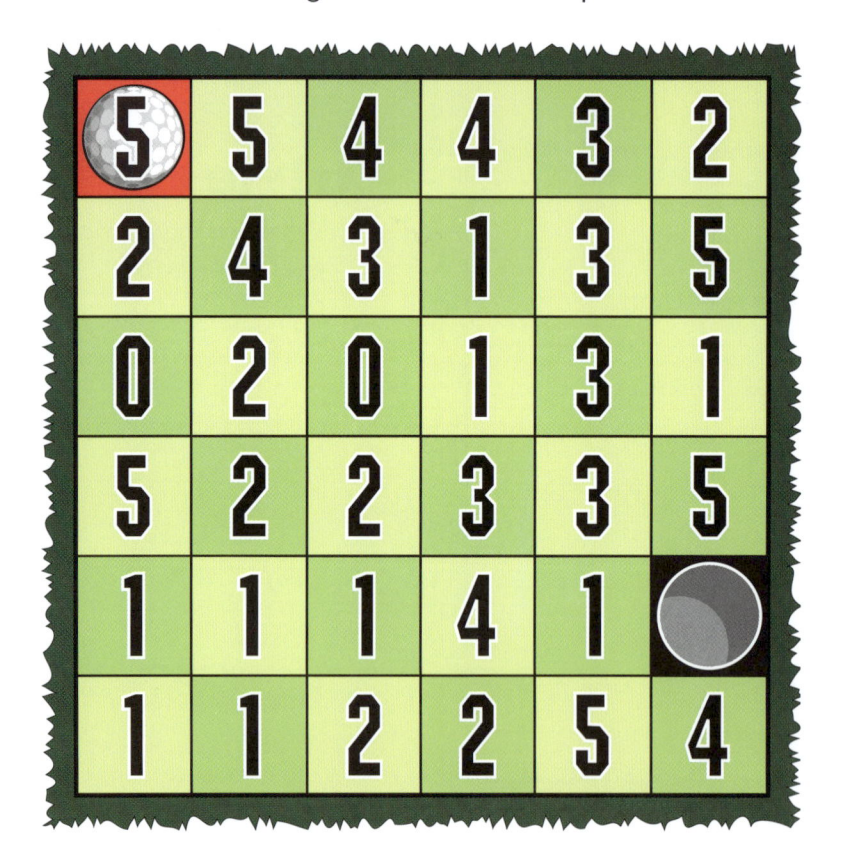

5	5	4	4	3	2
2	4	3	1	3	5
0	2	0	1	3	1
5	2	2	3	3	5
1	1	1	4	1	
1	1	2	2	5	4

do you KNOW?

Which country has the most universities?

REPOSITION PREPOSITION

Unscramble **MAN BY FOES** and find a three-word preposition.

WORD SEARCH: Europe

All the words are hidden vertically, horizontally, or diagonally—in both directions.

```
E U R R A T L A R B I G N O P
Y R A G N U H I T A L Y E E I
E S T O N I A D S T H A D E S
S M A C E D O N I A E W E M T
R E C D O N D A T D A R R O U
E E L N S N M L G A R O L N R
J C L A A L A E E E R N A A K
S N T L W M R C C O O N N C E
T A E O I M N I E N D R D O Y
A R I P A M O N T E N E G R O
I F E N G L A N D N A L N I F
R T Y I S N T I A I N A B L A
T H E W O O R L B A D A N I I
S W E D E N B D I R T I T S V
U P A I S S U R O K E A N L T
A Y A A B I T L A U O S R G A
E R T I H E C E E R G A N O L
C E A N N I A S C O T L A N D
```

- ALBANIA
- ANDORRA
- AUSTRIA
- BOSNIA
- CROATIA
- ENGLAND
- ESTONIA
- FINLAND
- FRANCE
- GEORGIA
- GERMANY
- GIBRALTAR
- GREECE
- HUNGARY
- ICELAND
- IRELAND
- ITALY
- JERSEY
- LATVIA
- MACEDONIA
- MALTA
- MONACO
- MONTENEGRO
- NEDERLAND
- NORWAY
- POLAND
- RUSSIA
- SCOTLAND
- SERBIA
- SPAIN
- SWEDEN
- TURKEY
- UKRAINE
- WALES

TRIVIAL PURSUIT: Country Comes to Broadway

Folks couldn't get enough of *Oklahoma!*, a classic love triangle set in farm country. Test your recall from the 1943 Broadway sensation that ran for a then-unprecedented 2,212 performances.

1 Richard Rodgers composed the songs. Name his new partner, who wrote the lyrics.

2 This female choreographer gets credit for the show's innovative dance numbers.

3 "All the sounds of the earth are like music," according to this jubilant song.

4 Who played Ado Annie in the original production?

5 Curly McLain boasts "Ain't no finer rig I'm a-thinkin'" in this catchy tune.

6 Who played Curly McLain in the original production?

7 An ensemble emphasizes "territory folks should stick together" in this rousing number.

8 Laurey Williams tells Curly, "Your eyes mustn't glow like mine" in this love ballad.

9 Curly claims that a brutish farmhand "had a heart of gold" in this dirge.

10 The musical is based on Lynn Riggs, 1931 play?

11 The musical opened on Broadway in 1943 at which theater?

12 Ado Annie laments, "But when I'm with a feller, I fergit!" as part of this ditty.

CROSSWORD: '60s Rock

ACROSS
1 Arctic Circle native
5 Johnny in *The Tourist*
9 Rafael Nadal's country
14 Bat lead-in
15 Organic compound
16 Brazen one
17 Creedence Clearwater Revival hit
19 Papal vestment
20 Shoot down a rocket
21 Bert or Ernie
22 NYC's first subway line
23 Tab
24 ///, to a kegler
28 Belief
32 Pronged
33 Beam
34 Cold coating
35 Tel ___
36 Bleachers
37 "Others" in a Latin phrase
38 Newspaper section
39 Float gently
40 Arkansas mountains
41 Firm
43 *Amadeus* setting
44 *Exodus* author
45 Electric fish
46 ___ Yonkers (1993)
49 Pennant
54 Anticipate
55 Ben E. King hit
56 *Roxana* author
57 Haydn sobriquet
58 $ dispensers
59 Heavenly places
60 City S of Moscow
61 "... ___ was my wife!"

DOWN
1 *Beverly Hills Cop* org.
2 *God's Little ___* Caldwell novel
3 "Aye" voters
4 Be sour
5 Begs to differ
6 Legislate
7 Fortified wine
8 Work at busily
9 "Auld Lang Syne" starter
10 Jimi Hendrix hit
11 "... and make it snappy!"
12 ... here on Gilligan's ___
13 "No way, Sergei!"
18 Like prunes
21 Airs
23 Edie of *Desperate Housewives*
24 Great balls of fire
25 Basketball maneuver
26 *West Side Story* girl
27 Beatles hit
28 Skill
29 *A Tree Grows in Brooklyn* family name
30 Terrier type
31 Eleniak of *Baywatch*
33 High and low
36 Beau
40 Drunk, in slang
42 Composes epistles
43 Springlike
45 A day's march
46 Bring on board
47 Came up short
48 Call at first
49 Hexagram
50 "...like ___ out of hell"
51 Don't believe it
52 Avenger Peel
53 Medical advice, often
55 Naval address: Abbr.

Sudoku

Fill in the grid so that each row, each column, and each 3 x 3 frame contains every number from 1 to 9.

8					9			
	5	3						
	2	9						
			4				2	
4	8				3	7		
5	1		7			9		
2			6	7				1
7		3		2		6	5	
9	6					2		

trivia

- What did Captain Cook call Hawaii?

BLOCK ANAGRAM

Form the word that is described in the parentheses, using the letters above the grid. Extra letters are already in the right place.

TISSUES   (portable rectangular containers)

				C	A			

BRAINSNACK® Skewered

Which kebab (1–5) is impossible to make knowing that the butcher only has five different types of meat?

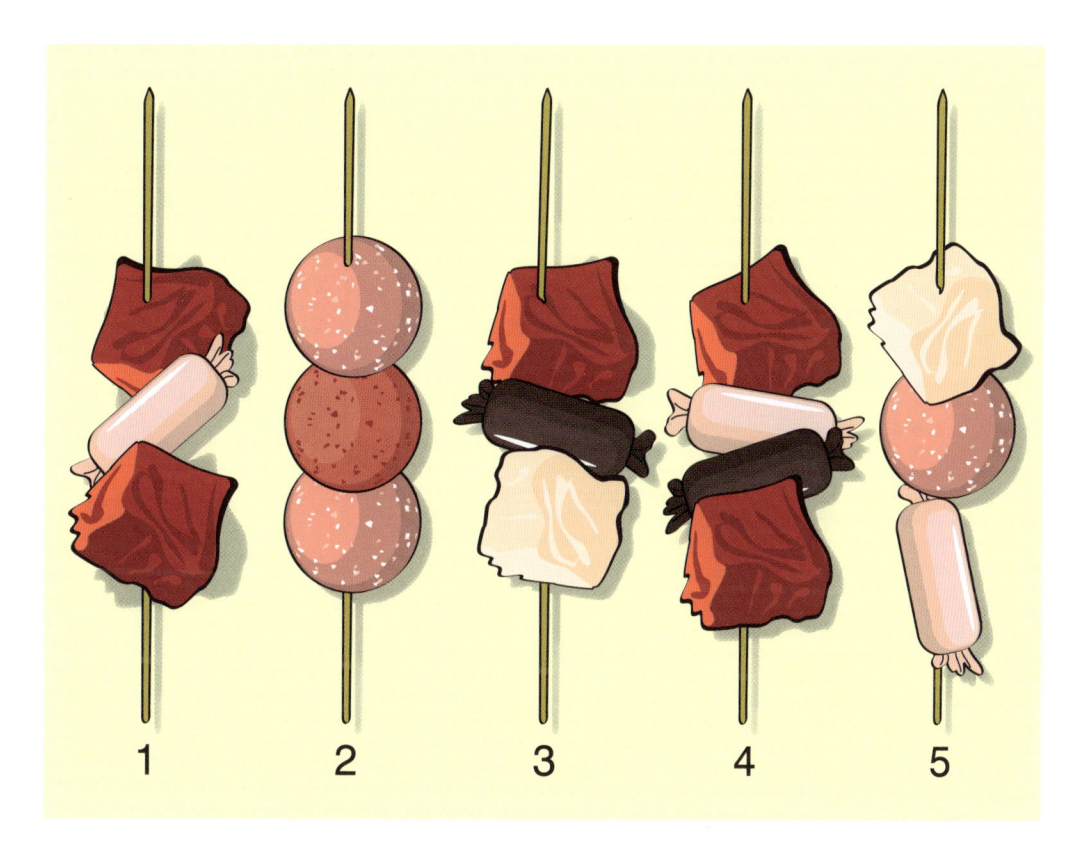

TRANSADDITION

Add one letter to the sequence below and rearrange the rest to create a set of rules.

I SIT NOT UNTO

CROSSWORD: Down Under

ACROSS
1 "The Pineapple King"
5 TV palomino
9 "... and the ___ are not cloudy all day"
14 "1000 Oceans" singer Tori
15 Air: Comb. form
16 Herding dog
17 Aussie hunting weapon
19 *Chinatown* director Polanski
20 At any hour
21 Gilbert & Sullivan operetta (with *The*)
22 "Elvis ___ left the building"
23 Rum cake
24 Infuriate
28 Achievement for a hasbeen
32 A watched pot is never this
33 Doofus
34 Jamaican tangelo
35 40 square rods
36 Inchon locale
37 Speakeasy risk
38 Wood finish oil
39 *Beverly Hills Cop* org.
40 9-to-5 drudgery
41 2009 Super Bowl champs
43 Cheap quarters
44 *American Pie* actress Tara
45 1959 Kingston Trio hit
46 Give out homework
49 Definitions
54 "Island" on the Atlantic Coast
55 Aussie oxbow lake
56 A writer's body of work
57 Give off fumes
58 Art school subj.
59 1977 John Denver film
60 *The Defiant ___* (1958)
61 Spoils

DOWN
1 Smidgens
2 *Typee* sequel
3 Appear imminent
4 *Babe* wife
5 *The Music Man* woman
6 500-sheet units of paper
7 Shore bird
8 Use a spade
9 Author
10 Aussie kingfisher
11 ___ la Douce
12 "Bejabbers!"
13 ___-Japanese War
18 *I Love Lucy* character
21 Venomous African snake
23 Disapproved of an act
24 Trading places
25 *10 Things I Hate ___ You* (1999)
26 Lorna ___
27 Aussie wind instrument
28 Cadet group
29 On the other hand
30 Eastwood in *Unforgiven*
31 Tot
33 Surfer's need
36 *Primary Colors* author
40 Accra is its capital
42 *The ___ of Bagger Vance*
43 Celery amounts
45 A beanball might lead to one
46 Exxon competitor
47 1979 Iranian exile
48 Air
49 Appearance
50 Beam in a bridge
51 Behavioral slip
52 Tiny pest
53 NCOs
55 "Don't tase me, ___!"

Pixel Fun

Color the correct squares black and discover the pixel image. The numbers on the outer border against the black or the white background indicate the total number of black or white squares on a column or row. The numbers on the inner border indicate the largest group of adjacent black or white squares to be found anywhere on that column or row. For instance, if there is a six on the outer ring and a two on the inner ring against a white background, then there are six white blocks in that row, and the biggest group or groups consist of a maximum of two adjacent white blocks.

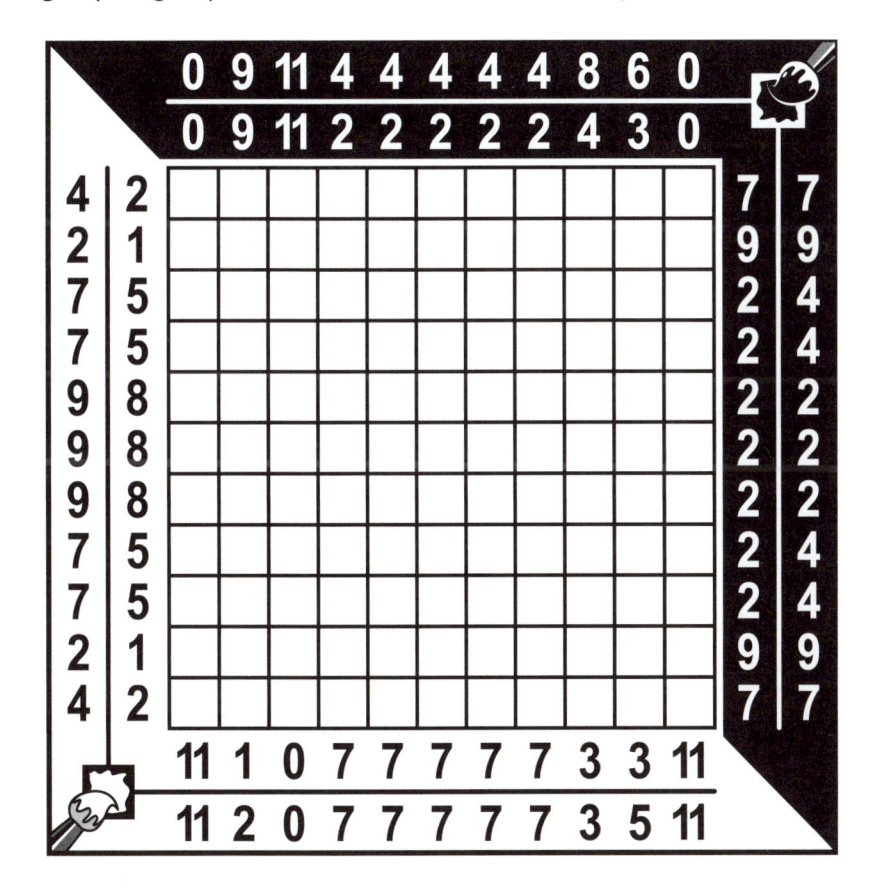

change ONE

Change one letter in each of these two words to form a common two-word phrase.

STRAY IN

Keep Going

Start on a blank square of your choice and connect as many blank squares as possible with one single continuous line. You can only connect squares along vertical and horizontal lines, not along diagonal lines. You must continue the connecting lineup until the next obstacle, i.e., the border of the box, a black square, or a square that already has been used. You can change direction at any obstacle you meet. Each square can only be used once. The number of blank squares that will be left unused is marked in the upper square. There is more than one solution. We only show one solution.

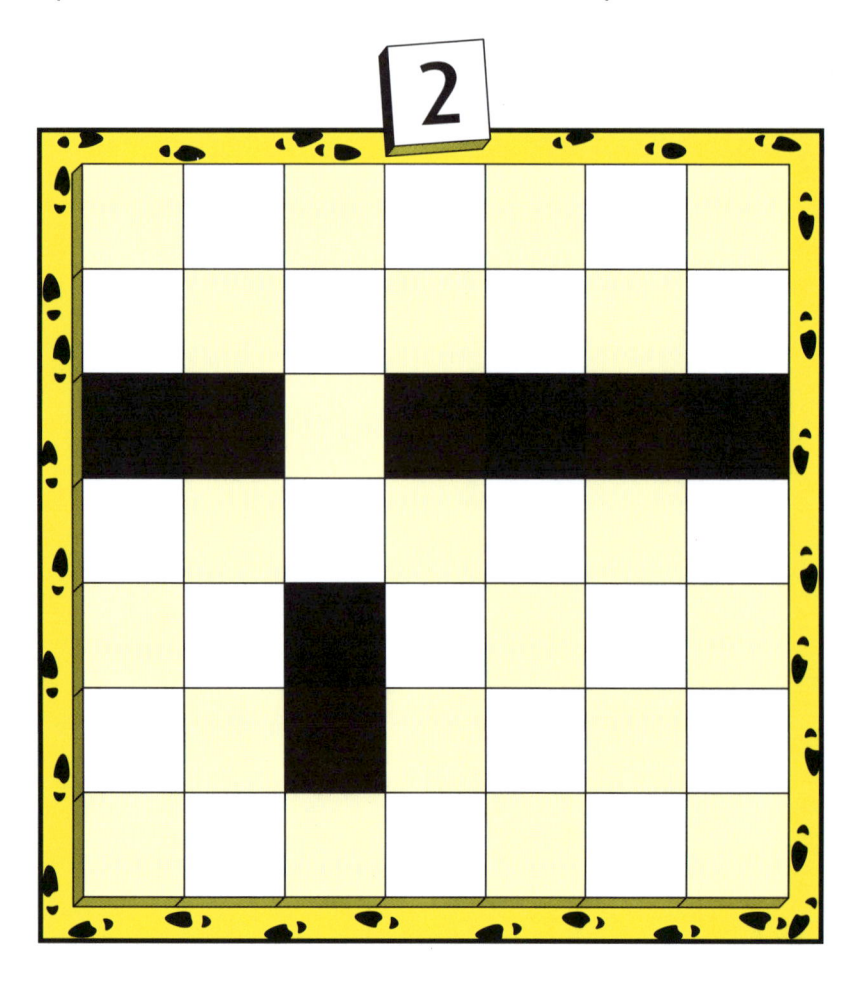

2

delete ONE

Delete one letter from the words

LIES LET'S RECOUNT

and rearrange the rest to get to the final outcome.

Binairo

Complete the grid with zeros and ones until there are 6 zeros and 6 ones in every row and every column. No more than two of the same number can be next to or under each other. Rows or columns with exactly the same content are not allowed. There is only one valid solution.

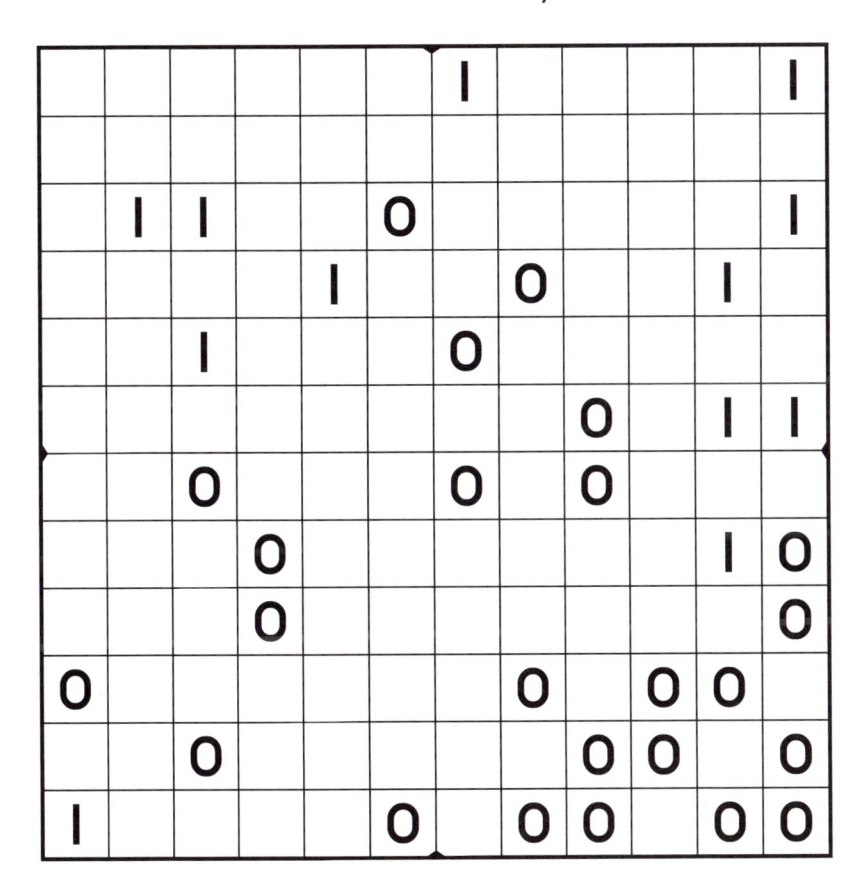

do you KNOW?

What is the fastest animal alive?

LETTERBLOCKS

Move the letterblocks around so that words associated with collections are formed on the top and bottom rows.

Top row: A L Y B I R R
Bottom row: A S E O T R G

WORD POWER: Magic

We've conjured up a page of magical words and phrases.
Step right up and test your vocabulary—then transport yourself into a world of wonder.

1. **levitate** ('le-vih-tayt) *v.*—
   A: defy gravity. B: weave spells.
   C: disappear.

2. **clairvoyant** (klayr-'voy-ent) *adj.*—
   A: in a trance. B: ghostly.
   C: seeing beyond ordinary
   perception.

3. **planchette** (plan-'shet) *n.*—
   A: sorcerer's cloak.
   B: Ouija board pointer.
   C: mischievous fairy.

4. **mojo** ('moh-joh) *n.*—
   A: book of secrets.
   B: magical spell. C: mantra.

5. **telekinetic** (te-leh-kih-'neh-tik)
   adj.—A: predicting the future.
   B: calling on ghosts.
   C: using mind over matter.

6. **voilà** (vwah-'lah) *interj.*—
   A: "Begone!" B: "There it is!"
   C: "Open!"

7. **whammy** ('wa-mee) *n.*—
   A: trapdoor. B: illusion.
   C: hex or curse.

8. **soothsaying** ('sooth-say-ing) *n.*—
   A: prophecy.
   B: recitation of chants.
   C: revelation of a trick.

9. **mesmerized** ('mez-meh-riyzd)
   adj.—A: sawed in half.
   B: hypnotized.
   C: turned to pixie dust.

10. **augur** ('ah-ger) *v.*—
    A: serve as an omen.
    B: bend a spoon without
    touching it.
    C: chant in a monotone.

11. **shaman** ('shah-men) *n.*—
    A: fake psychic.
    B: healer using magic.
    C: genie in a bottle.

12. **occult** (uh-'khult) *adj.*—
    A: sinister. B: miraculous.
    C: secret.

13. **invoke** (in-'vohk) *v.*—
    A: transform.
    B: use ventriloquism.
    C: summon up, as spirits.

14. **sibyl** ('si-buhl) *n.*—
    A: séance.
    B: fortune-teller.
    C: black cat.

15. **pentagram** ('pen-teh-gram) *n.*—
    A: elixir.
    B: five-pointed star.
    C: enchanted staff.

CROSSWORD

From B to B

ACROSS
1 Ninny
5 Crème ___ crème
9 Badmouth
14 "A-Tisket, A-Tasket" first name
15 Tel Aviv carrier
16 Calliope and Clio
17 Night stick
19 "Come here ___?"
20 Bewitched
21 Characterize
22 Col.'s superior
23 Sousaphone, for one
24 *The Love Bug* car
28 Aligned
32 Doozies
33 *Allure* competitor
34 Aisne's end
35 "Heads I win, tails you ___"
36 "Let's Get Away From It All" lyricist
37 Rottweiler in *Up*
38 "A Chapter on Ears" essayist
39 *Cat on the Scent* author ___ Mae Brown
40 Balcony sections
41 Monte Cristo, e.g.
43 "Addicted to Love" singer Palmer
44 "Country Gentleman" Atkins
45 "Red state" group
46 Bad looks
49 Apropos
54 Ancient Roman soothsayer
55 Devil
56 Infraction
57 *Breathing Lessons* author Tyler
58 "Another Pyramid" musical
59 Cabinet hardware

60 *American Graffiti* nerd
61 Insulting stare

DOWN
1 *Cheers* actress Neuwirth
2 *Alias* Emmy winner Lena
3 Tabasco pot
4 ChapStick, e.g.
5 Judicial decision
6 *Bat Out of Hell* singer Foley
7 Acclaim
8 Choirboy's wear
9 Tiny protozoan
10 Friend of Howdy Doody
11 ___ spumante
12 "... ___ and not heard"
13 A slave of crosswords?
18 Asana practicers
21 "Four Apostles" painter
23 *Rocky* actress Shire
24 Royal St. George's 18
25 *Waterworld* girl
26 *Jurassic Park* bug trapper
27 Ant's find
28 "Ariel" poet
29 Belgian burg
30 Poly follower
31 "... to say the ___"
33 ___ of Nantes
36 Russell Crowe's sign
40 *Anaconda* star Jennifer
42 "___ Waldo?"
43 Handmade, as cigars
45 *Commander in Chief* actress Davis
46 Bag
47 "No U-___"
48 Exchange premium
49 Escalator inventor
50 Wiener-schnitzel meat
51 "___ Baby" (*Hair* song)
52 In the altogether
53 Lift at Aspen
55 Cricket stick

Sudoku Twin

Fill in the grid so that each row, each column, and each 3 x 3 frame contains every number from 1 to 9. A sudoku twin is two connected 9 x 9 sudokus.

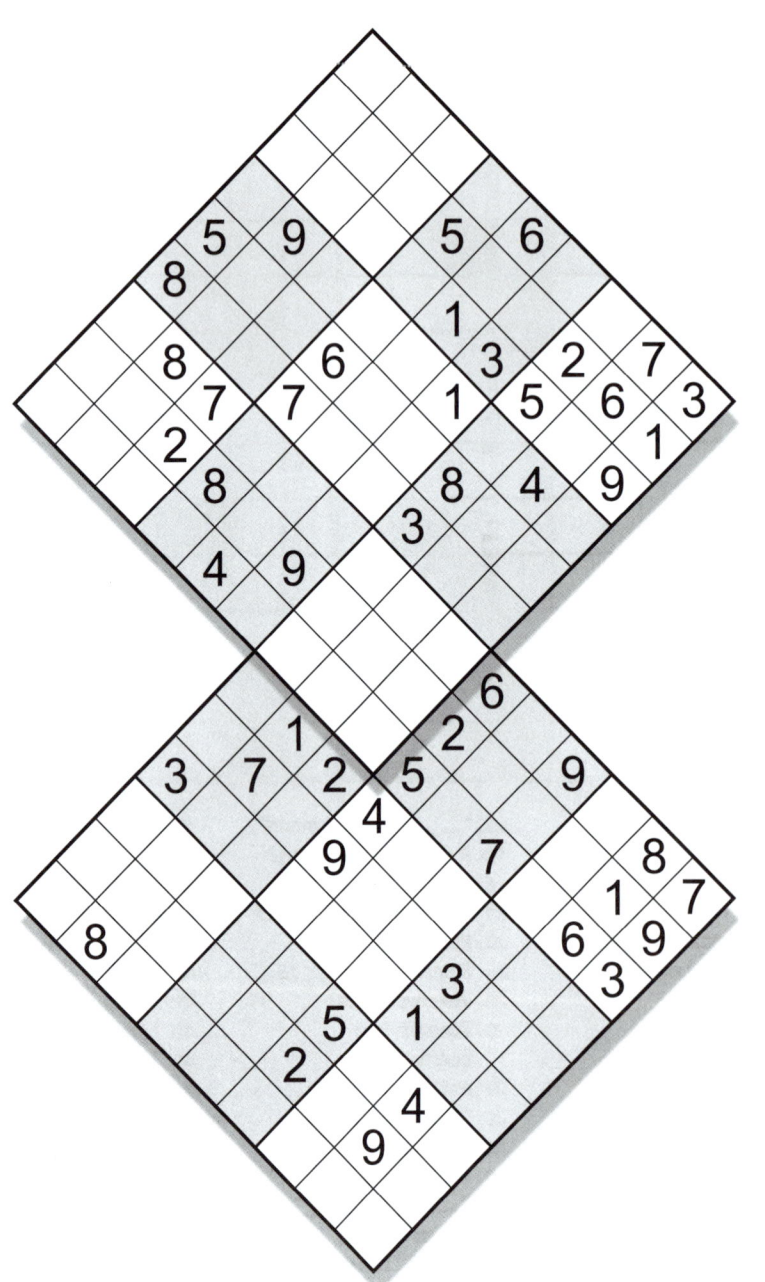

delete ONE

Delete one letter from the word **BEATERS** and rearrange the rest to get your money back.

_____

BRAINSNACK® Sign Language

Which number should replace the question mark?

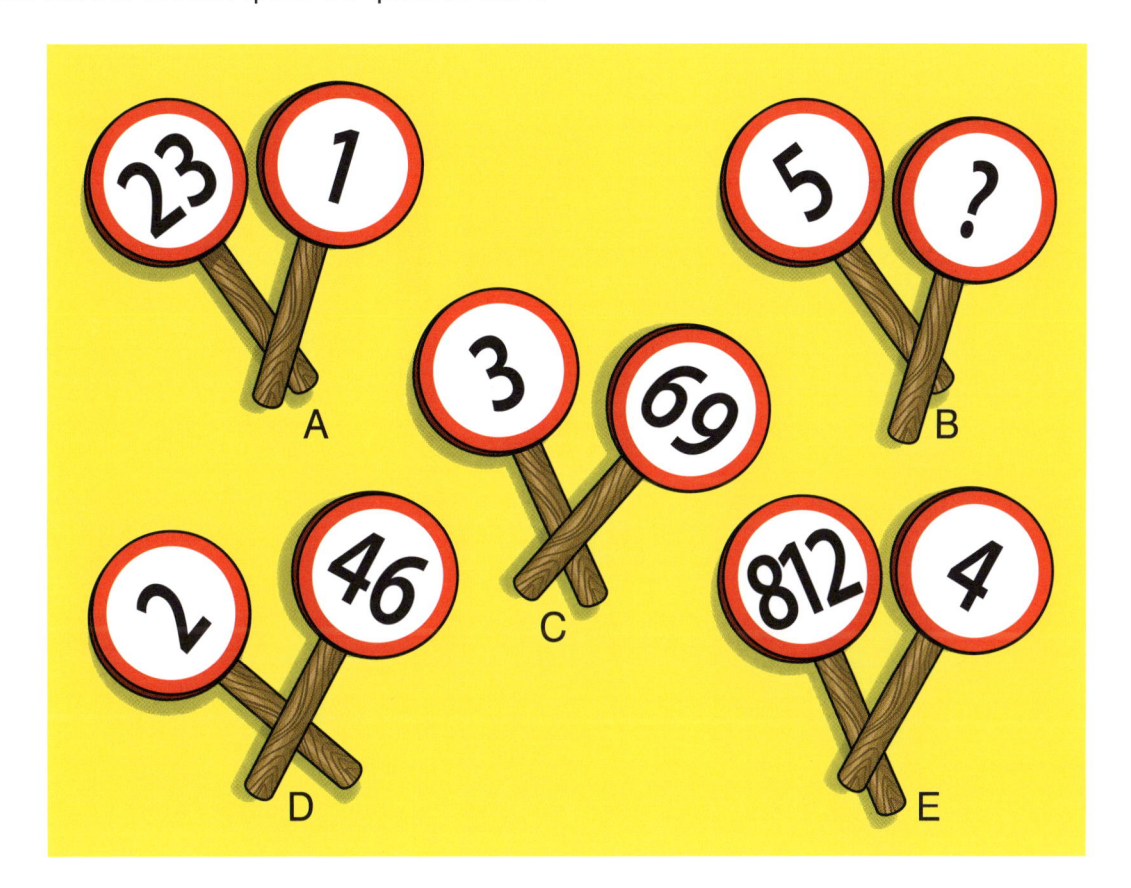

TRANSADDITION

Add one letter to the words below and rearrange the rest to be able to state the title and author of the novel.

NOVEL BY A SCOTTISH WRITER

Train Your Brain

An aptitude for visual tests indicates an analytical mind. If you like these puzzles, it implies that you are a logical person who thinks things through.

Lock in Place

Which of the pieces below marked A to E, when fitted to the red piece to the right, will form a perfect square?

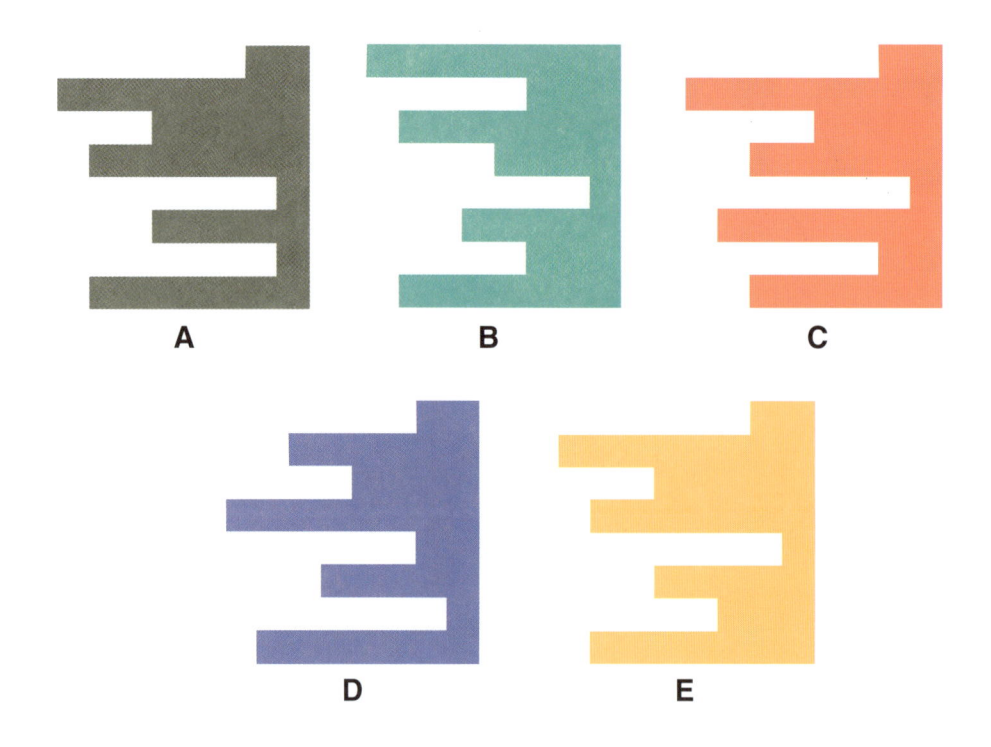

A

B

C

D

E

Patchwork

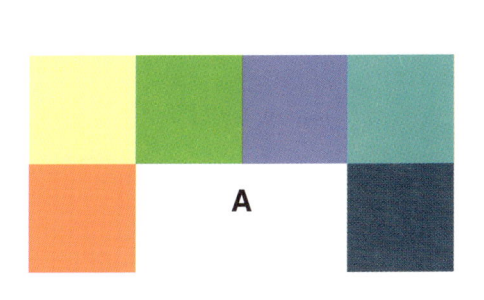

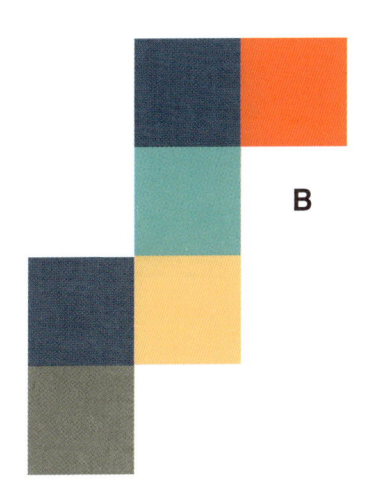

Which of the sequences (A through E) can be folded into a perfect cube?

Number Cluster

Cubes showing numbers have been placed on the grid below, with some spaces left empty. Can you complete the grid by creating runs of the same number and of the same length as the number? So, where a cube with number 5 has been included on the grid, you need to create a run of five number 5's, including the cube already shown. The run can be horizontal, vertical, or both horizontal and vertical.

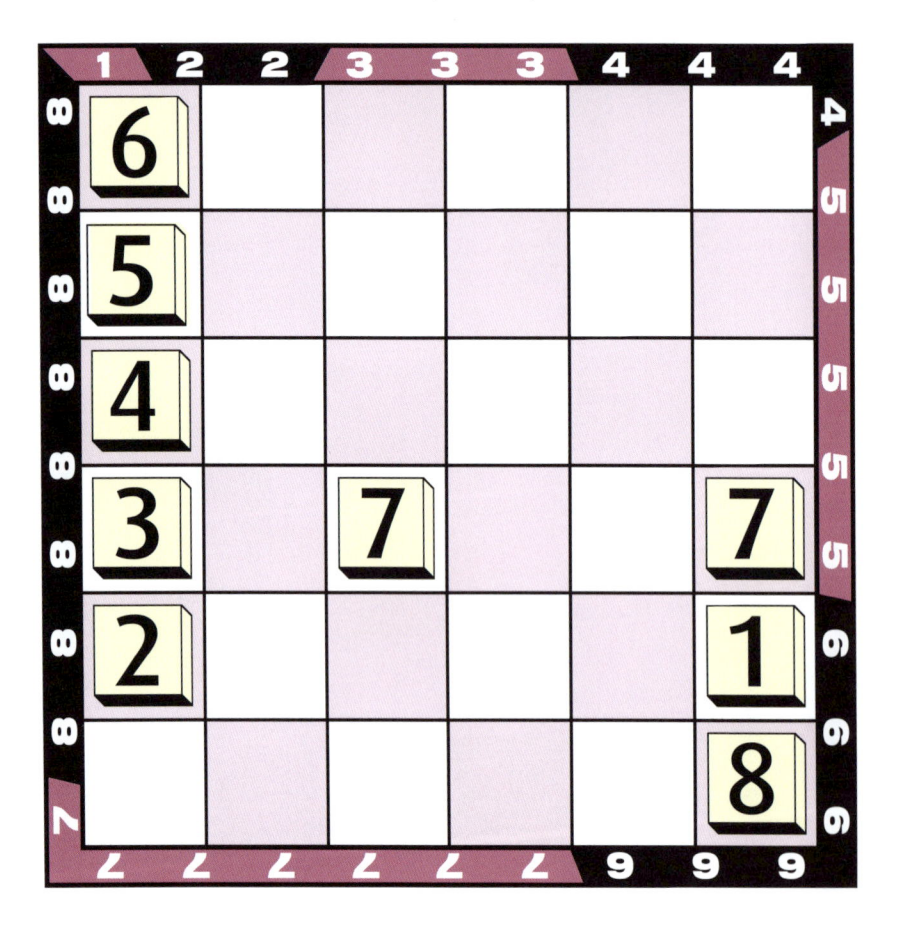

do you KNOW?

Which one is more buoyant, deep or shallow water?

_____

FRIENDS

What do the following words have in common?

ABLE EVEN FAST THROUGH DOWN AWAY WATER NECK

WORD SEARCH: Color

All the words are hidden vertically, horizontally, or diagonally—in both directions.

```
C O L O R A U B U R N T I S A
E S K Y B L U E N E D I E T T
U R E S E A G R E E N T R V T
L E M V I N A R E D V I N I O
B V I N D I G O B T L A B O C
N L Y T P E H E C T V N R L A
O I O E Z O M P O Y I R L E R
C S S N R C A C B T I E O T R
L N O A O H I L A F D D I F E
A R N K F R U E R L E N T W T
B G A H P E V N E L I V O R Y
E E N A G T O P U R P L E H S
T H A K T S D L A R E M E O G
L I E I M A G E N T A G H R O
P T C I C O T E L R A C S A L
I B R I G H T R E D N S I L D
N C U L T R A M A R I N E C E
K S T B R I C K R E D S O F N
```

- ALCON BLUE
- APRICOT
- AUBURN
- BRICK-RED
- BRIGHT RED
- BRONZE GREEN
- CLARO
- COBALT
- CRIMSON
- ECRU
- EMERALD
- GOLDEN
- INDIGO
- IVORY
- KHAKI
- LILAC
- MAGENTA
- NAVY BLUE
- OCHRE
- OLIVE
- ORANGE
- PINK
- PURPLE
- RAVEN
- SCARLET
- SEA GREEN
- SEPIA
- SILVER
- SKY BLUE
- TERRA COTTA
- TITIAN RED
- ULTRAMARINE
- VIOLET

TRIVIA QUIZ: Mostly Magazines

You have to be pretty sharp to make it in the magazine business. See if you have what it takes to stay in the game with this glossy round of riddles.

1. What weekly magazine debuted in 1923 and became legendary for its annual Man of the Year cover?

2. What popular men's magazine did Marilyn Monroe grace the cover of when it hit newsstands in 1953?

3. Who was on the cover of the very first *People* magazine in 1974?

4. In what country was the editor of *Vanity Fair*, Graydon Carter, born?

5. Who was 25 when she became editor-in-chief of England's oldest glossy, *The Tatler*?

6. In 1991 which photographer took the cover shot for *Vanity Fair* of a pregnant Demi Moore posing nude?

7. Who publishes *Rolling Stone* magazine?

8. At what women's magazine did Helen Gurley Brown serve at the helm for 32 years?

9. Which Canadian editor served as the editor-in-chief of *Us Weekly*, *Glamour*, *Cosmopolitan*, *Marie Claire*, and *YM*?

10. What was the name of the political magazine launched by the son of a U.S. president in 1995?

trivia

- *The Devil Wears Prada* was based on a 2003 bestseller by Lauren Weisberger and was inspired by her experiences as a personal assistant at what fashion magazine?

CROSSWORD: Hidden Gems

ACROSS
1 Banana stalk
5 *Arsenic and Old Lace* director
10 *Desire Under the* ___
14 *Rent* won one in 1996
15 Detail of a shoelace
16 *Chapter Two* playwright Simon
17 Type of bass
19 "Name of the ___": ABBA
20 Fantasts
21 Rich
23 Guidonian note
24 *Lulu* composer
25 .jpg and .gif files
29 Beat
33 Sub tracker
34 Strong wind
35 *I Was a ___ War Bride* (1949)
36 Pacer in *Cars 2*
37 "Done!"
38 10 million equal a joule
39 Starbuck's skipper
40 Skaneateles, e.g.
41 Act furtively
42 Companies of travelers
44 Spuds
45 Basic idea
46 "___ Rah": Fats Domino
47 Crèche figure
50 Became frosty
55 *Ararat* director Egoyan
56 Reiterate
58 "___ small world!"
59 "___ in the place, except ..."
60 Richard E. Byrd's alma mater
61 Hold a note
62 McFadden of *Star Trek: TNG*
63 "And when he had opened the second ___" (Rev. 6:3)

DOWN
1 "Deal!"
2 Vail transport
3 Hibernia
4 Prefix for bucks
5 *Ishtar* extras
6 Athenian square
7 Ne ___ ultra
8 Dampen flax
9 Bowl figures
10 Betrothal
11 "Get the ___ out!"
12 Silent actor
13 *Call of the Wild* vehicle
18 Abu Dhabi bigwig
22 Food scrap
24 Falsify
25 "Don't Let Go" singer Hayes
26 Arabian coffee
27 Lend ___ (listen)
28 Sanitation Department employee
29 *Mary Poppins* family
30 ___ show (street spectacle)
31 "Chanson de Matin" composer
32 Anchors' places
34 Mammoth
37 Like emergency lights
41 Jubail citizen
43 Big wheel
44 Movie melodies
46 "Daphne" division
47 "Go directly to ___"
48 *A Fish Called Wanda* character
49 *Scarface* drug lord
50 "___ Rhythm"
51 Burden
52 Amphora
53 Volcano known as Vulcan's Forge
54 Not virtual
57 "___ thousand times ..."

Sudoku

Fill in the grid so that each row, each column, and each 3 x 3 frame contains every number from 1 to 9.

				8	9	3		
				1	5	8	9	
	6							
	7	2						9
	3	9	4	2		6		7
		7			3		5	1
	9					7		
1		3		4				

trivia

- What was Bob Hope's real name?

_____

BLOCK ANAGRAM

Form the word that is described in the parentheses, using the letters above the grid. Extra letters are already in the right place.

JUNE BUG (it will get you suspended)

☐ ☐ ☐ ☐ ☐ **E**   ☐ ☐ **M** **P**

BRAINSNACK® **Gear Up**

Gear 1 can only turn clockwise. Knowing this can you determine in which direction gear 2 will turn? Will it turn clockwise (B), counterclockwise (A), or will it be locked and not turn at all? Answer 0 if you think gear 2 is locked.

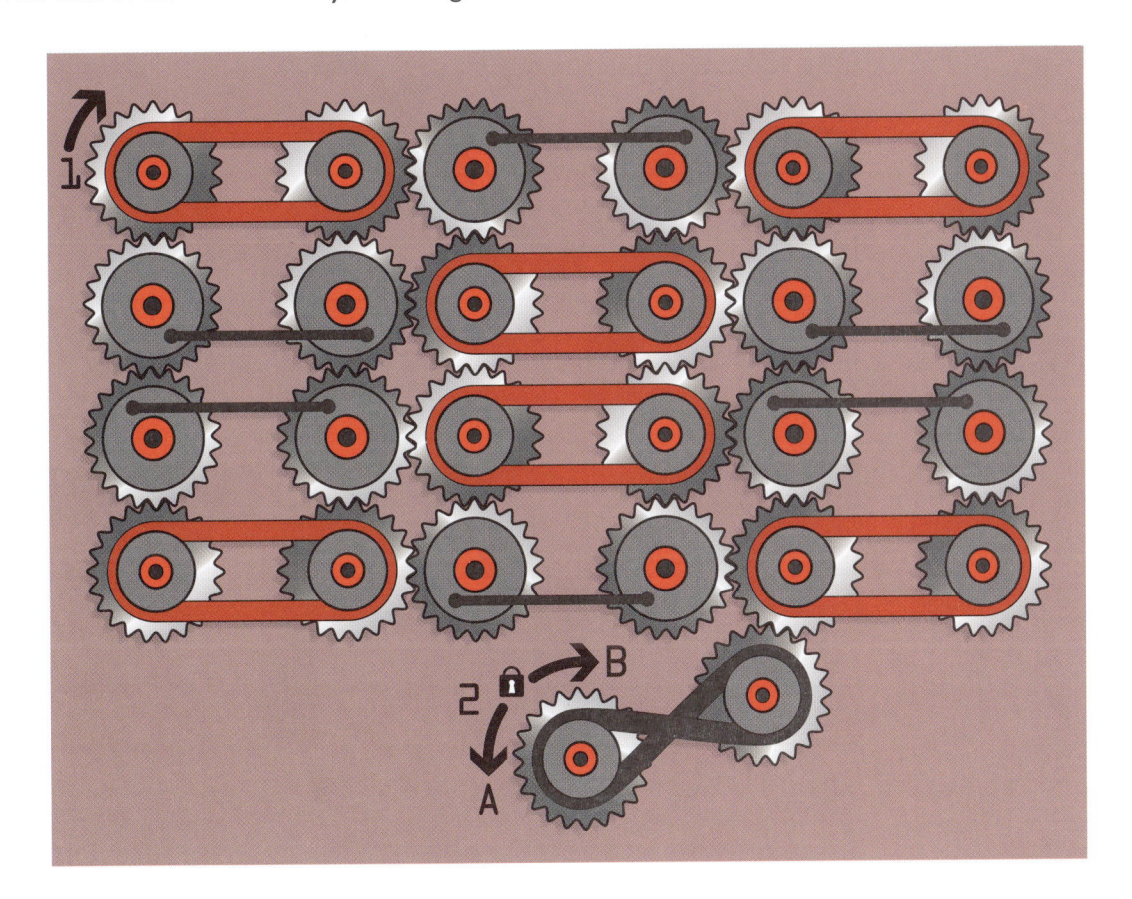

TRANSADDITION

Add two letters to the words below and rearrange the rest to form a newspaper headline that rocked the world.

DEATH STARTS IN ICE

CROSSWORD: High Cards

ACROSS
1. Account execs
5. Blowgun ammo
9. 7 to 10 on the Beaufort Scale
14. "C'est ___" ("it's his")
15. Wood stork
16. Angle that's smaller than 90
17. *Tropic Thunder* star
19. Lion's prey
20. Tavern
21. Breakwaters
22. Ultimate degree
23. Neuwirth of Broadway
24. Like milk glass
28. Wax the car
32. Part of M.O.
33. Blue-and-white shark
34. Very, in Verdun
35. Winglike petals
36. Add pep to (with "up")
37. Citi Field officials
38. Grayish goose
39. Commotions
40. Popsicle flavor
41. Color of Lee's Traveller
43. " 'Tis the ___ to be jolly ..."
44. Becomes baggy
45. "Eureka!" alternatives
46. Danny in *The Last Don*
49. Bête noire
54. Floridan snake
55. Extra-large
56. Bale binder
57. Cyclist LeMond
58. "... 15 miles on the ___ Canal"
59. *Grease* ballad
60. Stunning
61. Aykroyd and Fogelberg

DOWN
1. *Scooby-Doo* director Gosnell
2. Airline to Lod
3. Brownish purple
4. Turbaned Indian
5. Water down
6. Bring embarrassment to
7. Sushi ingredient
8. "Come, come!"
9. Backyard belvedere
10. 1994 Jim Carrey role
11. *Grease* job
12. Raison d' ___
13. Bering and Baltic
18. A little something extra
21. *Car Talk* subject
23. Tour de France racers
24. A Middle Easterner
25. Boatman on the Isis
26. Hersey bell town
27. Brisbane is its capital
28. "Stompin' at the ___": Goodman
29. La Douce et al.
30. A Marx brother
31. German food
33. Rorem's *King* ___
36. *Key* ___
40. *Adventures*
42. 747 kitchen
43. *Scooby-Doo* character
45. Building wing
46. *America's Got Talent* segments
47. *American Gothic* setting
48. The Auld Sod
49. Suffix for billion
50. Made tracks
51. Henry Aldrich player Stone
52. "Kiss ___ the Rain": Streisand
53. *Five Eliot Landscapes* composer
55. Metric wts.

Kakuro

Each number in a black area is the sum of the numbers that you have to enter in the next empty boxes. The empty boxes that make up the sum are called a run. The sum of the across run is written above the diagonal in the black area, and the sum of the down run is written below the diagonal. Runs can only contain the numbers 1 through 9, and each number in a run can only be used once. The gray boxes only contain odd numbers and the white only even numbers.

do you KNOW?

Who killed President Abraham Lincoln?

_____

SANDWICH
What five-letter word belongs between the word at left and the word at right, so that the first and second word, and the second and third word, each form a common compound word or phrase? JAIL _ _ _ _ _ BREAK

Sport Maze

Draw the shortest way from the ball to the goal. You can only move along vertical and horizontal lines, not along diagonal lines. The figure on each square indicates the number of squares the ball must move in the same direction. You can change direction at each stop.

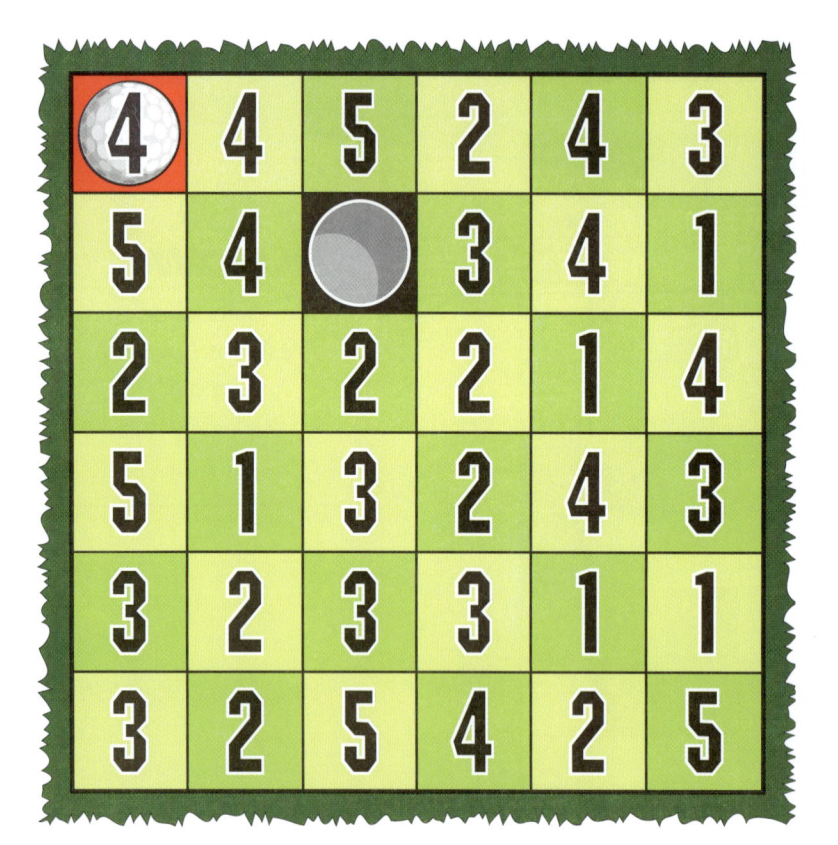

4	4	5	2	4	3
5	4		3	4	1
2	3	2	2	1	4
5	1	3	2	4	3
3	2	3	3	1	1
3	2	5	4	2	5

triVia

- What is the function of the USAF Thunderbirds?

REPOSITION PREPOSITION

Unscramble **TUTU APRONS** and find a two-word preposition.

Binairo

Complete the grid with zeros and ones until there are 5 zeros and 6 ones in every row and every column. No more than two of the same number can be next to or under each other. Rows or columns with exactly the same content are not allowed. There is only one valid solution.

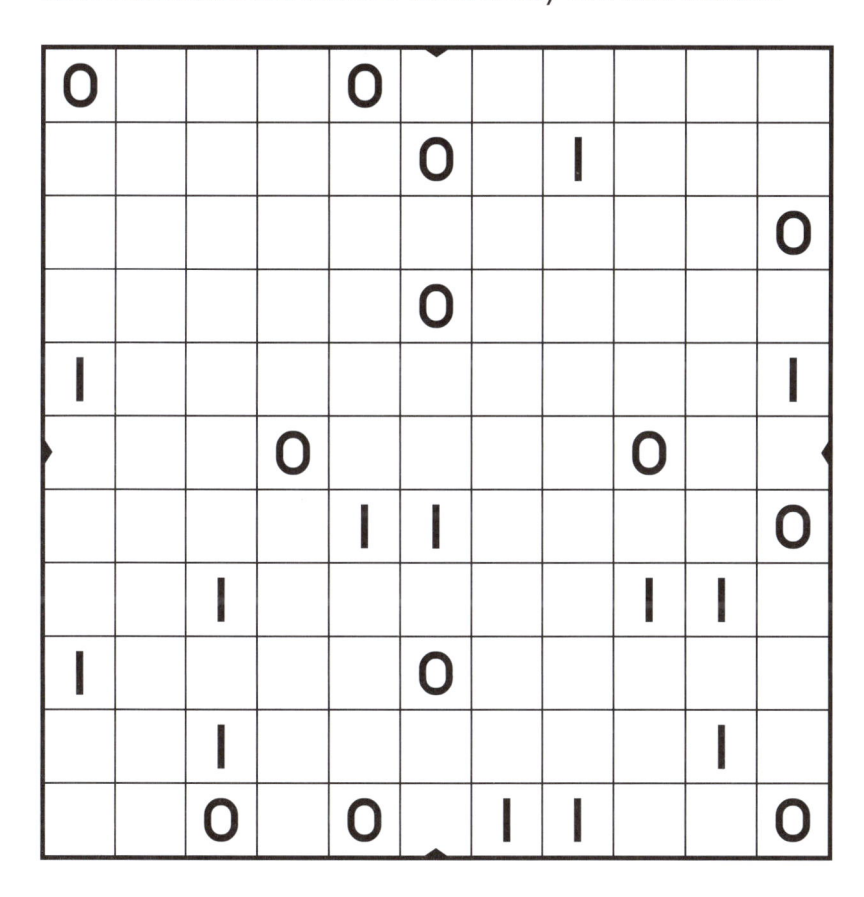

0			0							
				0		1				
										0
				0						
1										1
		0					0			
			1	1						0
	1						1	1		
1				0						
	1							1		
	0	0		1	1				0	

do you KNOW?

What was the capital of India until 1911?

LETTERBLOCKS

Move the letterblocks around so that words associated with marriage are formed on the top and bottom rows. In some blocks the letter from the top row has been switched with the letter from the bottom row.

```
N P T A N R R
I W D E E D G
```

TRIVIA QUIZ: All Iced Up

All answers in this round start with "ice." Can you answer them?

1. What name is given to a glacial period when ice sheets covered much of the Earth?

2. Name a North Atlantic island whose hot springs and volcanoes provide geothermal energy.

3. A mass of ice attached to land but projecting into the sea is called what?

4. What name is given to a large chunk of floating ice that's hazardous to ships?

5. What name is given to a steep part of a glacier resembling a frozen waterfall?

6. What name is given to the yellow-white glare in the sky caused by reflection from an ice field?

7. A vessel with a reinforced bow for cutting a channel through ice is called what?

8. What is a thick mass of ice permanently covering the polar regions?

9. What name is given to a buildup of ice on rivers that raises the water level, causing floods?

10. Ice crystals in polar skies that cause haloes and coronas are called what?

11. How would you describe something that is completely surrounded or covered by ice?

12. In the polar region a covering of ice over a large area is called what?

trivia

- The Arctic consists of the Arctic Ocean and parts of which eight continents?

CROSSWORD: Seeing Double

ACROSS
1 They lay green eggs
5 Atkinson in *Rat Race*
10 "Fiddle Fugue" composer
14 Not in the library
15 A safari quarry
16 Sheltered, at sea
17 Black Forest spa
19 Like streakers
20 Cute
21 Circulated, in a way
23 *Jersey Boys* director McAnuff
24 Postponement
25 Measly
29 Catamaran, for one
33 Tree
34 Hill by the sea
35 50-oared ship of myth
36 "I Just Wanna Stop" singer Vannelli
37 Le Moko et al.
38 Any of the Phillies, e.g.
39 Applied frosting
40 Something else
41 "___ Know How To Love Him"
42 Town & Country, for one
44 Burial chambers
45 Befitting a con man
46 ___ *Hear a Waltz?*
47 Arctic abodes
50 Apocalyptic quartet
55 Martian combiner
56 GI Joe's "Ooh la-la!"
58 Recover
59 Spam not in a can
60 Jump
61 Out, in baseball
62 Accepts a challenge
63 "___ sow, so shall …"

DOWN
1 Napoleon's 1814 address
2 *Beowulf* beverage
3 Rescind
4 An end to fun?
5 Second-story man
6 Academic hurdles
7 Like a Windsor tie
8 *Fish* star Vigoda
9 "Gay" decade
10 Black-and-white Australian snake
11 "*C'est* ___" ("it's his")
12 Decide not to keep
13 Take seriously
18 *Civic Arousal* author
22 ___ segno
24 Less loony
25 Criss Angel's art
26 Psychoanalyst Fromm
27 Daisy Mae's man
28 Smugly self-righteous
29 "Excellent!"
30 Ship deck
31 ICM employee
32 Actionable acts
34 Star in the Swan
37 Fine-tuned
41 Wolfhound breed
43 ___-mo
44 Florida snakes
46 *The Many Loves of* ___ *Gillis*
47 "___ Lonesome Hobo": Dylan
48 Mushroomed
49 Olin in *The Reader*
50 Construction piece
51 *Rooster Cogburn* heroine
52 Brit. awards
53 "Buy It Now" site
54 A barber may shave this
57 *Be Cool* actress Thurman

Word Sudoku

Complete the grid so that each row, each column, and each 3 x 3 frame contains the nine letters from the black box below. The hidden nine-letter word is in the diagonal from top left to bottom right.

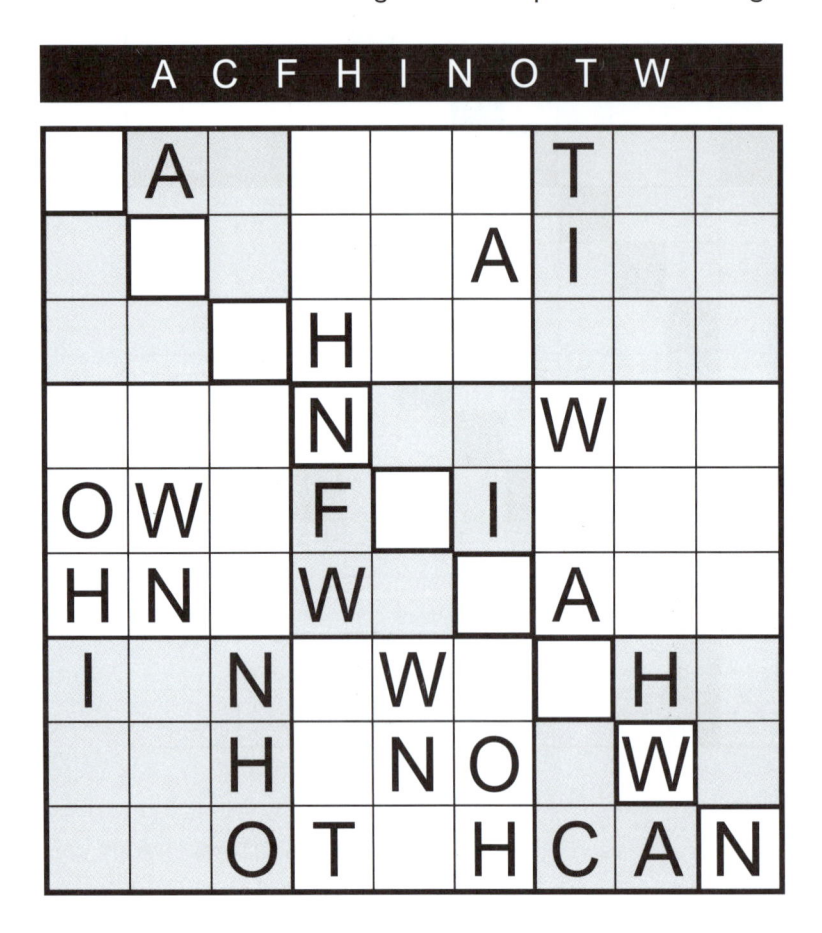

A C F H I N O T W

	A				T			
				A	I			
			H					
			N		W			
O	W		F		I			
H	N		W		A			
I		N	W			H		
		H		N	O		W	
		O	T		H	C	A	N

trivia

• What New York building is 1,047 feet high?

UNCANNY TURN

Rearrange the letters of the word below to form a cognate anagram, one that is related or connected in meaning to the original word. The answer can be one or more words.

LISTEN

BRAINSNACK® Getting Hot

Which temperature should replace the question mark?

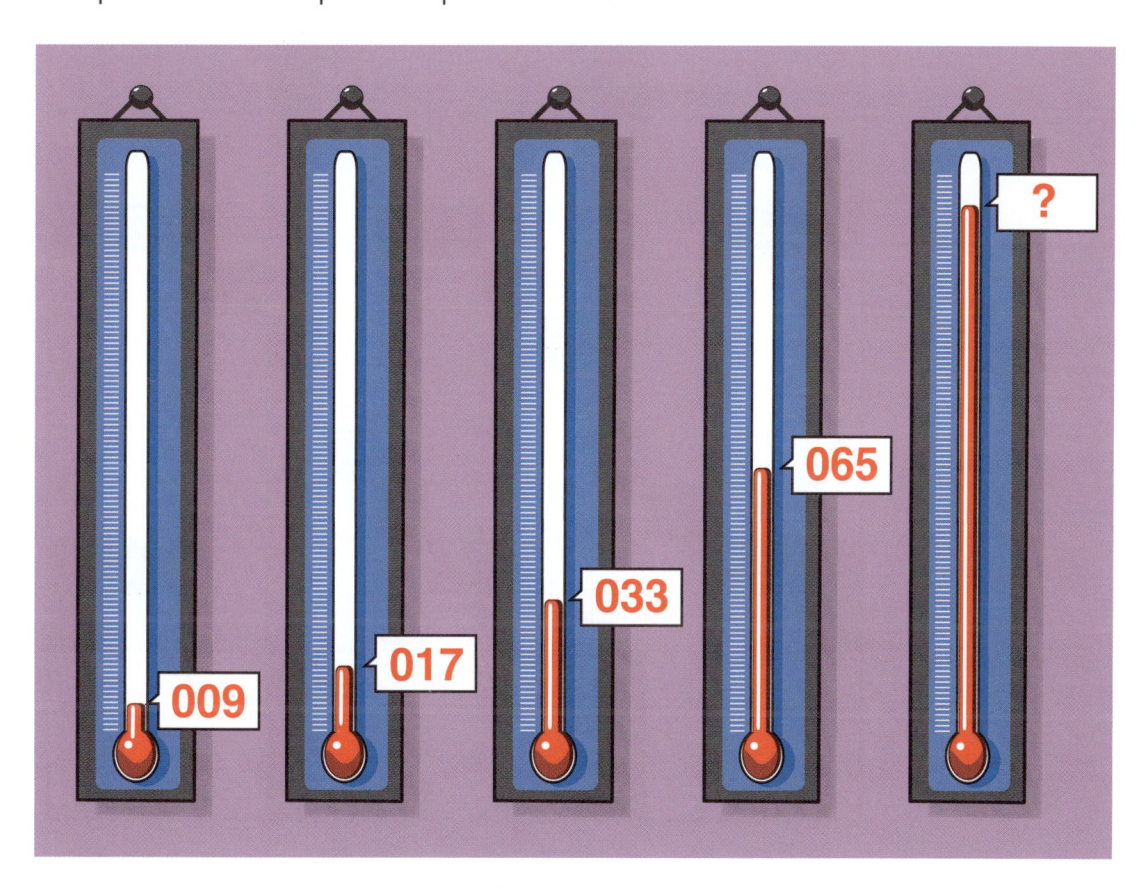

009 017 033 065 ?

WORD POWER

A collective noun is one that refers to a group of people, animals, or things considered as a whole. What is the collective noun for rhinoceroses?

_____

CROSSWORD: Superstars

ACROSS

1. Etel in *The Water Horse*
5. A Bordeaux wine
10. Above the ___
14. Take on cargo
15. *Nadja* actress Löwensohn
16. Tribal tales
17. Had ___ (knew someone)
18. A choir may stand on it
19. Arizona city
20. *The American* star
23. Banana throwaway
24. Chaney in *False Faces*
25. *Celebrity Mole* host Ahmad
28. "Take ___ from one who's tried ...": Dylan
30. Shriver of tennis
33. 10th-century German king
34. Straight ___ arrow
35. Prefix for wine lovers
36. *Meet the Fockers* star
39. Cheese with a rind
40. "Cool!"
41. Mountain detritus
42. Puppy's 2¢ worth
43. Almost closed
44. Julia in *Mona Lisa Smile*
45. "In a pig's ___!"
46. A convertiplane
47. *The Tourist* star
53. *Burlesque* star
54. "Image" combiner
55. Sandler in *Just Go With It*
57. Window sheet
58. Good manners
59. Rushed headlong
60. "It's ___!"
61. Williams of *Happy Days*
62. Grammy winner Fitzgerald

DOWN

1. ___ Provençale
2. k.d. of country
3. Singer Brickell
4. One who fears foreigners
5. Came together
6. Architect Gottlieb ___ Saarinen
7. 45 or 78
8. "The ___ lama, he's a priest ...": Nash
9. Monaco princess
10. Neil on *Scrubs*
11. Libertine
12. Salvation ___
13. "Indeed!"
21. Broadcast again
22. Ooola's husband
25. Benson in *Harry and Son*
26. *Asteroids* game company
27. Las Vegas main drag
28. "Hitch your wagon to ___": Emerson
29. Like cranberries
30. *The Good Earth* novelist Buck
31. Year in Paris
32. Statistical values
34. Between ports
35. Behave like some fans
37. Huston in *Agnes Browne*
38. "How much ___ much?"
43. Senate vote
44. Jill in *Diamonds Are Forever*
45. Wetlands wader
46. ___ Domingo
47. *Moby Dick* mariner
48. Honolulu Zoo bird
49. Windows symbol
50. Entre ___ (confidentially)
51. Not just a star
52. Tupper of Tupperware
53. Tax advisor
56. *Marry ___ Little*: Sondheim

Cage the Animals

Draw lines to completely divide up the grid into small squares, with exactly one animal per square. The squares should not overlap.

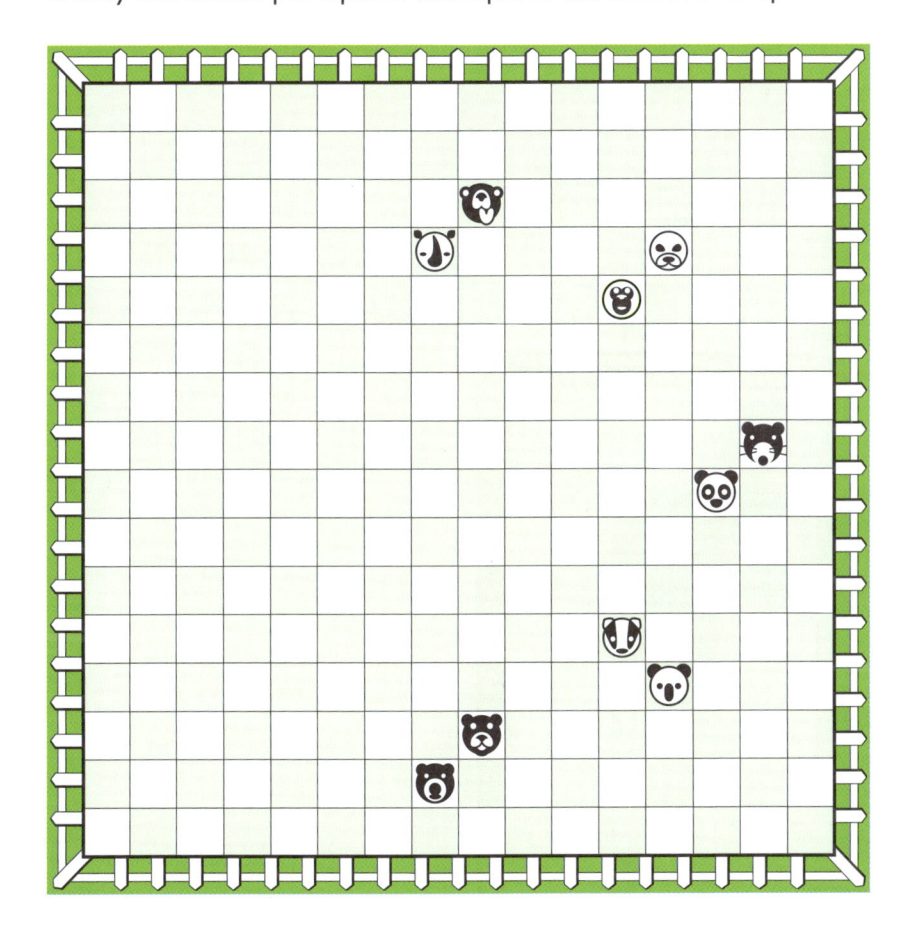

do you KNOW?

What name is given to a group of larks?

_____

DOODLE PUZZLE

A doodle puzzle is a combination of images, letters, and/or numbers that represent a word or a concept. If you cannot solve a doodle puzzle, do not look at the answer right away. Think hard—and outside the box.

ED (surrounded by SUR SUR SUR SUR SUR SUR SUR SUR)

Keep Going

Start on a blank square of your choice and connect as many blank squares as possible with one single continuous line. You can only connect squares along vertical and horizontal lines, not along diagonal lines. You must continue the connecting lineup until the next obstacle, i.e., the border of the box, a black square, or a square that already has been used. You can change direction at any obstacle you meet. Each square can only be used once. The number of blank squares that will be left unused is marked in the upper square. There is more than one solution. We only show one solution.

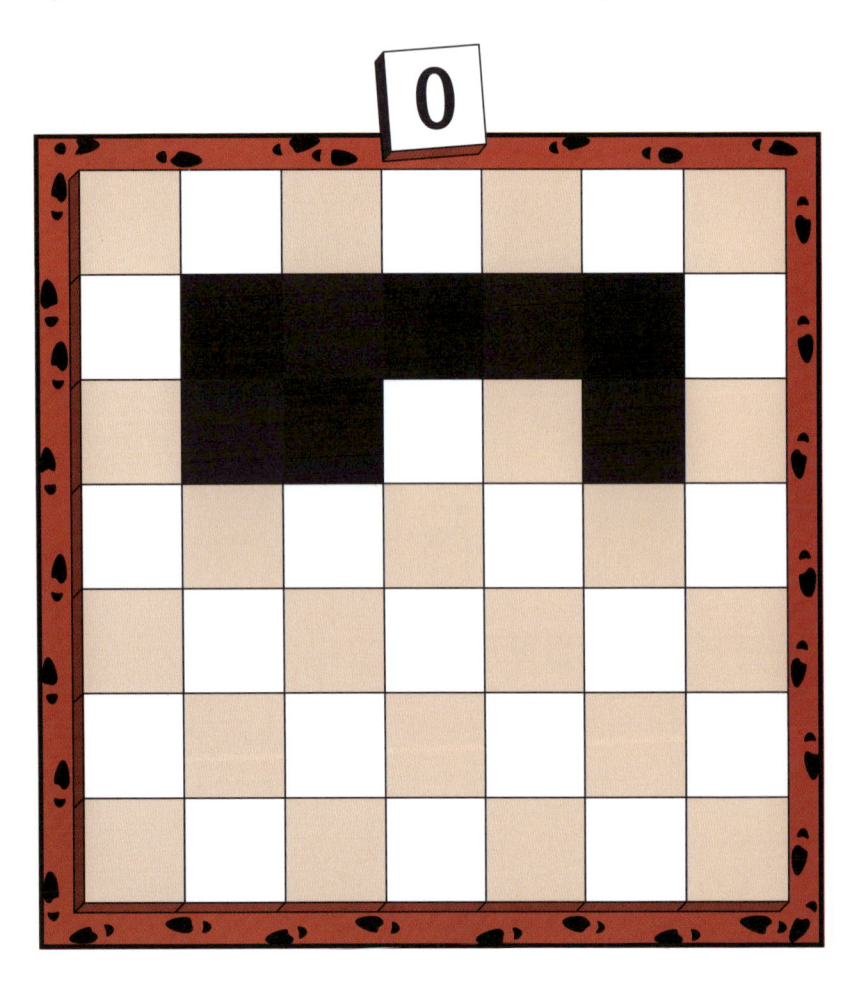

0

delete ONE

Delete one letter from the word below
SAGITTARIUS
and rearrange the rest to find players.

WORD SEARCH: The Rolling Stones

All the words are hidden vertically, horizontally, or diagonally—in both directions.

```
T H E S T O N E R S L A S T T
O G J E R R Y E N O M U R W A
S U T H E E G I T R G M O S T
L I U G D G C R A C R O T I V
E T G T A R R E S T E D L H E
Y A T J R R C S E H C P A V C
E R E L A L I E L D O T S H B
S H R O P X S L T A R W A U U
U U G H T E U S A E D R S U S
W R C I I F M O E P I N E A I
O O E R H U K S B S N G A I N
M S O T I Y C A M A G N N C E
E W I D A C O A D T S H W A S
N A A L C D R U G S T E Y U S
F T S I N G E R T N U I M T E
S T E W A R T E D H D S A T N
A S A T I S F A C T I O N T O
S E U L B E S L O H O C L A J
```

- ALCOHOL
- ANGIE
- ARRESTED
- BEATLES
- BIANCA
- BLUES
- BUSINESS
- CHARISMA
- CIRCUS
- DRUGS
- FAITHFULL
- GUITAR
- HIT PARADE
- JAGGER
- JERRY
- JONES
- LOGO
- MONEY
- RECORDING STUDIO
- REGGAE
- ROCK MUSIC
- SATISFACTION
- SCANDALS
- SHOWS
- SINGER
- SIXTIES
- STADIUMS
- STEWART
- SUSPECT
- WATTS
- WILD
- WOMEN
- WOOD
- WYMAN
- YOUTH

WORD POWER **News**

The folks at merriam-webster.com/news-trend-watch highlight words that are in the news. Test yourself to see how well informed you are.

1. **amnesty** ('am-neh-stee) *n.*—
   A: treason. B: pardon.
   C: safe haven.

2. **harridan** ('har-eh-den) *n.*—
   A: brief, wild storm.
   B: mercenary soldier.
   C: haggard, old woman.

3. **repudiate** (rih-'pyu-dee-ayt) *v.*—
   A: overthrow.
   B: refuse to accept or support.
   C: divulge.

4. **indict** (en-'diyt) *v.*—
   A: point out.
   B: charge with a crime.
   C: vote.

5. **gentrification** (jen-treh-feh-'kay-shehn) *n.*—A: gender switch.
   B: uncultured upbringing.
   C: displacement of the poor by the affluent.

6. **sovereignty** ('sahv-er-en-tee) *n.*—
   A: full knowledge.
   B: supreme power.
   C: communal state.

7. **conflate** (kon-'flayt) *v.*—
   A: barter or deal. B: ignore.
   C: confuse or combine into a whole.

8. **solipsistic** (soh-lep-'sis-tik) *adj.*—
   A: highly egocentric. B: slick.
   C: applied to the lips.

9. **intransigence** (in-'tran-sih-jents) *n.*—A: stubbornness. B: hard travel.
   C: secret information.

10. **subterfuge** ('sub-ter-fyewj) *n.*—
    A: deceptive stratagem.
    B: underwater dwelling.
    C: cheap replica.

11. **inherent** (in-'hir-ent) *adj.*—
    A: inborn. B: granted by a will.
    C: leased for low cost.

12. **eponymous** (ih-'pah-neh-mes) *adj.*—A: unsigned.
    B: opposite in meaning.
    C: named for a person.

13. **intrepid** (in-'treh-pid) *adj.*—
    A: stumbling. B: unpleasantly hot.
    C: fearless.

14. **sectarian** (sek-'ter-ee-an) *adj.*—
    A: related to a horse.
    B: of religious factions.
    C: having six parts.

15. **culpable** ('kuhl-peh-buhl) *adj.*—
    A: blameworthy. B: likely to happen.
    C: not competent.

CROSSWORD: Take It Easy

ACROSS

1. Way not to run
5. Gillette ___ II Plus
9. Rocker Stefani
13. Drug clinic
15. *State Fair* state
16. Foofaraw
17. Green Giant product
19. Around
20. Gunther's granny
21. Brief biography
23. Author Deighton
24. "Beat it!"
28. Kind of bed
30. Longoria of *Desperate Housewives*
31. Play parts
33. They're out of their mines
34. Ill-fated Heyerdahl craft
35. Book after Micah
37. "Just ___!" ("Hold on!")
39. Adhere
41. Move your mum
43. London streetcar
45. Half-day exam, briefly
47. Artifact
49. "Michael Collins" org.
50. Stop
52. Art ___
53. Temporal expanse
54. Big name on Broadway
57. Visits, briefly
59. Digit
60. Copperfield's first wife
62. Total
63. Ripening need
65. He was Basil Fawlty
70. Mideast strip
71. Opposite of sans
72. Connecticut Bulldog
73. Dagger of yore
74. Verne submariner
75. Great dog

DOWN

1. Husky sound
2. Debussy's *La* ___
3. "So there you are!"
4. Primitive musical instrument
5. Tout's offering
6. ___ Wade
7. Mark time
8. Cuban dictator
9. Pontiac of song
10. The Red Sox won the 100th one
11. Ford with no future
12. Peter who was Herman
14. Lament
18. Kind of races Petty won
22. Surrounding glow
24. Dictionary designation
25. To no ___ (uselessly)
26. Significant other
27. Upper regions of space
29. Robin's home
32. Improve, in a way (with "up")
36. Subterranean pests
38. Chocolate alternative
40. Paint with a sponge
42. Toe preceders
44. Oodles
46. Even-steven
48. In a reserved manner
51. War Achilles fought in
54. Fawn fathers
55. *Crocodile Dundee* star
56. Treasure
58. Petition
61. "Excuse me ..."
64. Actress Dawn Chong
66. Sgt. or Cpl.
67. Guido's high note
68. Commandment violation
69. Width for Bigfoot

Sudoku

Fill in the grid so that each row, each column, and each 3 x 3 frame contains every number from 1 to 9.

9			4				5	7
3	4		1				2	
	2				3			
				5		4		8
2			3		9			6
5		6		7				
			9				8	
	3				8		4	5
6	5				1			3

do you KNOW?

Which river flows through the Grand Canyon?

_____

BLOCK ANAGRAM

Form the word that is described in the parentheses, using the letters above the grid. Extra letters are already in the right place.

MINOR   (Narcotic extracted from opium used to relieve pain)

			P	**H**		**E**

Ages Apart

Peter Out and Gail Force first met 16 years ago. At that time, Peter was twice Gail's age, but now Gail is two-thirds of Peter's age. How old was Peter when he first met Gail? Use the graph below to help you solve this puzzle.

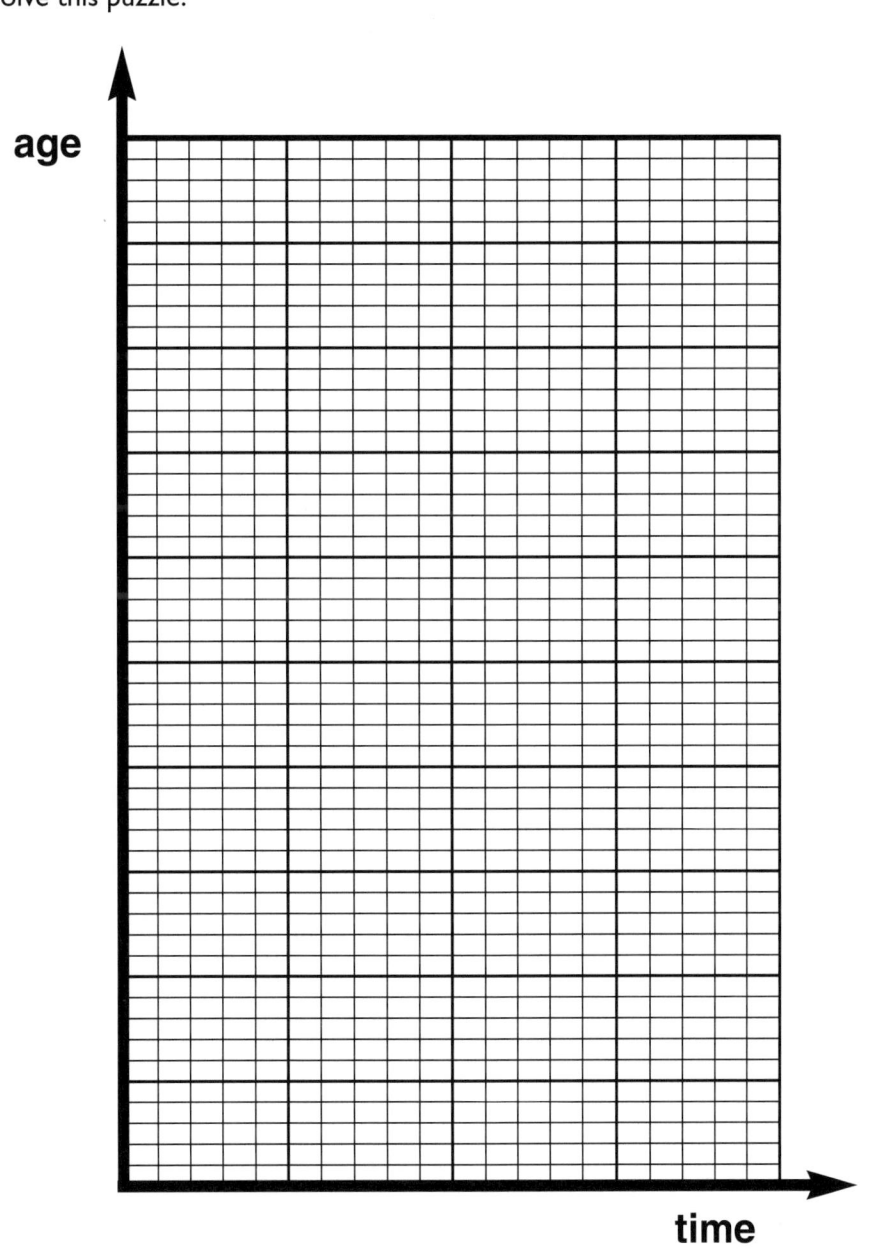

CROSSWORD: Tree-Huggers

ACROSS

1. Org. cofounded by Helen Keller
5. Exodus plague
9. Roll up
14. *Daily Planet* reporter
15. "Kookie" Byrnes et al.
16. Quebec peninsula
17. *Freddy's Dead* setting
19. Beelike
20. Like newborns
21. *Cast Away* setting
22. Prevaricate
23. *As I Lay Dying* character
24. *Peanuts* character
28. "Greater" Caribbean islands
32. Lei Day greeting
33. Arabic commander
34. All-Star game side
35. Dutch singer DeLange
36. *All My Children* vixen
37. *The Thin Man* canine
38. Monte Carlo roulette bet
39. Oasis fruit
40. "Come here ___?"
41. Forever and a day
43. Cleared tables
44. City near Tokyo
45. "___ a problem"
46. Irrational fear
49. Battle of Tours locale
54. 100-cent coins
55. *Huffington Post* senior editor
56. ___ brûlée
57. Major ending
58. ___ for one's money
59. No neat freaks
60. Got a load of
61. Dover fish

DOWN

1. *Guantanamera* director
2. "Common" ailment
3. Prom night rental
4. Cold War superpower
5. *The Love Bug* car
6. "Chasing Pavements" singer
7. Henri's thought
8. *Saving Private Ryan* carrier
9. 2001 Australian Open winner
10. Toronto skaters
11. Argento in *XXX*
12. 9-inch measure
13. Forward
18. Shire in *Chantilly Lace*
21. "Inter" opposite
23. "Have ___ day!"
24. "Dirigo" is its motto
25. Allocate
26. *Bye Bye Birdie* girl
27. 1988 John Mellencamp song
28. *Jaws* setting
29. Cobblers' forms
30. *Teen Wolf Too* actress Chandler
31. Vendor's booth
33. "The Lovely" Muse
36. Jennifer's *Ab Fab* role
40. "They're ___ get me!"
42. Attention getters
43. A l'anglaise
45. *48 HRS* actor
46. Above the abs
47. Be a pitcher
48. Chocolate cookie
49. Compassion
50. "As ___ saying …"
51. 470-mile Spanish river
52. *The Addams Family* star Julia
53. "… auld lang ___"
55. Flea-size

BRAINSNACK® Cheese Escape

What is the minimum number of cheese cubes the mouse has to eat to escape from the maze?

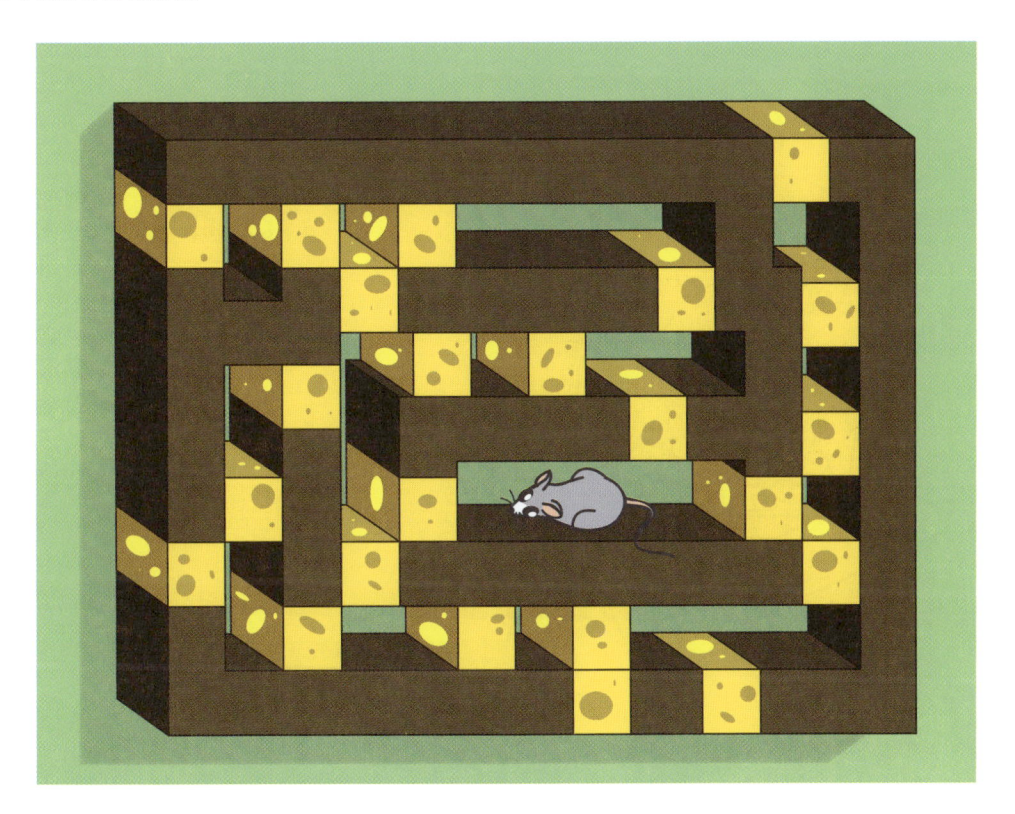

LETTER LINE

Put a letter in each of the squares below to make a word that means "yielded." The number clues refer to other words that can be made from the whole.

3 5 2 PRONOUN • 8 5 1 7 4 GULLED
6 5 1 VESSEL

1	2	3	4	5	6	7	8

Spot the Differences

Find the nine differences in the image on the bottom right.

do you KNOW?

What is the fear of spiders called?

_____

trivia

- What was the name of King Arthur's sword?

_____

Binairo

Complete the grid with zeros and ones until there are 6 zeros and 6 ones in every row and every column. No more than two of the same number can be next to or under each other. Rows or columns with exactly the same content are not allowed. There is only one valid solution.

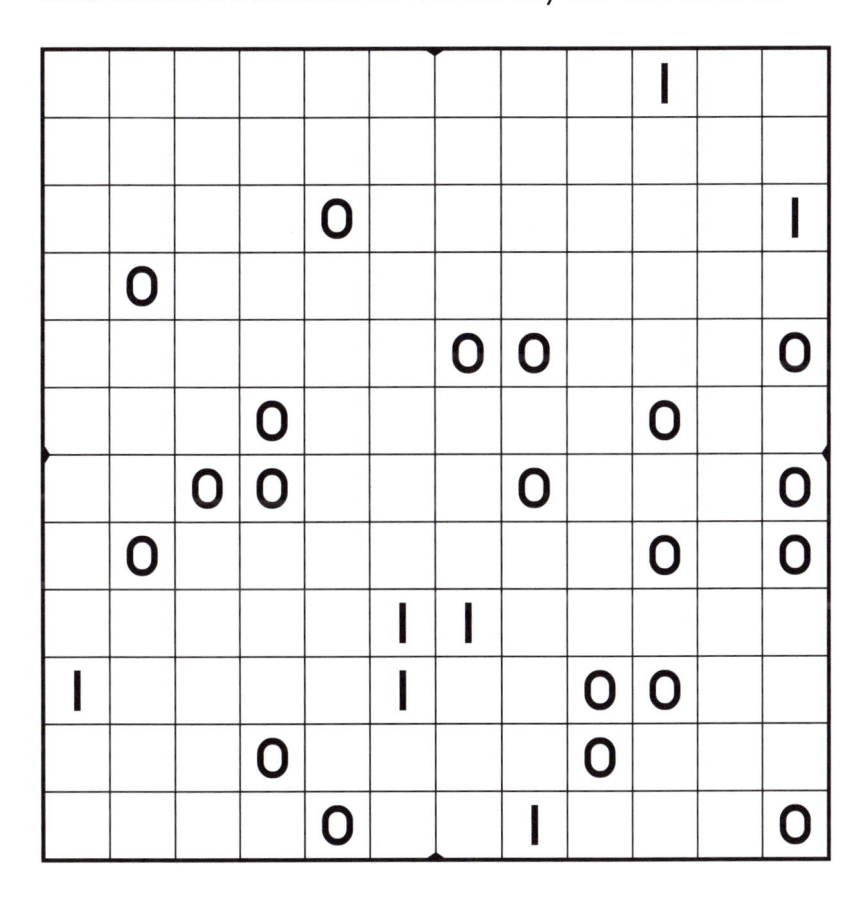

do you KNOW?

Which ocean is to the east of Africa?

_____

LETTERBLOCKS

Move the letterblocks around so that words associated with marriage are formed on the top and bottom rows. In some blocks the letter from the top row has been switched with the letter from the bottom row.

L L S Y A P O
M C D B A A A

TRIVIA QUIZ — Short for...

LOL (lots of luck) with these three-letter acronyms!

1. In the world of computers and the Internet, what does FTP stand for?

2. In the British police force, what does CID stand for?

3. In the world of stamp-collecting, what is an FDC?

4. The underground network of which city includes a service called the RER?

5. What does RMS stand for when referring to a ship—as in the RMS *Queen Mary 2*?

6. In the world of accident and emergency, what does SAR stand for?

7. In the jargon of the advertising world, what does USP stand for?

8. What does FBI stand for?

9. In an airport, what important function is known by the acronym ATC?

10. The Soviet secret police was the Komitet Gosudarstvennoi Bezopasnosti (KGB). What does that mean in English?

11. In home technology, what does the acronym VCR stand for?

12. In text messages and emails, what do the initials BTW mean?

13. The military forces of which country are known as the PLA?

14. What does the first D in DVD stand for?

15. Which airport has the code LHR?

16. What do the initials of the elite force SAS stand for?

CROSSWORD: School Clubs

ACROSS

1. You might have searched for Bobby Fischer here, 2 words
6. Club for those who love numbers
9. BBQ item
11. Subjects for discussion in Chem Club
12. Club for those who make a good case
13. Grown-up kitten
14. Vintage
16. High _____, Gary Cooper movie
17. Winter sports gear
18. A in Austria
20. Vote into office
22. Japanese currency
23. Frank Herbert sci-fi classic
25. Club for budding actors and actresses
27. _____ Crackers, Marx brothers movie
28. Either's partner
30. Sports judge
32. GoodFellas actress Mazar
34. Club for choral songs
35. Middling grade
37. Spelling contest
38. Club made up of the major interscholastic winners
39. Up to, for short
41. Bond's foe in Goldfinger
42. Popular band club for stepping in time

DOWN

1. They perform organized chants and dances at games
2. Chris of tennis fame
3. Make sure of something, 3 words
4. Dance club for rumba and samba or ancient language
5. Actress Derek
6. Get together
7. With 31 down, athletic club for hurdles, high jump, etc., 3 words
8. Top of the charts
10. "Heavens to _____!"
12. _____ Ackroyd of The Blues Brothers fame
13. Student _____, leadership group
15. Remote button
19. Charlie McCarthy and _____ Bergen
21. Little _____, who sang "Loco-Motion"
22. Annual roundup of students and their achievements and qualities
24. Expression of goodwill
26. Hawkeye Pierce actor
29. Reunion attendees
31. See 7 down
33. One section of a relay race
35. Setting of a Barry Manilow hit
36. Singer Clapton
37. Signal at Sotheby's
39. Gift-tag word
40. St. Louis arch state (abbr.)

Word Sudoku

Complete the grid so that each row, each column, and each 3 x 3 frame contains the nine letters from the black box below. The hidden nine-letter word is in the diagonal from top left to bottom right.

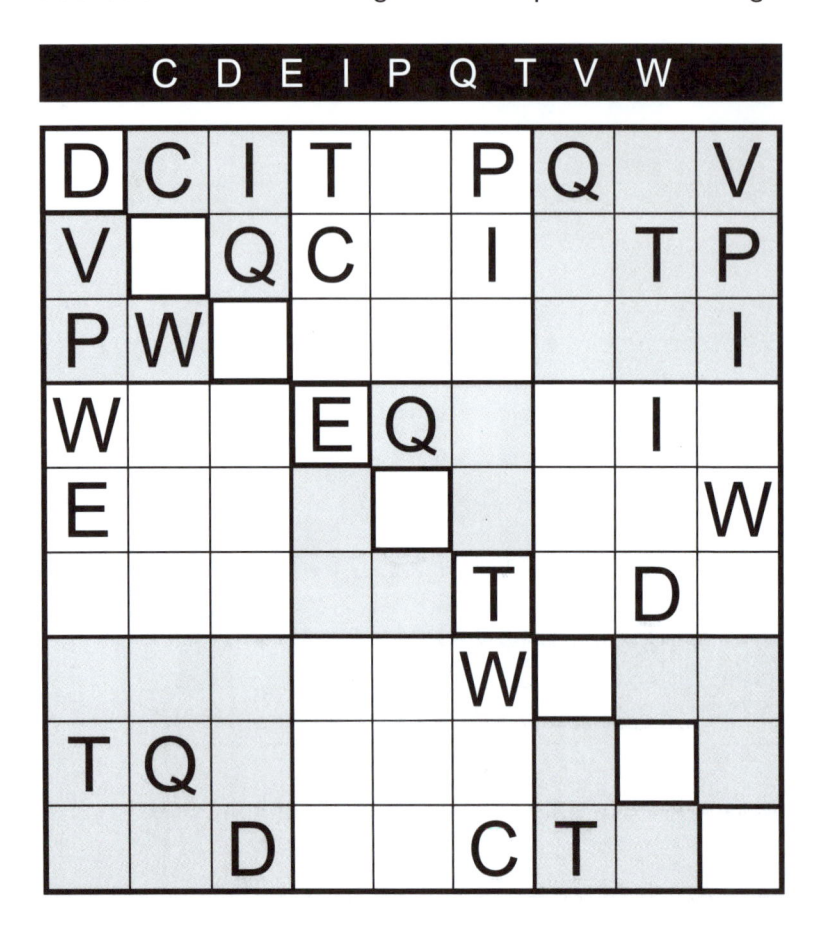

C D E I P Q T V W

D	C	I	T		P	Q		V
V		Q	C		I		T	P
P	W							I
W			E	Q			I	
E								W
					T		D	
				W				
T	Q							
		D			C	T		

trivia

- Which U.S. territory drives on the left?

UNCANNY TURN

Rearrange the letters of the phrase below to form a cognate anagram, one that is related or connected in meaning to the original phrase. The answer can be one or more words.

HERE COME DOTS

BRAINSNACK® Cubed

Which piece (1–6) completes the cube?

INHERITANCE TEST

A family had a piece of land. It was decided that a will would be made so that the two sons and two daughters would each inherit equal amounts of land of similar shape. The triangular part had already been sold to a developer. How was the land shared?

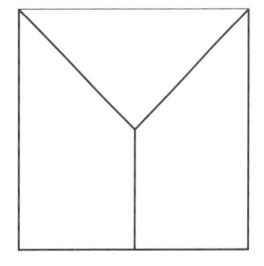

CROSSWORD: Wet Set

ACROSS
1. Henry VIII's sixth
5. Appeared
10. Aerobic gait
13. Hatred
15. Campus group
16. Conquistador's cache
17. Legendary blues singer (1915–1983)
19. Rhine feeder
20. Cordoba coin
21. Before
22. ___ Christum
23. Thin wedge
25. Bound by oath
27. Amount so far
31. Rani's robe
32. Chi follower
33. Gannet
35. "Nevermore" bird
38. Loaf
40. Big wheel
42. Helen of Troy's mother
43. Sum
45. Himalayan humanoids?
47. Periphery
48. "None of ___ business!"
50. Permit holder
52. Tear
55. Billionth: Comb. form
56. Marathon
57. Hawaiian dish
59. Scotch-and-vermouth cocktail
63. Oahu music maker
64. "Wild Horses" singer
66. Arthur in *Maude*
67. ___ *World Turns*
68. Confuse
69. Taxpayer's ID: Abbr.
70. Submerge
71. It's 88 days on Mercury

DOWN
1. Magnificence
2. Together, musically
3. Eliminates
4. Most impolite
5. Hard-rock links
6. Learning method
7. Ernani is one
8. Makes coleslaw
9. Car finish?
10. *The Celebrity Apprentice 2* winner
11. Address the multitude
12. Like some Pamplona runners
14. Legendry
18. Work as a garçon
22. Acoustic
24. Indian Ocean archipelago
26. Shake up
27. Brochette
28. 4-H Club sponsor: Abbr.
29. "Loverboy" singer
30. Classify
34. Out
36. Falco of *Nurse Jackie*
37. Handle
39. Marry cheaply
41. Stomach soother
44. Brynner in *Taras Bulba*
46. Lady of "la casa"
49. Banquet
51. "I Ain't Got ___": Williams
52. Thrashes
53. Roués
54. Flourless cake
58. ___ *Jury*: Spillane
60. Took the train
61. Norman locale: Abbr.
62. River to the North Sea
64. Petrol
65. Wise to

WEATHER CHART **Sunny**

Where will the sun shine? With the knowledge that each arrow points to a place where a symbol should be, can you locate the sunny spots? The symbols cannot be next to each other vertically, horizontally, or diagonally. A symbol cannot be placed on top of an arrow. We show one symbol.

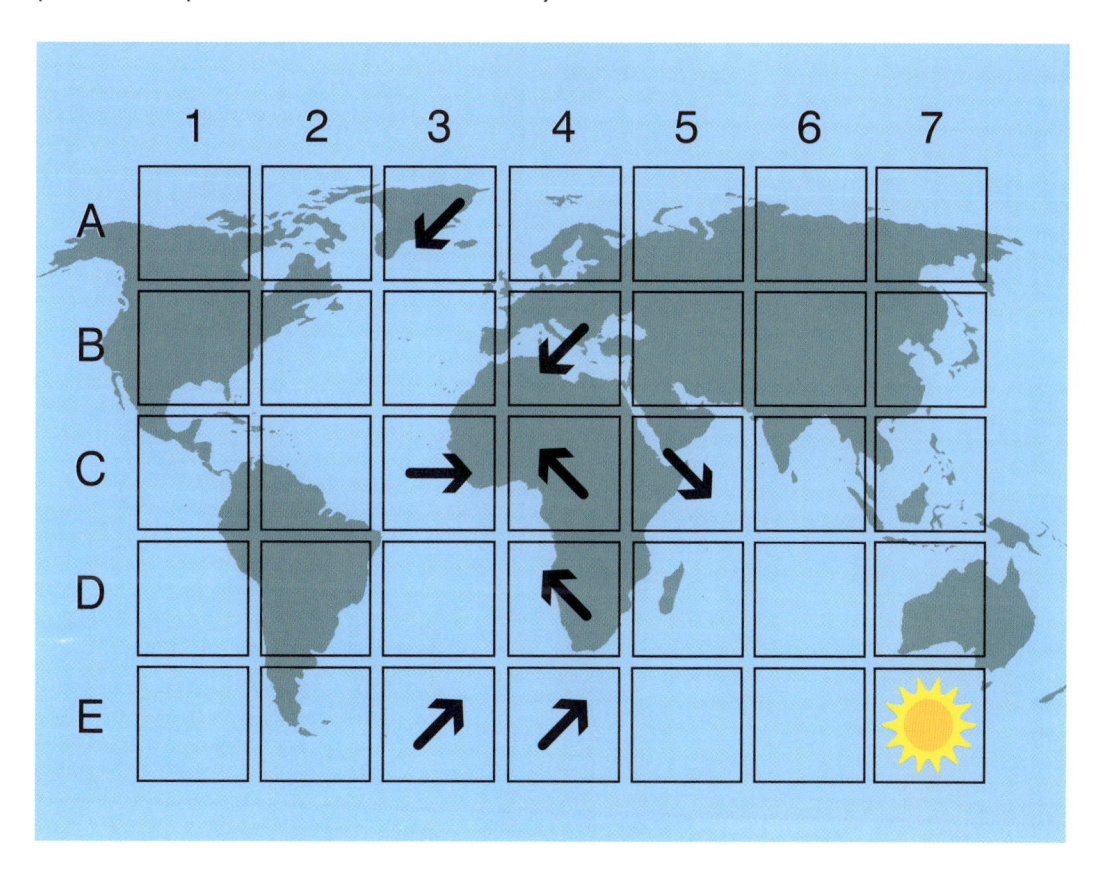

DOUBLETALK

What seven-letter word is satisfied, yet often needs an index?

Sport Maze

Draw the shortest way from the ball to the goal. You can only move along vertical and horizontal lines, not along diagonal lines. The figure on each square indicates the number of squares the ball must move in the same direction. You can change direction at each stop.

4	1	1	5	3	1
4	3	4	3	2	
1	3	3	1	4	5
2	2	2	1	2	3
2	3	2	2	2	5
1	1	2	2	2	2

trivia
- Where does Charles Foster Kane live?

REPOSITION PREPOSITION

Unscramble **SEAWALLS** and find a three-word preposition.

WORD SEARCH: Reptiles

All the words are hidden vertically, horizontally, or diagonally—in both directions.

```
R E P T I L D S E A S N A K E
E X O T I C E N S L R S I R R
V E D I A N D H A U E B P O O
L A E C E N C R A L S T O T V
V H R A T E A S A A R R E C I
E M M E E U O C N Z E A G I N
R U I L T N S T O P I R E R R
T I S I I A C T I N I L C T A
E R M D S A T V V O D E K S C
B A O O G N O F O E R A O N G
R R N C N A R E F L E X O O T
A R E O U U T G H E E R R C L
T E V R L G O A O M N F I W M
E T A C L I I M S A S U A C H
A S D E S E S A R H N R T S A
N D M O U N E M T C C N A I N
O N O H T Y P B U S R E A G I
O N S T U A T A R A T O A D S
```

- ANACONDA
- ANOLIS
- CARNIVORE
- CHAMELEON
- COBRA
- CONSTRICTOR
- CRAWL
- CROCODILE
- DERMIS
- DINOSAUR
- EXOTIC
- FROG
- GECKO
- GOANNA
- IGUANA
- LAND
- LEECH
- LIZARD
- LUNGS
- MAMBA
- PYTHON
- REFLEX
- SCALES
- SEA SNAKE
- TERRARIUM
- TOADS
- TORTOISE
- TUATARA
- VENOM
- VERTEBRATE
- VIPER

TRIVIAL PURSUIT # Gotta Dance!

Each year of the 1950s offered movie musicals filled with catchy songs and spectacular dancing—with 1954 being especially tuneful.

TAP YOUR MEMORY OF THE MELODIC DELIGHTS THAT GRACED SCREENS THAT YEAR.

1 Vincente Minnelli directed this story of two Americans who find a mystical Scottish town.

2 This star revolutionized the movie musical in the 1950s with innovative choreography and complex dance sequences.

3 Judy Garland starred in this remake of a 1937 drama about an actress who becomes more famous than her mentor.

4 Michael Kidd put dancers through their paces in this musical set in the wilds of Oregon.

5 This seasonal favorite has Bing Crosby singing the top-selling holiday song of all time.

6 Can you name the redheaded comedian who was Bing's co-star in that holiday musical?

7 Dorothy Dandridge was the first African American to be nominated for Best Actress for this take on a French opera.

8 Ethel Merman belted out what was one of her signature tunes in this musical about vaudeville.

trivia

- Many believed it was Mitzi Gaynor who played Judy Haynes in the musical movie *White Christmas*, but in fact it was an American dancer/actress known for her solo performances as well as her work with partners.

CROSSWORD: U.S. History

ACROSS
1 Fancy-schmancy
5 *Hardball* network
10 Headless cabbage
14 Eye layer
15 "That's ___ excuse for ..."
16 In the thick of
17 Vice President in 1804
18 Engine booster
19 Off-white
20 U.S. President who spoke Dutch
23 Derek Jeter, for one
24 ___ Kan
25 Apian groups
28 *You've Got* ___ (1998)
30 The woman yonder
33 The ends of the earth
34 *True Grit* star
36 Urbi et ___
37 Aristae
38 Chef's wear
39 Subject of an 1857 Supreme Court decision
41 First U.S. President to marry in office
42 Cyclone center
43 Grow faint
44 With kindness
45 *For Me and My* ___
46 Irish ___ bread
47 U.S. President from New Hampshire
54 Composer Schifrin
55 Gold medalists, often
56 Like Granny Smith apples
58 "___ my wit's end"
59 Hardy in *A Chump at Oxford*
60 Friend of Coleridge
61 *High Noon* hero Will
62 ___-foot oil
63 "Take Me Or Leave Me" musical

DOWN
1 Tavern
2 Egg
3 "*Buona* ___" (Italian greeting)
4 Nevada statesman
5 Morning prayer
6 Mettle
7 NFL coach Turner
8 ___ Fett (*Star Wars* bounty hunter)
9 Former CBS anchor
10 Afghanistan capital
11 Cupid
12 Ancestry
13 First lady's garden
21 Flat hats
22 Like old tires
25 English potter
26 Brood
27 *Seascape* playwright
28 Unglossy finish
29 Rat-___ (drumbeat)
30 The Joker's expression
31 "___ California" (Eagles hit)
32 Gateway
34 "Are you putting ___?"
35 First Family member in 1980
37 Salad ingredient
40 Love letters?
41 Almanac topic
44 Auditory assaults
45 Yard
46 Banana ___
47 Hopper's nemesis
48 Vishnu incarnate
49 Mathematician Turing
50 Do nothing
51 Spike Lee heroine
52 NASCAR legend Yarborough
53 The Old Sod
57 Make a doily

Sudoku X

Fill in the grid so that each row, each column, and each 3 x 3 frame contains every number from 1 to 9. The two main diagonals of the grid also contain every number from 1 to 9.

								1
				6				
	9		1		4		5	2
		1	8		5		4	3
	8			4				
		9	2	1		7		5
		8	5					
	6	2					9	4
					5			

do you KNOW?

Castries is the capital of which Caribbean nation?

_____

GREEDY LETTER

Which is the only letter in the alphabet that has three syllables?

_____

BRAINSNACK® Party Time

Where (1–6) is the item that is located across from the item that is 3 places counterclockwise from the item that is across from the item to the left of the champagne cork?

LONELY WORDS

There are four words in the English language with which no word rhymes. What are they?

_____   _____   _____   _____

CROSSWORD: Oscar Winners

ACROSS
1 Rowlands in Hope Floats
5 Thumper's friend
10 "His Master's Voice" co.
13 *The Good Earth* heroine
14 Matriculate
15 Virtuous
16 *Schindler's* ___ (1993)
17 Conductor Doráti
18 1970 Paul Newman film
19 *Faith of Our* ___
21 Favorite of Scrooge
23 "___ bodkins!"
24 A Bobbsey twin
25 *Weekend at* ___ (1989)
29 Edgar Allan Poe poem
33 Daisy that's a weed
34 King's Plymouth Fury
36 Merit-badge holder
37 Saint of baseball
38 Mandlikova of tennis
39 Oscar-winning Elizabeth Taylor film
41 Vernal month
42 Leave for a while
43 "Bam!" chef Emeril
45 "Plop" preceder
46 Salon goo
47 Great Red Spot planet
51 "___ in the Air": Don McLean
55 Pianist Feinberg
56 Dunn and Charles
58 Razzed
59 D.C. team
60 Puzzle parts
61 Olive genus
62 Some dashes
63 "Maybe, Yes" singer Mandell
64 *What Women* ___ (2000)

DOWN
1 Sawgrass sport
2 *Baby Doll* director Kazan
3 GOP Elephant creator
4 *The Silence of the Lambs* Oscar winner
5 Amanda of *Married… With Children*
6 Murray and Beattie
7 "Pity the fool!" guy
8 Venice transportation
9 Monopoly avenue
10 One-sided victory
11 "___ fan tutte": Mozart
12 Singer Lambert
15 *Shakespeare in Love* Oscar winner
20 Warhol companion Sedgwick
22 Slangy negatives
25 Autumn pears
26 Raise on high
27 View anew
28 Caan of *Hawaii Five-O*
29 *Perry Mason* event
30 They're unbelievable
31 *Brokeback Mountain* hero
32 Football great "Greasy"
35 Lew Wallace's *Ben-*___
37 Fishburne in *The Matrix Revolutions*
40 Cecil Day Lewis, e.g.
41 *Rock of* ___
44 1992 Wimbledon winner
47 "Fascination" singer Morgan
48 Polish lancer
49 Butter squares
50 Shoot dice
51 Normandy city
52 Johnson in *A Prairie Home Companion*
53 Garden snake locale?
54 Do an usher's job
57 *Golden Girl* McClanahan

Cage the Animals

Draw lines to completely divide up the grid into small squares, with exactly one animal per square. The squares should not overlap.

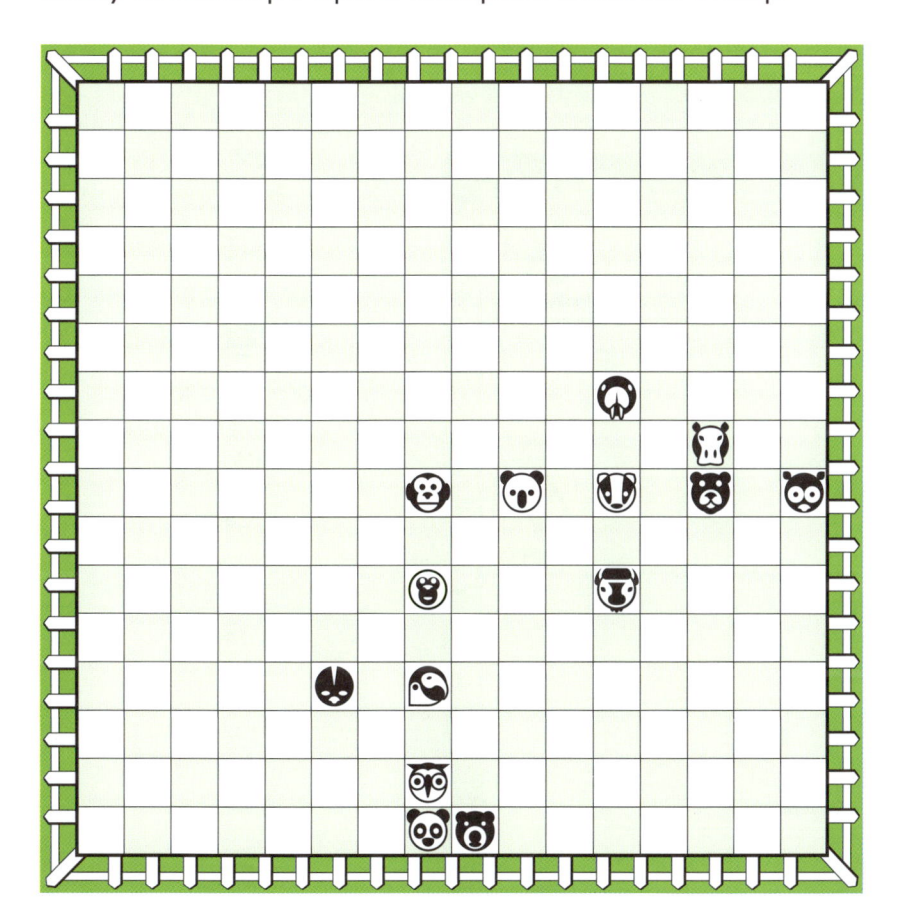

do you KNOW?

Which planet is Triton a moon of?

_____

DOODLE PUZZLE

A doodle puzzle is a combination of images, letters, and/or numbers that represent a word or a concept. If you cannot solve a doodle puzzle, do not look at the answer right away. Think hard—and outside the box.

Number Cluster

Cubes showing numbers have been placed on the grid below, with some spaces left empty. Can you complete the grid by creating runs of the same number and of the same length as the number? So, where a cube with number 5 has been included on the grid, you need to create a run of five number 5's, including the cube already shown. The run can be horizontal, vertical, or both horizontal and vertical.

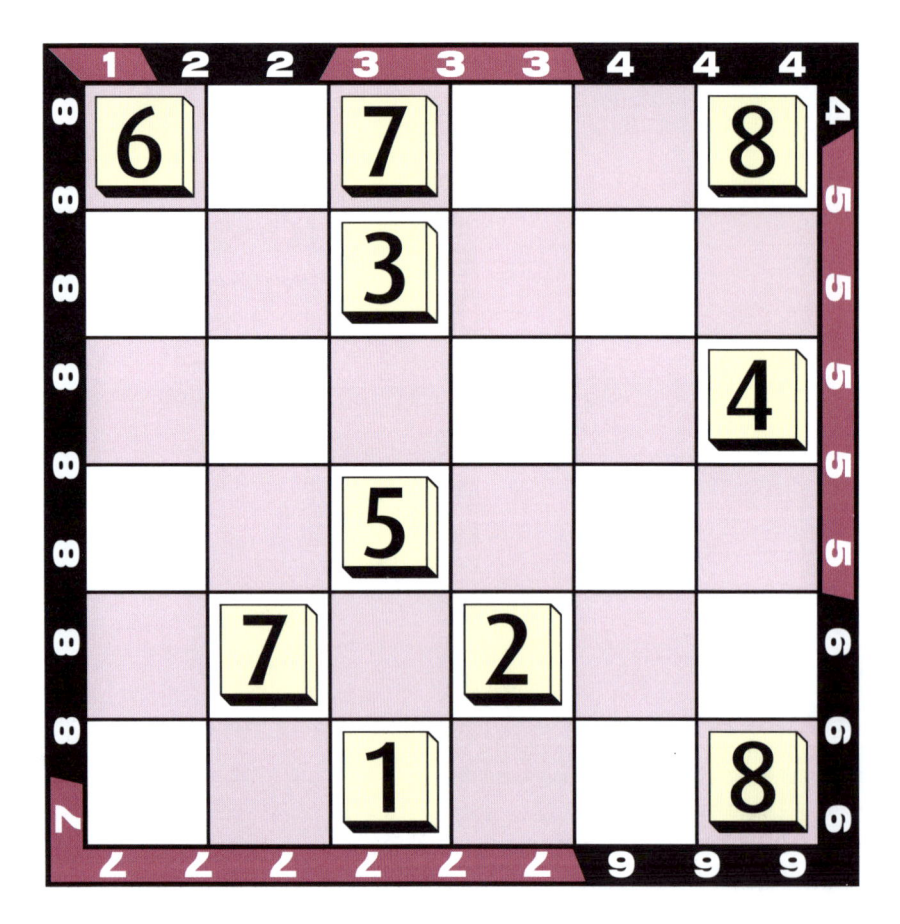

do you KNOW?

Which country is Lake Thingvalla located?

_____

FRIENDS

What do the following words have in common?

FOIL CRACKER CARBON PLANE SKIS LOGICAL

Binairo

Complete the grid with zeros and ones until there are 5 zeros and 6 ones in every row and every column. No more than two of the same number can be next to or under each other. Rows or columns with exactly the same content are not allowed. There is only one valid solution.

trivia

- Name the shipping line which owned the *Titanic*?

_____

LETTERBLOCKS

Move the letterblocks around so that words associated with marriage are formed on the top and bottom rows. In some blocks the letter from the top row has been switched with the letter from the bottom row.

```
I U M S U S U
L S N E R C U
```

TRIVIA QUIZ: Getting the Runaround

Do you know the most direct route for this round? If you're passionate about running, you will!

1. In 1975, which New Zealand athlete became the first man to run the mile in under 3 minutes 50 seconds?

2. In 1999, who smashed the men's 100-meter world record at a meet in Athens?

3. Which 1927 invention enabled sprinters to start faster?

4. In a 110-meter hurdles race, how many hurdles are negotiated?

5. Which well-known American won his second Olympic title in the 400-meter hurdles in 1984?

6. How many laps of the track are run for a 400-meter outdoor race in the Olympics?

7. Who won an Olympic gold medal for the 100 meters in 1924 and was portrayed in the film Chariots of Fire?

8. In what year were women's track and field events added to the Summer Olympics?

9. What distance is the longest track event in the women's heptathlon?

10. How many lanes are there on an Olympic running track?

11. Who claimed nine Olympic gold medals by winning the long jump in Atlanta?

12. Which American gold-medal winner of 1968 gave his name to a style of high jumping?

13. Which American gold-medal winner in the 1960 Olympics suffered from polio and wore leg braces until she was nine?

14. What company did Phil Knight and Bill Bowerman form in 1964 to market a lighter and more comfortable shoe?

CROSSWORD: Presidential Runners

ACROSS
1 "Brandenburg Concertos" composer
5 Super Bowl XXXIV winners
9 Lake Tuscawilla locale
14 Snoopy's original owner
15 Buck heroine
16 Spanish tennis star
17 River that joins the Neisse
18 Theda of silents
19 AOL message
20 He ran against Richard Nixon in 1972
23 *Netsuke* container
24 Spirit's shout
25 Communications satellite
28 Give an edge to
30 Fertility drug
33 Kurosawa's *The ___*
34 Boehner may try to pass it
36 Sean in *The Tree of Life*
37 Like a Bigfoot encounter
38 Langston Hughes poem
39 He ran for president four times
41 Endow with talent
42 Add-___ (extras)
43 How vichyssoise is served
44 Hannity's former debater
45 Kiev locale: Abbr.
46 Gloom's partner
47 He ran against George Bush in 1988
54 Palo Alto car company
55 *Maude* producer
56 Jekyll's alter ego
57 Turkic people of China
58 Installs carpeting
59 Scat singer Fitzgerald
60 Herbivore's snack
61 Where starter
62 Projectionist's unit

DOWN
1 Internet column
2 Home-care employee
3 Singer Laine
4 First Family of 1889
5 Downey or Kennedy
6 San Antonio landmark
7 "You Sang to Me" singer Anthony
8 Hose woe
9 Elections have been won by this
10 Small part for a big star
11 Purim month
12 Stretched out
13 "___ I Want to Do": Sugarland
21 Tiny pest
22 Stout
25 Anthrax antibiotic
26 Cinema name
27 Son of Zeus and Europa
28 Part of WHO
29 Eight, in Paris
30 "___ where they ain't": Willie Keeler
31 Like extra-inning games
32 Lip cosmetic
34 Canine command
35 HBO's *Real Time with ___*
37 Portuguese city
40 Aaron of *Thank You for Smoking*
41 Bibliophile's love
44 Heading
45 Bruin on the field
46 Attack times
47 Siesta preceder
48 Fisher in *Wedding Crashers*
49 She, in Cherbourg
50 Faithful
51 *South Park* kid
52 Thumb-twiddling
53 Easter ___
54 Recipe abbr.

Sudoku

Fill in the grid so that each row, each column, and each 3 x 3 frame contains every number from 1 to 9.

4			6			9	8	
		1	3	7				
	8		4	1				
	1					7	3	
							1	5
8	6							2
5								
	9	3		5				
						6		

trivia

- Who wrote *Pinocchio*?

_____

BLOCK ANAGRAM

Form the word that is described in the parentheses, using the letters above the grid. Extra letters are already in the right place.

Morons   (secretion of an endocrine gland)

H					E	

BRAINSNACK® # Ping-Pong

Which stroke (A–I) to the other table tennis player is wrong?

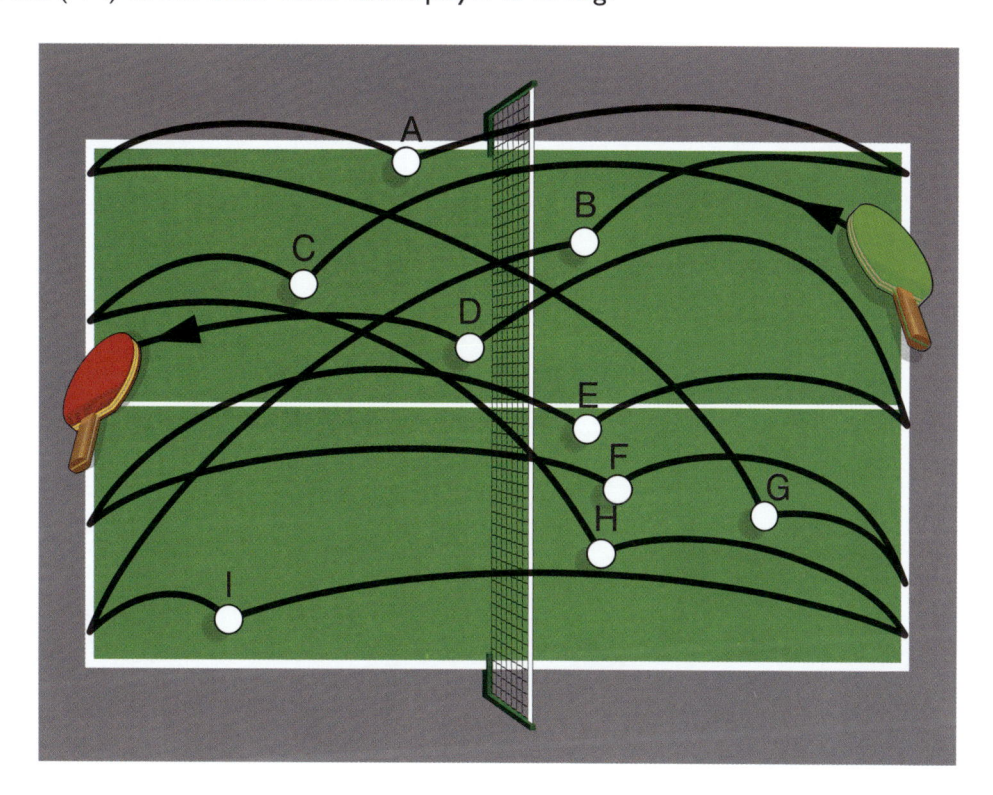

DOODLE PUZZLE

A doodle puzzle is a combination of images, letters, and/or numbers that represent a word or a concept. If you cannot solve a doodle puzzle, do not look at the answer right away. Think hard—and outside the box.

CROSSWORD: Hizzoner

ACROSS
1. Water dogs
5. Shinbones
11. Catherine Bell series
14. Tasteless
15. Go to extremes
16. Oaxaca "whoopee!"
17. New York City mayor in 1926
19. Luke Skywalker's friend
20. Bids first
21. Use a thurible
23. Irish oath
26. "Super!"
28. Bowls over
29. Close call
32. Coward's *Private* ___
33. Dawdle
34. Teachers' union
35. Avoided a tag
36. Debra in *Love Me Tender*
37. Tots up
38. Rhone tributary
39. Tennis cup
40. Badlands scenery
41. Troubadour instrument
43. Tongue-lash
44. Caught congers
45. Decked out
46. "Do You Want To Play" singer
48. At the ready
49. Mayor Koch et al.
50. Atlanta mayor in 1989
56. Ambient music pioneer
57. Resuscitate
58. *Hurlyburly* playwright
59. *The Office* receptionist
60. Arachnid
61. Dog-paddled

DOWN
1. JFK's successor
2. Jerry Quarry's 1970 opponent
3. Emeril's shout
4. Chatted
5. Skyline sights
6. Eric Trump's mom
7. Loudness units
8. Tick off
9. Picnic drink
10. Black magic
11. New York City mayor in 1973
12. "Oh, dear!"
13. Mapping subject
18. Belgian battlefield of WWI
22. Nightmarish street
23. Christmas tree
24. Iago's wife
25. San Francisco mayor in 2010
26. Monica of tennis
27. Poet Whitman
29. New Orleans mayor in 2009
30. Tranquilize
31. Mouthed off
33. Ex-NYC mayor Dinkins
36. Pasty
37. Aquarium bubblers
39. *A Fistful of* ___ (1964)
40. Like Robin Hood's men
42. Sandra in *Gidget*
43. Milwaukee slugger
45. Tylenol rival
46. Grand Cherokee, for one
47. Mode in *The Incredibles*
48. Like dust bowls
51. Cotton knot
52. Caesar's 506
53. Motor City union
54. Rajon Rondo's org.
55. Pink Panther, e.g.

Umbrella Trouble

A math teacher bought herself two umbrella which, when folded out, looked like this from above. Can you help her identify the missing number on her umbrellas? Study the numerical patterns and sequences, and fill in the absent figure. You will find that X often marks the spot.

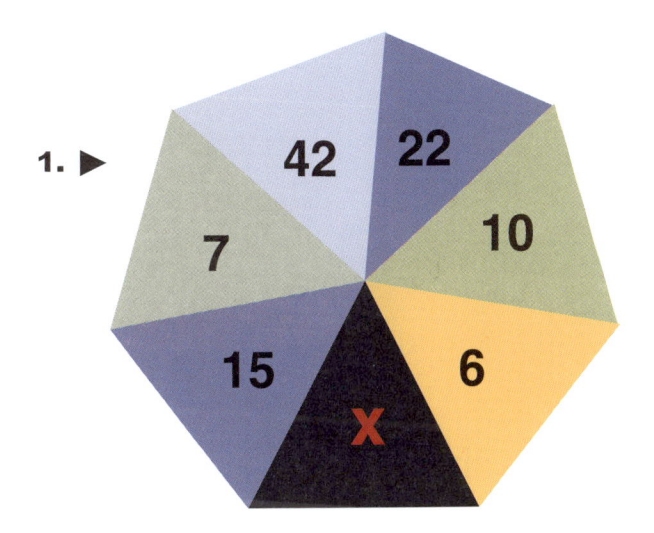

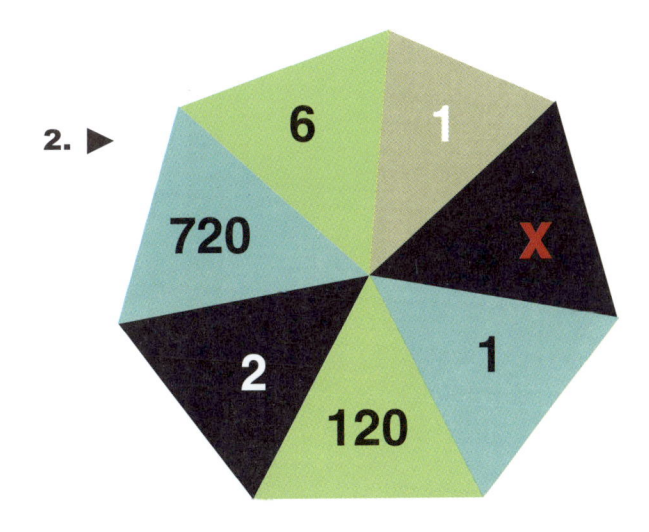

1. ▶

   42, 22, 10, 7, 15, 6, X

2. ▶

   6, 1, X, 1, 120, 2, 720

do you KNOW?

What is the cube root of 1728?

Keep Going

Start on a blank square of your choice and connect as many blank squares as possible with one single continuous line. You can only connect squares along vertical and horizontal lines, not along diagonal lines. You must continue the connecting lineup until the next obstacle, i.e., the border of the box, a black square, or a square that already has been used. You can change direction at any obstacle you meet. Each square can only be used once. The number of blank squares that will be left unused is marked in the upper square. There is more than one solution. We only show one solution.

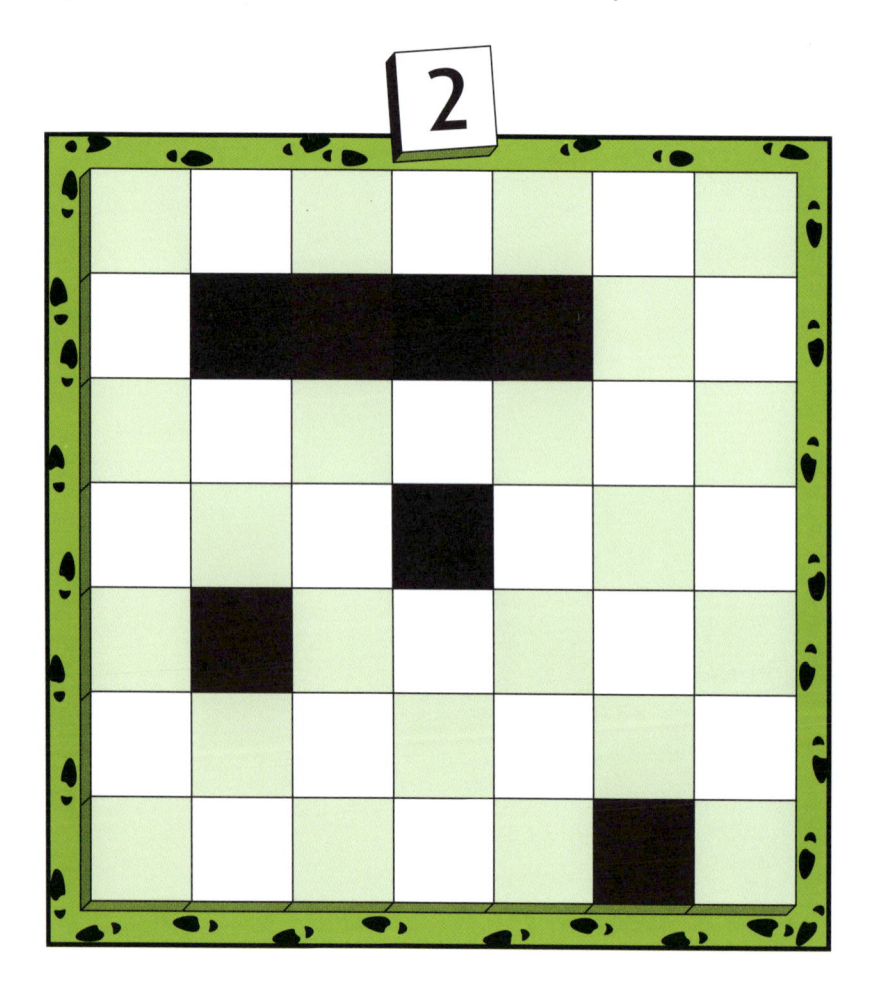

2

delete ONE

Delete one letter from **DESTINATION** and rearrange the rest to develop a limp.

_____

WORD SEARCH: Airplanes

All the words are hidden vertically, horizontally, or diagonally—in both directions.

```
S U I T C A S E D R O C N O C
T L T R O P R I A H O C E E U
S I E O F S E A I N R R P R L
R A A N U D K E T A S H A I A
E T S B I S K R S O M D E F M
T U R L C H O H G R A V I T Y
S I G D I L F S C R U S P I S
A E A N T O N O V D N E A P G
S A T O S T E W A R D E S S T
I V W R U N W A Y T I D S V R
D E A E A C O C T N N O E O A
R L V B S V A E O A Q U N E N
I O I U O T E E L N C G G G S
A P A E E M S L I O N L E A P
W U T R O L B T P H E A R G O
I T I T E E N S V I R S O G R
N N O N M U C U S T O M S U T
G R N E N F T A I R F I E L D
```

- AIR DISASTER
- AIRBUS
- AIRFIELD
- AIRPORT
- ANTONOV
- AVIATION
- BOMBS
- CATERING
- CONCORDE
- CONTROL TOWER
- CRASH
- CUSTOMS
- DOUGLAS
- FOKKER
- FUEL
- GLIDE
- GRAVITY
- LAND
- LUGGAGE
- MOTOR
- NOSE
- PASSENGER
- PILOT
- RADAR
- RUNWAY
- SPITFIRE
- STEWARDESS
- SUITCASE
- TAIL
- TRANSPORT
- TRAVEL
- TUPOLEV
- WING

WORD POWER — On the Job

Employment comes in many shapes and forms.
Roll up your sleeves and punch in for this quiz of on-the-job vocabulary.

1. **oeuvre** ('oo-vruh) *n.*—
   A: job opening. B: body of work.
   C: French chef.

2. **arduous** ('ar-je-wus) *adj.*—
   A: passionate. B: cheap. C: difficult.

3. **bum's rush** (bumz rush) *n.*—
   A: mass retail markdown.
   B: five-o'clock traffic.
   C: forcible eviction or firing.

4. **functionary** ('funk-sheh-nar-ee) *n.*—
   A: jack-of-all-trades.
   B: number cruncher. C: one who
   works in a specified capacity or
   as a government official.

5. **remunerate** (ri-'myu-neh-rayt) *v.*—
   A: pay for work.
   B: do the same job repeatedly.
   C: break a contract.

6. **proletariat** (proh-leh-'ter-ee-et)
   n.—A: working class.
   B: head honcho.
   C: cowboy skilled with a lasso.

7. **indolent** ('in-doh-lent) *adj.*—
   A: unpaid. B: averse to work, lazy.
   C: migratory.

8. **Luddite** ('luh-diyt) *n.*—A: one who
   opposes technological change.
   B: freelancer. C: bigwig.

9. **on spec** (on spek) *adv.*—
   A: with no assurance of payment.
   B: exactly as planned.
   C: in a supervisor's role.

10. **trouper** ('troo-per) *n.*—
    A: traveling theater actor.
    B: infantry soldier.
    C: temp-agency worker.

11. **sinecure** ('siy-nih-kyur) *n.*—
    A: herbal healer.
    B: math faculty.
    C: cushy job.

12. **métier** ('met-yay) *n.*—
    A: fee for services.
    B: oath of office.
    C: area of expertise.

13. **sedentary** ('se-den-ter-ee) *adj.*—
    A: multitasking.
    B: mindlessly obedient.
    C: not physically active.

14. **garnishment** ('gar-nish-ment) *n.*—
    A: extra pay.
    B: withholding of wages.
    C: job in name only.

15. **indentured** (in-'den-sherd) *adj.*—
    A: having perks.
    B: bound to work.
    C: illegally employed.

CROSSWORD: Men of Letters

ACROSS
1. Half a Hawaiian fish
5. Sleepy, e.g.
10. Way off
14. Jordan of Jordan-Marsh
15. Harder to come by
16. Angler's delight
17. *The Forsyte Saga* author
19. Doe beau
20. In la-la land
21. Oil-can letters
22. Poet Pound
23. New Mexican ski spot
25. Render a verdict
27. Annex
30. Paris streets
32. Satisfy
33. *The Matrix* hero
34. Runway
36. Pierre's thank-you
39. Part of YWCA
41. Khartoum locale
43. Nobleman
44. Giant
46. Excellence
48. Floral necklace
49. Mesabi yield
51. Ten: Comb. form
52. *A Summer Place* star
53. Palate cleanser
56. Short satire
58. ___ Scotia
59. Activate
61. Bolivian beasts
65. Little helper?
66. "The Necklace" author
68. Small dog
69. Goodbye, Gabrielle
70. Goodbye, Reginald
71. Comes out with
72. Dweebs
73. Radiate

DOWN
1. Lotsa
2. "___ le Roi!": Bastille cry
3. *Mutiny on the Bounty* co-author
4. Map feature
5. Quitters
6. Realm of Mars
7. Knacks
8. Detox center
9. Young chickens
10. No-show
11. *The Last Tycoon* author
12. Video-game name
13. Shakespearean princess
18. Dons
24. Vaccine
26. "___ Woman": Reddy
27. Physical-therapy subj.
28. He loved Lucy
29. *The Brothers Karamazov* author
31. Did a vinyl house job
35. Prunes
37. Summer on TV
38. Nastase of tennis
40. Recounts
42. Golden Bear of golf
45. Tortoise beak
47. Monkey suit
50. Deckhand
53. Loses it
54. Biblical prophet
55. FTC concern
57. Liking
60. Sierra Club founder John
62. Drawled address
63. Con
64. RN's "at once!"
67. Foot: Comb. form

Sudoku Twin

Fill in the grid so that each row, each column, and each 3 x 3 frame contains every number from 1 to 9. A sudoku twin is two connected 9 x 9 sudokus.

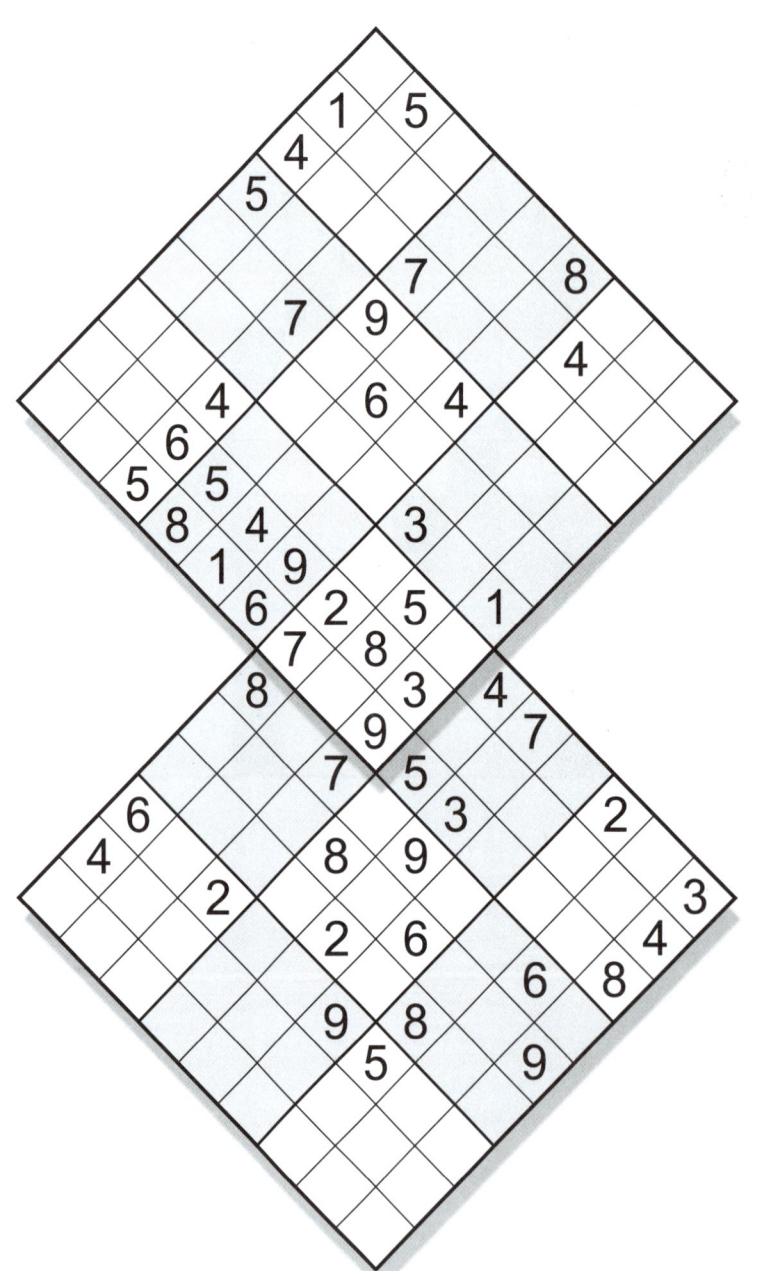

delete ONE

Delete one letter from **RIM STY TIN** and rearrange the rest to come up with a vocation.

_____

NAME THAT CAR

Memorable Model

The car is a dream to drive. It has coil springs in the front for an easy ride. The 93-horsepower, six-cylinder engine is equipped with an optional overdrive transmission the manufacturer aptly called the "gas saver." The overdrive boosts the coupe's top speed. It'll do 65 mph very nicely. What is its name?

tips

1. This make was founded in 1928, three years after Chrysler Corp. was reorganized from Maxwell Motor Co.
2. The brand was named after a conquistador who reached the Mississippi River.
3. This coupe has no backseat. Instead, shelves provide interior storage space.
4. The maker designated this year's model lineup the Series S3.
5. During this model year, Chrysler signed its first labor contract with the United Auto Workers.

CHANGELINGS

Each of the three lines of letters below spell the name of a well-known English poet, but some of the letters have been mixed up. Four letters from the first name are now in the third line, four letters from the third name are in the second line, and four letters from the second name are in the first line. The remaining letters are in their original places. What are the poets' names?

L R N G H E O L O S
W O F D E W A R T Z
W I T L G O R F L D

CROSSWORD: State Mottoes

ACROSS
1 Cartoonist MacNelly
5 Sings like Ella
10 Caroline of *Sabrina, the Teenage Witch*
14 "It's ___!"
15 Fencing thrust
16 Maul
17 "I have found it!" state
19 Merely
20 *The Spanish Tragedy* dramatist
21 Exchange allowance
22 Gil of baseball
24 "See you, Pasquale!"
25 Supplemental
26 State U. in Lorman, Mississippi
29 "Thus always to tyrants" state
33 Times Square lights
34 Scoundrels
35 Ditty
36 Bluto or Pluto
37 Bum
38 Letterhead symbol
39 Birthplace of Yeats
40 Pierre's notion
41 James in *The Blue Max*
42 Visa rival
44 North Pole's latitude
45 Gibe at
46 Hawked
47 Radcliffe or Craig
50 Twice tetra-
51 Jacuzzi
54 Baldwin of *30 Rock*
55 "By and by" state
58 Carte
59 San Antonio shrine
60 Hammer head
61 Amanda in *Syriana*
62 Cellulose fabric
63 Prefix for room

DOWN
1 Hill climber of rhyme
2 PayPal parent
3 Crease
4 Murphy Brown's show
5 Catchphrase
6 Flea-market item
7 12 *mesi*
8 ___ Friday's
9 Aquarium favorite
10 "Hope" state
11 Put up drapes
12 A.A. Fair's real first name
13 Irving and Grant
18 Blue-ribbon events
23 Part of NATO
24 "He who transplanted sustains" state
25 Gnat
26 Went to pot?
27 Pope in 682
28 Colorado Rockies field
29 Princess Leia's dad
30 Grafton's *N Is for ___*
31 Fort Knox bar
32 Newspaper column
34 Citadel student
37 Subject of a 1990 Ken Burns documentary
41 Where to see "The Last Supper"
43 IOU segment
44 Caprice
46 Noodlehead
47 Like some cellars
48 Not aweather
49 Honolulu Zoo bird
50 Anthem starter
51 Compact Chevy pickup
52 Sonneteer
53 Hathaway in *Get Smart*
56 Chicken ___ king
57 Class rank fig.

Kakuro

Each number in a black area is the sum of the numbers that you have to enter in the next empty boxes. The empty boxes that make up the sum are called a run. The sum of the across run is written above the diagonal in the black area, and the sum of the down run is written below the diagonal. Runs can only contain the numbers 1 through 9, and each number in a run can only be used once. The gray boxes only contain odd numbers and the white only even numbers.

do you KNOW?

What is a mammothrept?

_____

SANDWICH

What five-letter word belongs between the word at left and the word at right, so that the first and second word, and the second and third word, each form a common compound word or phrase?

CANDLE _ _ _ _ _ WEIGHT

Word Pyramid

Each word in the pyramid has the letters of the word above it, plus a new letter.

I
(1) Rhode Island
(2) Gentle wind
(3) Water falling in drops
(4) Fairy bluebird
(5) Aviators
(6) Vivid red
(7) Inhabitant of the U.S.

do you KNOW?

What happened on Griffin's Wharf in December 1773?

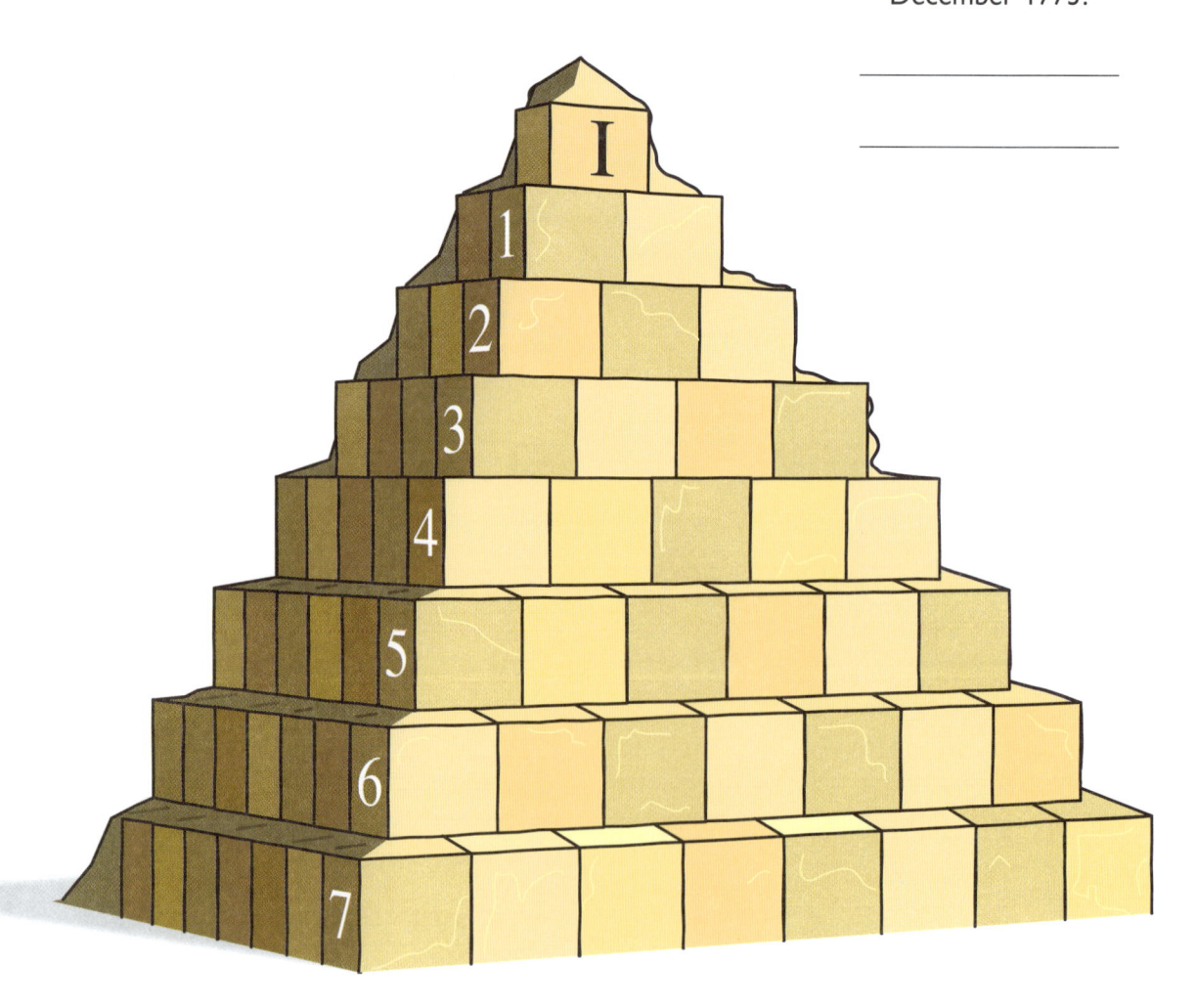

_____
_____

Binairo

Complete the grid with zeros and ones until there are 6 zeros and 6 ones in every row and every column. No more than two of the same number can be next to or under each other. Rows or columns with exactly the same content are not allowed. There is only one valid solution.

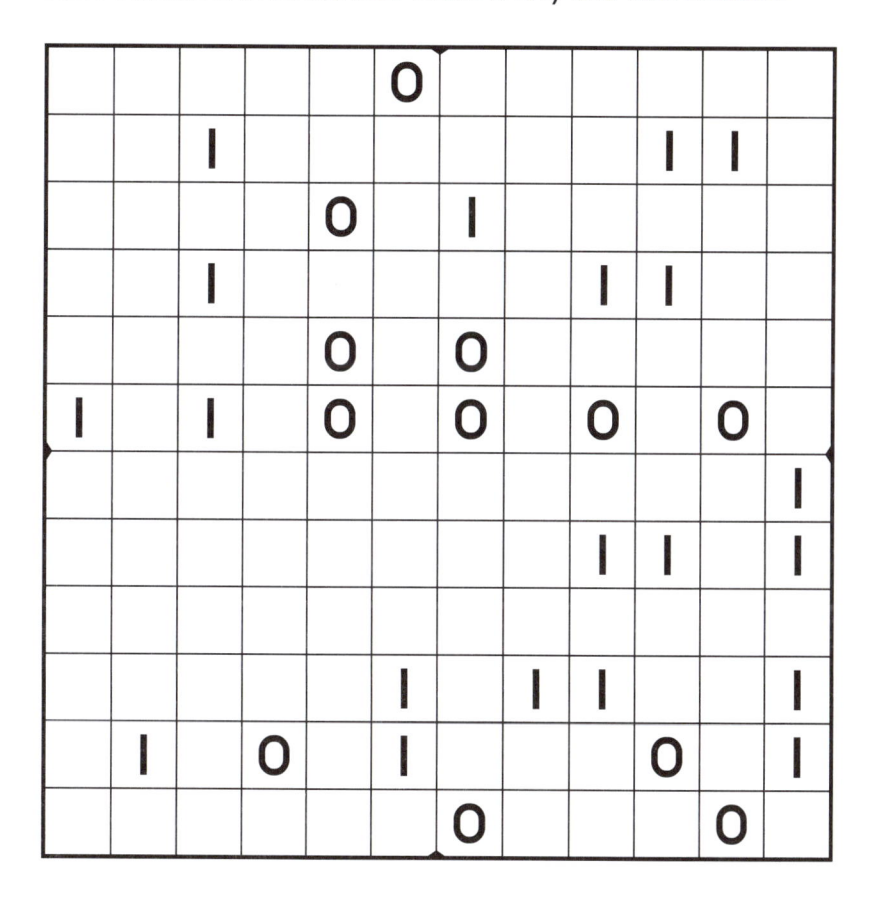

			O								
	I						I	I			
		O		I							
	I					I	I				
			O		O						
I		I	O		O		O				
								I			
					I	I		I			
			I		I	I			I		
	I	O		I			O		I		
				O				O			

trivia

- Where were potato chips invented?

LETTERBLOCKS

Move the letterblocks around so that words associated with crime are formed on the top and bottom rows.

Top: A L S A U S T
Bottom: P I R S U U T

TRIVIA QUIZ — Myths of the Americas

Many civilizations flourished in North and South America, and long before the arrival of the Europeans, there were highly developed religious and mythological beliefs. What do you know about these cultures?

1. Which Native American chief of the 18th century, whose name is recalled in a famous American car, united the Indians of the Great Lakes against the European invaders?

2. Which civilization came first: the Toltecs or Aztecs?

3. On which continent did the native people believe in a great spirit called Manitou?

4. Which Mexican people worshiped a god in the form of a plumed serpent, a god previously worshiped by the Toltecs?

5. Which South American civilization built Machu Picchu?

6. Which northern people once revered a goddess named Sedna?

7. What is the ritualistic item *peyote*: a heraldic emblem, a hallucinogenic drug, or a magic wand?

8. What is the proper term for a medicine man who is believed to interact with a spirit world through altered states of consciousness, such as a trance.

9. Which Central American people worshiped a god called Itzamna?

10. What was the term for the pipe smoked by the North American Plains Indians in honor of the Great Spirit?

11. In Aztec myth, who is the brother of the principal deity Quetzalcoatl: Xolotl or Zolotl?

12. Which celestial feature was called the World Tree or the White-Boned Serpent by the Maya of Central America?

13. Inti Raymi was a feast dedicated to a god in which civilization?

14. Which animal was most commonly sacrificed by the Incas?

CROSSWORD: Themeless

ACROSS
1 Campaign tactics
8 Went postal
15 Festoon
16 Like pegged pants
17 Allows
18 Backing
19 Breakage
20 Barely flow
21 "Fair!" or "Foul!"
23 Argues logically
26 Flavor
29 Worth a ten
31 "Riddle-me-___" ("Guess!")
32 "And ___ fine fiddle had he"
33 Alternatives to suspenders
34 ___ Aviv
35 Weary
36 Royal reception
37 Beauvais department
38 50-cent piece
39 "Beyond the Sea" singer Bobby
40 ___ River Anthology
41 Devoured
42 Angled
43 Al dente order
44 Fragrant flower
46 Hoopla
48 Component
49 Moon color, at times
53 Novice
56 Guess Who's Coming to Dinner star
57 "Waltzing ___"
58 Aerial
59 Fontina and Colby
60 Renters

DOWN
1 Added years
2 Blue Nile source
3 Airport conveyance
4 Popular tuna
5 Stampede Park site
6 Use a prayer rug
7 Radical '60s group: Abbr.
8 Matthew and Mark
9 Gross out
10 Takes to a higher court
11 Le Moko and Le Pew
12 Ratio
13 Eternally, in verse
14 Silent Spring killer
22 Africa's oldest republic
23 Caves in
24 Liam in The A-Team
25 Moon goddess
26 Ancient Persian governor
27 Get some airtime?
28 Keep going
30 Faust character
36 Equator's is zero
37 Makes it go
39 Jeff in Sweet Hearts Dance
40 Alcohol
45 Loosen a skate
47 Fifty ___ (long odds)
50 What a stitch in time saves
51 Star Trek producer Roddenberry
52 Stats at Cooperstown
53 Mad Men network
54 ___-jongg
55 Dorm mentors: Abbr.
56 Homey

Word Sudoku

Complete the grid so that each row, each column, and each 3 x 3 frame contains the nine letters from the black box below. The hidden nine-letter word is in the diagonal from top left to bottom right.

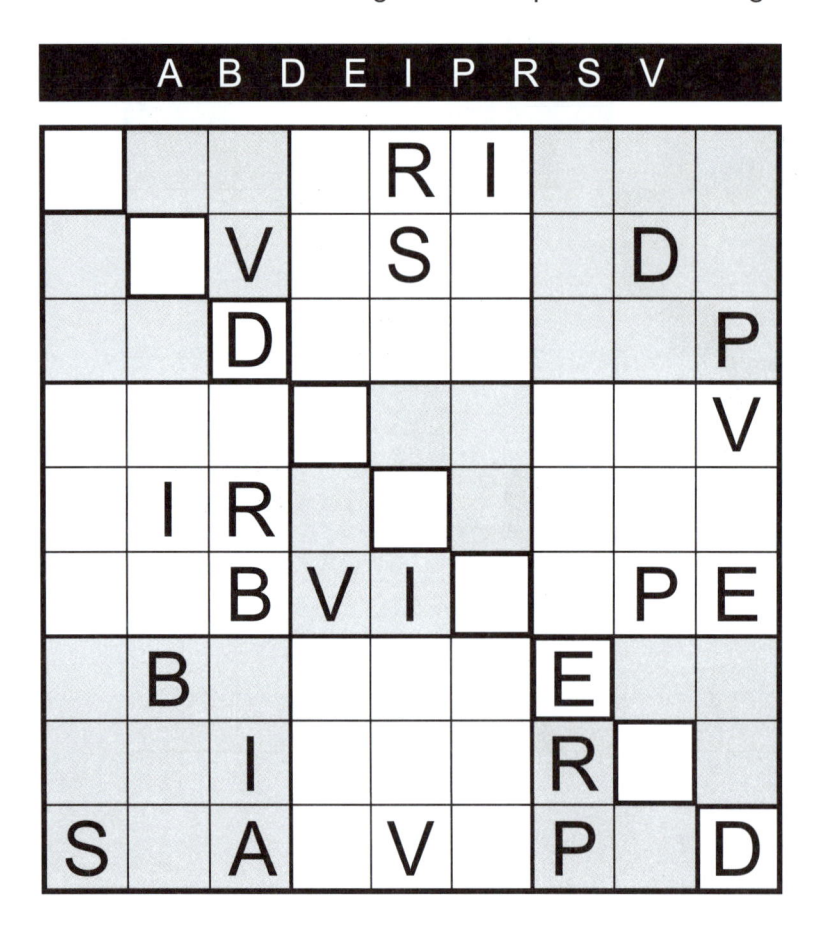

A B D E I P R S V

				R	I			
		V		S			D	
		D						P
								V
	I	R						
		B	V	I			P	E
	B					E		
		I				R		
S		A		V		P		D

do you KNOW?

The Welland Canal is part of what seaway?

UNCANNY TURN

Rearrange the letters of the word below to form a cognate anagram, one that is related or connected in meaning to the original word. The answer can be one or more words.

DORMITORY

BRAINSNACK® Golf Holes

Where is the sixth hole if you start at hole D9? There are no holes in the blue ponds.
Answer like this: C3. (Tip: Think diagonally.)

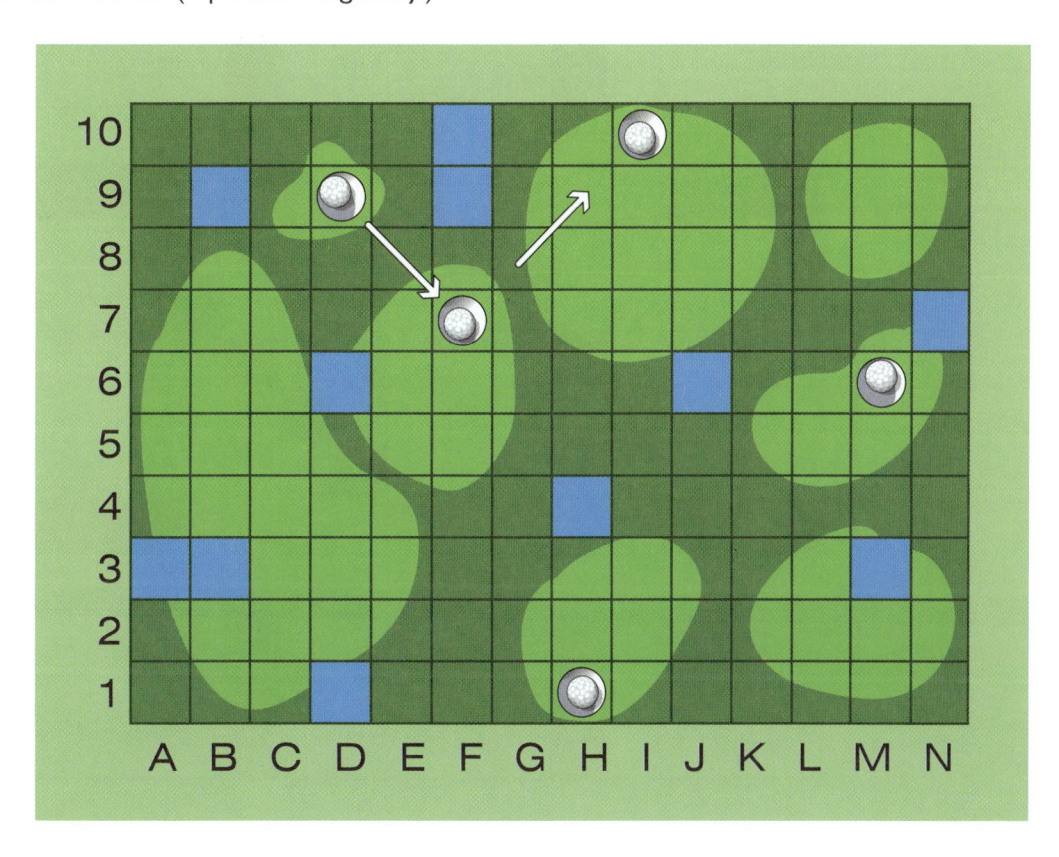

LETTER LINE

Put a letter in each of the squares below to make a word that means "out of work."
The number clues refer to other words that can be made from the whole.

4 2 10 6 9 8 TUNES • 10 3 5 6 7 8 EXTEND
4 7 2 9 8 CASH • 6 3 4 7 2 FRUIT

1	2	3	4	5	6	7	8	9	10

CROSSWORD: A+ Novels

ACROSS
1. "Please respond"
5. Ranchero's rope
10. Acoma Pueblo is on one
14. Anatomical aqueduct
15. Fire remnant
16. Duck genus
17. Andean land
18. *The Crucible* setting
19. Flood guard
20. E.M. Forster novel
23. Han of *Star Wars*
24. Seine tributary
25. Live
28. Went the full monty
32. Killer whales
33. Billie Holiday's music
34. Always, in verse
35. Cloud seeding result
36. Sombrero features
37. Au naturel
38. Ike's WWII command
39. They all lead to Rome
40. Andrea ___
41. Rikki-Tikki-Tavi, for one
43. Globetrotters' home
44. NASDAQ quotes
45. Bang-up
46. Ernest Hemingway novel
53. Spinning-wheel product
54. Papal vestment
55. "No way, Sergei!"
56. Ashtabula's lake
57. Adversary
58. Indigo plant
59. Bed support
60. Stands for
61. *Beetle Bailey* boob

DOWN
1. Kelly of talk TV
2. One of baby's firsts
3. *Laura* author Caspary
4. Waterloo fighter
5. Flea-market deal
6. Adult insect
7. ___-bodied
8. Tops used in gambling
9. Boudoir furniture pieces
10. Wild parsnip
11. City WNW of Tulsa
12. H.H. Munro's pen name
13. Between ports
21. Adds turf to
22. Cow-headed goddess
25. "Air Music" composer
26. A Muse
27. Grafting shoot
28. Playground sight
29. Cultured gem
30. Like *The X-Files*
31. Dorothy's Oz visit, e.g.
33. French restaurant
36. Library regular
37. David of *Bones*
39. American Beauty
40. "Book 'em ___!"
42. January birthstone
43. They have their reservations
45. Detective Pinkerton
46. "Yes" votes
47. Take a spill
48. Song from *La Tosca*
49. Volcanic rock
50. Sandberg of baseball
51. Israeli premier (1969–74)

Duel on the Green

Three men are playing a tournament of "match play"-style golf, where the greatest number of holes won determines the winner. A player wins a hole by completing it in at least one stroke fewer than his partner, regardless of how many strokes that is. Tied holes are, effectively, ignored. You'll notice that someone has erased some of the current standings from the clubhouse blackboard. It now shows the following:

	PLAYED	MATCHES won	MATCHES lost	MATCHES drawn	HOLES won	HOLES lost
Archie						3
Bernard						6
Chris		1		0	5	0

The three men in question have agreed to play each other once in games consisting of two players. You do not know whether some or all of these matches have been played. See if you can fill in the missing figures.
Can you work out how each two-player match panned out?

trivia

- What is an "epithalamium"?

Sport Maze

Draw the shortest way from the ball to the goal. You can only move along vertical and horizontal lines, not along diagonal lines. The figure on each square indicates the number of squares the ball must move in the same direction. You can change direction at each stop.

5	5	3	2	4	3
2	4	3	3	1	5
5	4	1	3	1	4
1	3	3	3	4	5
5	4	4	●	2	3
5	5	1	5	5	1

trivia

- What were Bonnie and Clyde's surnames?

REPOSITION PREPOSITION

Unscramble **HATING OWL** and find a two-word preposition.

WORD SEARCH: Fruit Salad

All the words are hidden vertically, horizontally, or diagonally— in both directions.

```
P J O J K S N N M T S C O S C M K C T
I S N N I G R V N A M N U P R E M J S
I T I U R F R A T S O A E R X K O C R
S M U L P O W A C M P A N W R V C Z N
E O K C M W J H M R C K N D G A V Y D
I R N N X V E I I H O U O G A V N D Y
R A F C D R S C K H P M L Q P R P T Z
R N E I R R O L O M A Q E A P N I L S
E G D I E T P N I O P U M Z L Y N N C
B E E P I S E O N C A A R B E J E B A
W S A K K Y E Z F H Y T E B S N A L N
A Y A H D V K O Y J A H T H Y F P U T
R S B E K D V B G C M I A Z Q G P E A
T U W M F W A D I N W G W I M U L B L
S J T O F N I T Y X A U R I L P E E O
Y W V F A C R J T W A M X A K A G R U
J C O N P E A R R D S R Z I P S V R P
V O A J N T S E M S K I V X Q E T Y E
D T X V E U N R A I S I N S D Q S W H
```

- APPLES
- APRICOT
- BANANA
- BLUEBERRY
- CANTALOUPE
- CHERRIES
- CURRANTS
- GRAPES
- HONEYDEW
- KIWI
- KUMQUAT
- ORANGES
- MANDARIN
- MANGOES
- PAPAYA
- PEACH
- PEAR
- PERSIMMON
- PINEAPPLE
- PLUM
- RAISINS
- STARFRUIT
- STRAWBERRIES
- WATERMELON

TRIVIA QUIZ — Who Said It?

Famous words, famous speakers. Can you figure out who uttered the following statements?

1. "I only regret that I have but one life to lose for my country!"

2. "Let me assert my firm belief that the only thing we have to fear is fear itself...."

3. "There are no second acts in American lives."

4. "Nobody ever went broke underestimating the taste of the American public."

5. "These are the times that try men's souls."

6. "Senator, you're no Jack Kennedy."

7. "Sic semper tyrannis!"

8. "The British are coming!"

9. "When you come to a fork in the road, take it."

10. "Genius is 1 percent inspiration and 99 percent perspiration."

11. "Everyone wants to be Cary Grant. Even I want to be Cary Grant."

12. "Remember that time is money."

13. "A house divided against itself cannot stand."

14. "Man is the only animal that blushes. Or needs to."

15. "Take my wife, please."

16. "That's one small step for (a) man, one giant leap for mankind."

CROSSWORD: National Parks

ACROSS

1. Famous gorge formed by the Colorado River, 2 words
7. Color
9. Iconic landscape photographer
10. Half Dome's home
11. Effigy Mounds National Monument's state, abbr.
12. Outcropping
14. _____ Cave, South Dakota, where you can see bison herds
18. Part of Leonardo's last name
19. Fox's home
20. Unusual
22. _____ Cave, part of world's longest known cave system
24. Compass point
25. Container
26. National bird
27. National park that includes part of the Blue Ridge Mountains
29. Mount Rainier's state, abbr.
31. Florida's iconic national park
33. _____ Capitan
34. _____ Gang
35. Famed Utah national park
37. Spanish explorer of the Pacific
38. Coloring liquid
39. Lacking feeling
40. It's before beauty
41. Bond opponent
42. _____ Lake, national park in Oregon with an immense blue lake

DOWN

1. Montana national park that is home to grizzly bears, lynx and 700 lakes.
2. From a distance
3. Mojave or Great Basin
4. Vanderbilt of etiquette fame
5. Not no
6. Propose for
7. Ancient dwellings
8. Former partner
13. Wyoming national park named after towering mountain, 2 words
15. Wedding words
16. The first national park, formed in 1872
17. Beech or birch
21. Tall spreading tree
22. What a boy grows up to be
23. Hee _____, TV show
25. Cod or Hatteras
27. Tranquil national park with some of the oldest and tallest trees in the world
28. Summer mo.
30. Mesa _____, where you can see cliff dwellings in Colorado
32. Airline, competitor to American
35. Meditative school of Buddhism
36. Squirrel's find
37. U.K. broadcaster, abbr.

Sudoku

Fill in the grid so that each row, each column, and each 3 x 3 frame contains every number from 1 to 9.

1								
			9				3	
		2		7				
4				1		5		
	9					1		7
	8							
8			6	2		4		
	5	7		9			2	
	6							9

trivia

- What does defenestrate mean?

___

BLOCK ANAGRAM

Form the word that is described in the parentheses, using the letters above the grid. Extra letters are already in the right place.

ATHLETE (communication from one mind to another)

☐ ☐ ☐ ☐ **P** ☐ ☐ **Y**

126

BRAINSNACK® **Web of Intrigue**

The yellow zones are closely monitored by the spider. Which zone (1–16) should also be yellow?

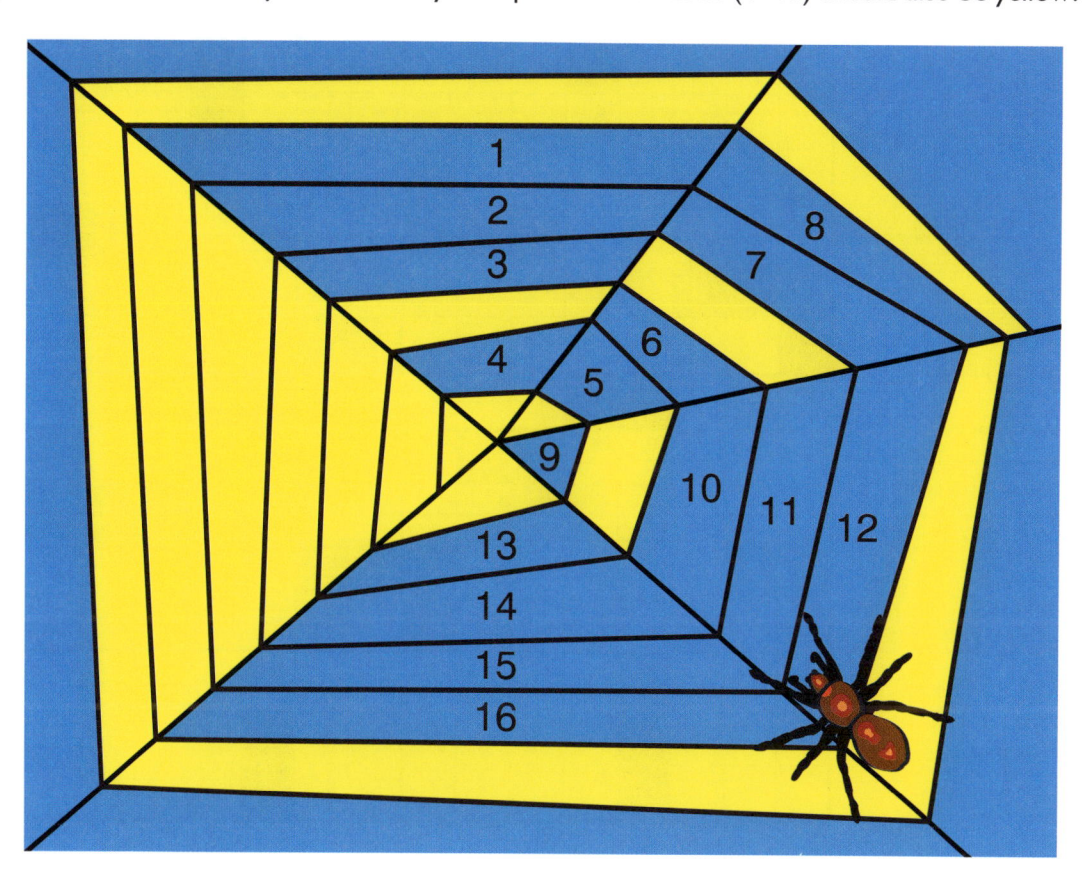

ECONOMICAL

There is only one word that is made using only two different letters, each used three times. What is it?

CROSSWORD: Shipwrecks

ACROSS
1 Bard
5 Goes with the flow
11 Threatened tree
14 Big prefix
15 U.S. surface-to-air missile
16 Tacitus' 12
17 It sank on 7/25/1956
19 Ruff, to Dennis the Menace
20 Move furtively
21 Most energetic
23 Mahatma Gandhi, for one
24 Striped antelope
25 It sank on 12/15/1917
31 Tax assessor's concern
33 Look after
34 Austrian "alas!"
35 Opening night
38 Just purchased
39 Cookbook verb
42 I specialists
45 It sank on 12/15/1976
48 *La sonnambula* heroine
49 North Carolina's ___ Banks
53 Sources of caviar
55 Synthetic
57 End of some URLs
58 It sank on 1/24/1909
60 Pedal pumper
61 Kingklip catchers
62 Fast time?
63 Problem's sol.
64 Record holder
65 Baseball card stats

DOWN
1 Total
2 Meter starter
3 Wasatch Mountains city
4 March 17th marcher
5 Blind as ___
6 Bye-bye birdie?
7 What Antony told Cleopatra
8 Did Latin homework
9 Threesome
10 Sacred beetles
11 Means to an end
12 Rough positions
13 Bench had a hand in it
18 Lose one's tail
22 Memo opener
26 Crumple up
27 Mellow
28 Medieval instrument
29 Map lines: Abbr.
30 Painful shout
31 Rent-___
32 Drinks in one gulp
34 Entomologist Fitch
36 "E-e-ww! Gross!"
37 ___ fare-thee-well
40 Japanese director Uchida
41 Displaced persons
43 Former Turkish premier
44 Blunder
46 Tooth part
47 Emulate Hulk Hogan
50 Old German coin
51 Mall of America site
52 Sales slips, for short
53 Fleck of jazz
54 Tree of Knowledge locale
55 First name in game shows
56 Vaulted recess
59 Eurasian sandpiper

Cage the Animals

Draw lines to completely divide up the grid into small squares, with exactly one animal per square. The squares should not overlap.

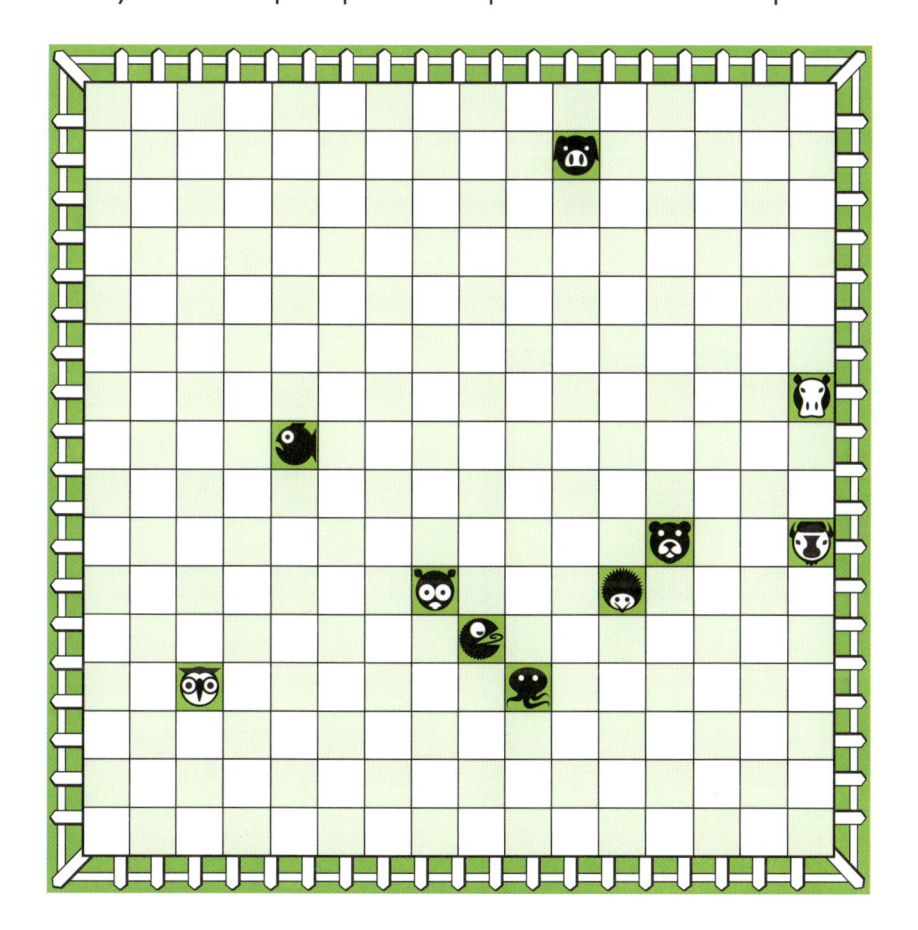

trivia
- Which logo is based on a Norse woodcut of a mermaid?

DOODLE PUZZLE

A doodle puzzle is a combination of images, letters, and/or numbers that represent a word or a concept. If you cannot solve a doodle puzzle, do not look at the answer right away. Think hard—and outside the box.

Keep Going

Start on a blank square of your choice and connect as many blank squares as possible with one single continuous line. You can only connect squares along vertical and horizontal lines, not along diagonal lines. You must continue the connecting lineup until the next obstacle, i.e., the border of the box, a black square, or a square that already has been used. You can change direction at any obstacle you meet. Each square can only be used once. The number of blank squares that will be left unused is marked in the upper square. There is more than one solution. We only show one solution.

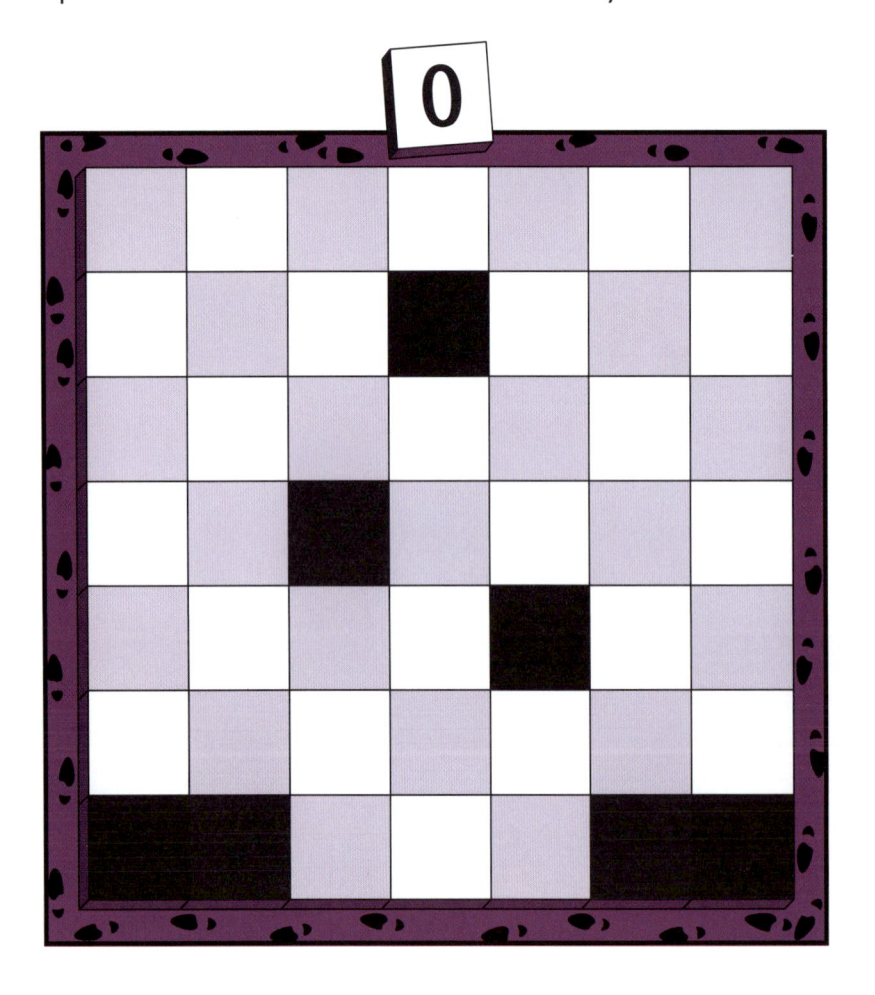

0

delete TWO

Delete two letters from **ORCHESTRATE** and rearrange the rest to get some pulling power.

_____

Binairo

Complete the grid with zeros and ones until there are 6 zeros and 6 ones in every row and every column. No more than two of the same number can be next to or under each other. Rows or columns with exactly the same content are not allowed. There is only one valid solution.

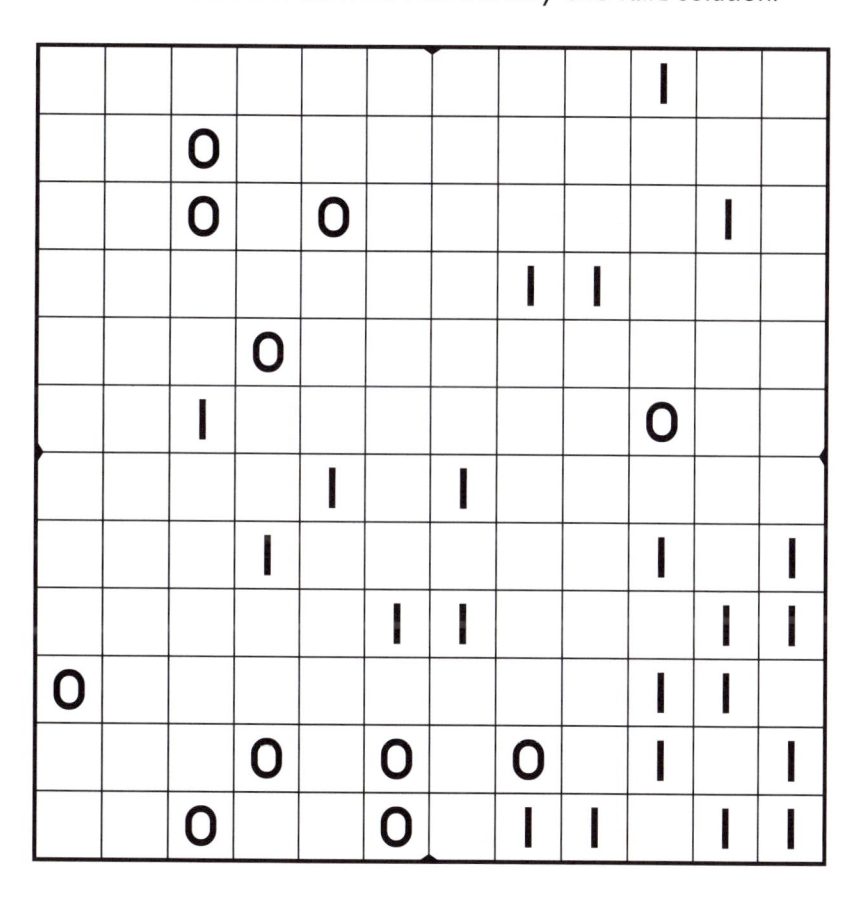

							1				
	0										
	0		0					1			
					1	1					
		0									
	1						0				
			1		1						
	1							1		1	
				1	1			1	1		
0											
		0		0		0		1		1	
		0		0		1	1			1	

do you KNOW?

Name the only rock that floats in water.

_____

MISSING LETTER PROVERB

Fill in each missing letter, indicated by an X, to make a well-known proverb.

XXITHXX X XXRROXER XOX X XEXDEX XE

WORD POWER — Favorite Words

The words in this quiz come from the book *Favorite Words of Famous People* by Lewis Burke Frumkes. Try to determine the meanings, but in addition, guess which notable names used these terms.

1. **plangent** ('plan-jent) *adj.*—
   A: flexible. B: very loud.
   C: carefully detailed.

2. **ruckus** ('ruh-kuhs) *n.*—
   A: backpack. B: melee.
   C: dry gully.

3. **vermilion** (ver-'mil-yun) *n.*—
   A: ten-figure number.
   B: moth larva. C: bright red.

4. **chthonic** ('thah-nik) *adj.*—
   A: of the underworld.
   B: frozen solid.
   C: having sharp claws.

5. **gormless** ('gorm-les) *adj.*—
   A: nonflowering.
   B: lacking firm shape. C: stupid.

6. **interstitial** (ihn-ter-'stih-shuhl) *adj.*—
   A: beyond our solar system.
   B: in the spaces between.
   C: joined by stitches.

7. **unilateral** (yoo-nih-'la-tuh-ruhl) *adj.*—
   A: one-sided. B: in alliance with.
   C: flat.

8. **palimpsest** ('pa-lehmp-sehst) *n.*—
   A: spotted pony. B: leg brace.
   C: written-over document.

9. **beguiling** (bih-'guy-ling) *adj.*—
   A: twisted together.
   B: complementary.
   C: cleverly deceptive.

10. **lambent** ('lam-buhnt) *adj.*—
    A: easily dissolved.
    B: submissive. C: luminous.

11. **incarnadine** (ihn-'kar-nuh-dine) *adj.*—A: flesh-colored.
    B: reborn.
    C: not digestible.

12. **phosphorescent** (fos-fuh-'reh-sent) *adj.*—A: of ocean depths.
    B: glittering.
    C: soapy.

13. **ramshackle** ('ram-sha-kuhl) *adj.*—
    A: barnlike.
    B: rickety-looking.
    C: falsely imprisoned.

14. **pixilated** (pick-suh-'lay-ted) *adj.*—
    A: grainy or blurry. B: elfin.
    C: mentally unbalanced.

15. **qua** ('kwah) *prep.*—
    A: in the capacity of.
    B: starting from.
    C: in the immediate neighborhood of.

CROSSWORD: Fall Fun

ACROSS
1. Fresh fall drink: apple ___
6. 1st and ___ (football term)
9. Roker and Pacino
12. Make amends
13. Four score and 7 years ___
14. Feline
15. Black and white bear
16. Blazing fall activity
18. Shade tree
20. Chocolate treat
21. Fall apples get covered in this
25. Landscape photographer Adams
26. Somewhere ___ the Rainbow
27. Diplomacy
29. Places for flowers
30. Bull's-___
31. Large rodents
35. Popular cologne
36. Beige
37. Crystal-banded rock
41. Fall is the time to visit the ___ patch
43. Desi Arnaz, for one
44. My Gal ___
45. Fall fun behind a tractor
48. Has supper
52. Hospital areas (abbr.)
53. Fuel
54. Several computers (specific brand)
55. Initials for a dentist
56. Biggest city in U.S. (abbr.)
57. Labyrinths

DOWN
1. Top of the toothpaste tube
2. Call ___ day (2 words)
3. ___ Quixote
4. Makes lovable
5. Domain
6. Projection on a file folder
7. Inflated feeling of pride
8. Type of milk
9. Amino and nucleic
10. Big
11. Heavy metal
17. Enjoyable
19. 3.28 feet
21. Corn on the ___
22. ___ Maria
23. Crimson
24. Basketball move (hyphenated)
28. Constellation of the Whale
31. Copy
32. Expression of dismay
33. Cycle prefix
34. Our daytime star
35. Not malignant
37. Felt sore
38. Protect
39. Bottomless pit
40. Black paving goo
42. "Dear Sir or ___"
46. 24 hours
47. Computer key
49. ___ Perce Indians
50. Before, poetically
51. Leaky tire sound

Sudoku

Fill in the grid so that each row, each column, and each 3 x 3 frame contains every number from 1 to 9.

	3		1					5
2		6		5			1	
				9	4		6	3
		5	8	2				4
	2	9				5	8	
6				3	5	1		
8	1		3	4				
	9			1		2		8
4					2		9	

trivia

- In which 1967 film was Mrs. Robinson featured?

ANAGRAM

Unscramble the letters in the phrase BATTERED SPORRANS to form four words with the same or similar meanings.

Mismatched Cards

From a conventional pack of cards, the numbers 2, 3, 4, and 5 of each suit have been selected. Can you lay out the 16 cards in a 4 × 4 grid so that no row, column, or (corner to corner) diagonal contains cards of the same number or the same suit? Four cards have been put in place already.

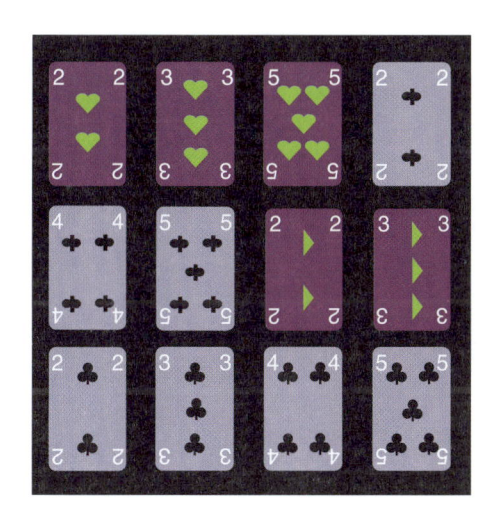

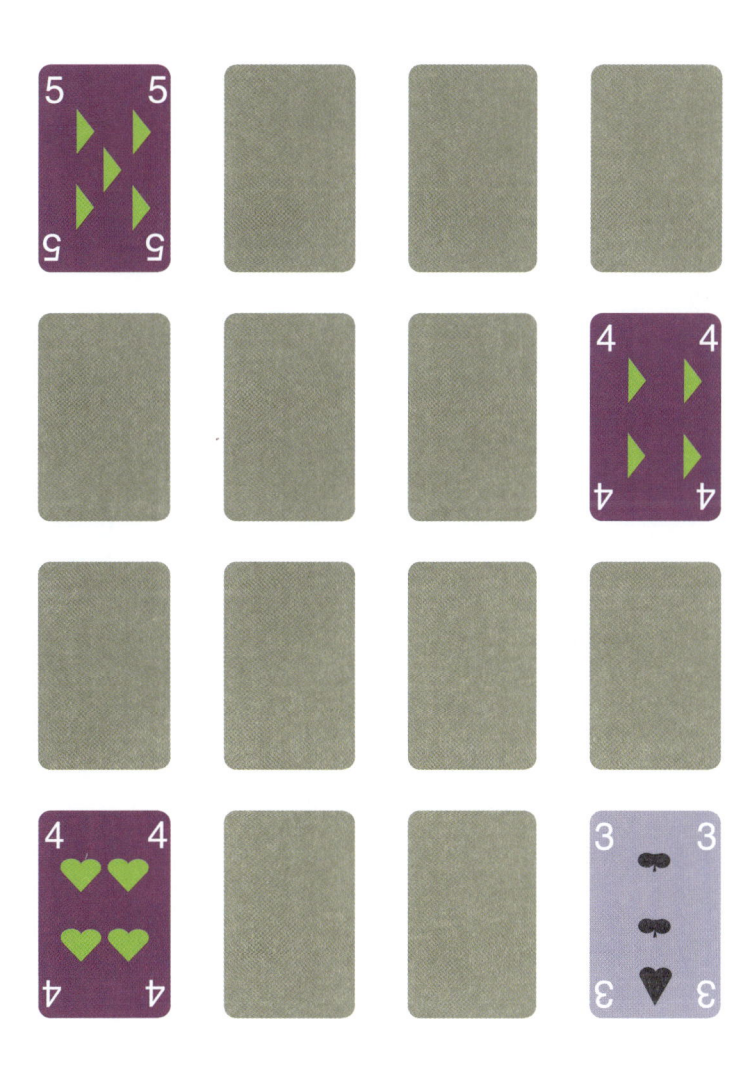

CROSSWORD: Flying Colors 1

The clues are standard, but the letters in the colored squares are an anagram of a famous 34 down.

ACROSS
- **1** Crept quietly
- **6** Common practice
- **9** 34 Down who hasn't taken vows
- **10** Confidential comment
- **11** Rendezvous
- **12** Short beginning
- **13** Primp
- **16** Slow mollusc
- **19** Stir
- **22** Sticks out
- **23** South African prairie
- **24** Overshadow
- **28** Stringed instrument
- **30** Press together
- **32** More spacious
- **33** Goddess of the moon
- **35** German city in the Ruhr
- **37** Substitute
- **38** Correct
- **39** Legends

DOWN
- **2** Yellow-green color
- **3** Young man
- **4** Glancing at
- **5** Order or decree
- **6** Greatest
- **7** View
- **8** Concert venue
- **14** Awaken
- **15** Artist's stand
- **17** At no time
- **18** Relation by marriage
- **20** Not well
- **21** Electrical unit
- **25** Noel ___, British songwriter
- **26** Situated within a building
- **27** Piercing cry
- **29** Rental contract
- **31** Beginning
- **34** Member of religious order
- **36** Filthy place

CROSSWORD: American History

ACROSS

1. Flip side
5. High-ranking NCOs
10. Vesuvian slag
14. "Unattractive" Jamaican fruit
15. Geometric abstract
16. Ex of Tiger Woods
17. Adjudge
18. Olympic decathlete Johnson
19. More than want
20. U.S. Attorney General (1961-64)
23. Ashtabula's lake
24. 180° turn, slangily
25. Brushes off
28. Bringing up the rear
30. 16-oz. units
33. Seed coverings
34. Dermal opening
35. Poky
36. Obama's Secretary of Homeland Security
39. "Esq." user
40. Decorated a cake
41. Be opposed
42. Mauna ___
43. 1998 animated bug film
44. "Aw, c'mon!"
45. *Sesame Street* watcher
46. "Where the Sidewalk Ends" poet Silverstein
47. Independent candidate for President in 1976
54. Like ___ of bricks
55. Scruffs
56. Jeopardy
58. Like sourballs
59. Male wasp
60. Zone
61. "___ a Woman": Beatles
62. Boots
63. Cute and sassy

DOWN

1. Pal
2. "Happy Days Are Here Again" composer
3. *Pinocchio* goldfish
4. Walsh of Girls Aloud
5. 9Lives cat
6. Avalanche
7. Butcher's hook
8. Lance Armstrong's bike
9. Coffeecake topping
10. *Shark Tale* shark
11. On the safe side, at sea
12. Enrich, in a way
13. Rooney of *60 Minutes*
21. Artist Max
22. After expenses
25. *Wheel of Fortune* host
26. Chatter
27. Beehive State range
28. Jennifer in *Shall We Dance*
29. Teammate of Jeter
30. Andean grazer
31. A little something extra
32. Cussed
34. Agreement
35. Mind comparison
37. *Donkey Kong* creator
38. Ambitionless one
43. Chicago's ___ Center
44. Sci-fi weapon
45. *Dances With Wolves* shelters
46. Public display
47. Beanery sign
48. Four Corners corner
49. 2007 Peace Nobelist
50. Mother of Hermes
51. Suffix for pluto
52. Put on
53. 1914 Belgian battle line
57. "Over It" singer McPhee

Number Cluster

Cubes showing numbers have been placed on the grid below, with some spaces left empty. Can you complete the grid by creating runs of the same number and of the same length as the number? So, where a cube with number 5 has been included on the grid, you need to create a run of five number 5's, including the cube already shown. The run can be horizontal, vertical, or both horizontal and vertical.

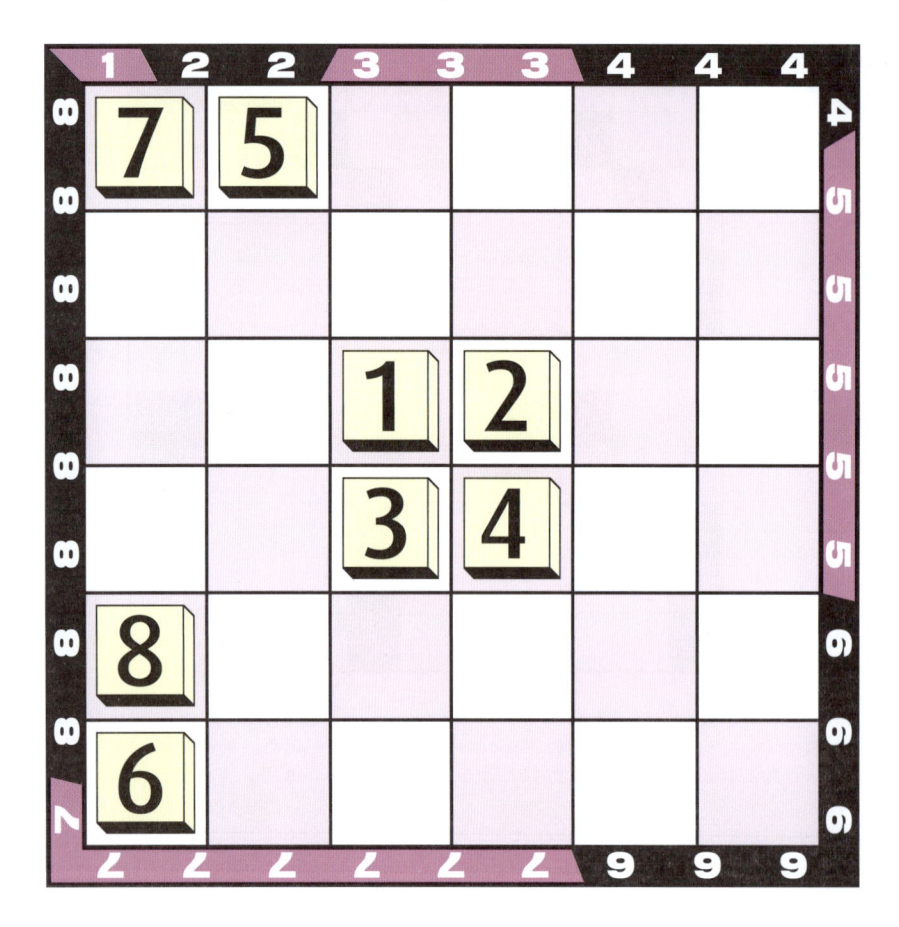

do you KNOW?

What is basophobia?

_____

FRIENDS

What do the following words have in common?

TREAT   GOVERN   DEVELOP   MANAGE   DEPART

WORD SEARCH: Science

All the words are hidden vertically, horizontally, or diagonally—in both directions.

```
T G E O M E T R Y S C I E N C
H E I T S T D G H A T S P Y A
E R T O B A O Y O F S C O M Y
O C I P I L E G N T C I S O R
L Y W O O G G O H A O T C N T
O O S N L E E L P N M S I O S
G E I Y O B O O H T P I T R I
Y S G M G R L H Y H O L C T M
G O A Y Y A O C S R S L A S E
O N T O L O G Y I O I A D A H
L L L I S T Y S C P T B I O C
O O S Y S T E P S O I M D A R
E G D E R M A T O L O G Y A S
L I T I C A L E C O N O M Y L
E C M Y T H O L O G Y M N Y A
P S Y C H I A T R Y A T C Q U
S I R E K N O H E R A L D R Y
Y M O T A N A W G X L E D G E
```

- ALGEBRA
- ANATOMY
- ANTHROPOLOGY
- ASTRONOMY
- BALLISTICS
- BIOLOGY
- CHEMISTRY
- COMPOSITION
- DERMATOLOGY
- DIDACTICS
- DYNAMICS
- ECONOMY
- GEOLOGY
- GEOMETRY
- GRAMMAR
- HERALDRY
- LOGIC
- MYTHOLOGY
- ONTOLOGY
- PHYSICS
- PSYCHIATRY
- PSYCHOLOGY
- SINOLOGY
- SPELEOLOGY
- SYNTAX
- THEOLOGY
- TOPONYMY

TRIVIAL PURSUIT But Cerealously

Breakfast cereal was invented to provide a grain-fueled start to the day. In the 1950s, demand grew for ready-to-eat breakfasts. Heavily sweetened versions of the old standby grains were marketed to kids.

WHICH COLD CEREALS DO YOU REMEMBER DROWNING IN MILK?

1. A 1958 TV commercial told kids this multigrain cereal was "A-B-C-Delicious!"

2. Two decades after its 1942 debut, the wheat-based cereal boasted of two scoops of dried fruit in every box.

3. What's the corn, oat and rice concoction that made people go cuckoo?

4. Marketed as an aid to digestive health, these high-fiber flakes came out in 1915.

5. Chocolaty bits of oven-toasted rice have been turning milk brown since 1958.

6. Kids loved sugary corn puffs in raspberry red, lemony yellow and orangey orange.

7. One of the sweetest, this puffy wheat cereal was 46% sugar by weight. (What do you expect? Sugar's in the name.)

8. Tony the Tiger arrived with a G-r-r-reat corn cereal in 1952.

trivia

- What was the mascot Kellogg used before Tony the Tiger?

CROSSWORD: End Rhyme

ACROSS

1. Kung fu master Po, e.g.
6. Pearl, essentially
11. Pulled off
14. "___ the loneliest number ..."
15. *For Better or For Worse* kid
16. Central Florida?
17. Hand off to someone else
19. Social-page word
20. Occupational hazard for supermodels?
21. It's often taken on the whole
23. Remote button
24. *The Black Cat* author
25. Sub in a tub
26. Norwegian Folk Museum site
29. Loafer
31. Put in a lawn
32. Pixies
34. Vanocur of TV
37. Wednesday's cousin
38. Released
40. Mod or nod ender
41. Cutting some slack
43. Mexican musician
45. Word in old oaths
46. Like white Bengal tigers
47. Pelt
48. Skinny
50. High rnk.
51. Kind of browser
53. McCallum's *NCIS* role
55. Piano men?
58. Outback denizen
59. Something to fall off of?
62. Nick Adams, for short
63. Employ anew
64. Young
65. "___ Ann Landers"
66. Frau Mahler and others
67. Pelota basket

DOWN

1. Short report?
2. Literary tidbits
3. Nutcracker suite
4. Repudiate
5. Kind of "naut"
6. Glasgow negatives
7. NYPD notice
8. Defoe hero
9. Nouveau ___
10. Napa winery known for its Pinot Noir
11. Irascible Disney toon in a sailor suit
12. Sherlock's Adler
13. *Ice Age* tiger
18. He stuck it to Dracula
22. Kind of companion
24. He always rings twice?
26. Drama award
27. Madrid miss: Abbr.
28. Best wishes
30. Cock and bull, e.g.
31. *Reginald* author
33. Carmelites
34. Blunderer
35. Lower ed.?
36. Curb
39. Nasser's state
42. Hero
44. Malign
46. Scary word from *The Shining*
48. Ciardi's ___ *Man*
49. John and Jane
50. Oliver Twist's dinner
52. Silly little trick
54. Wet shaver
55. Musical curves
56. *Broom Hilda*'s creator
57. Rabbit tail
60. Hush-hush gp.
61. World's tallest mountain

Word Sudoku

Complete the grid so that each row, each column, and each 3 x 3 frame contains the nine letters from the black box below. The hidden nine-letter word is in the diagonal from top left to bottom right.

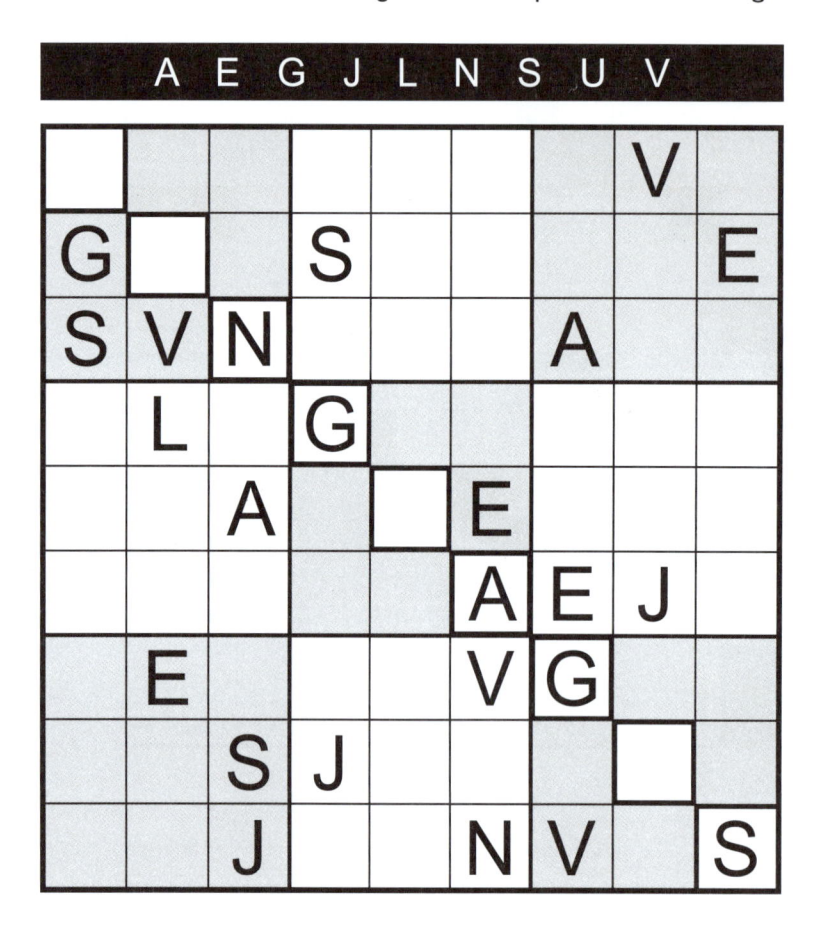

A E G J L N S U V

						V		
G			S					E
S	V	N				A		
	L		G					
		A			E			
					A	E	J	
	E				V	G		
		S	J					
		J			N	V		S

trivia
- What does VSOP on a brandy bottle mean?

UNCANNY TURN

Rearrange the letters of the phrase below to form a cognate anagram, one that is related or connected in meaning to the original phrase. The answer can be one or more words.

REAL FUN

BRAINSNACK® Cherry-picking

Which card (1–11) is the other cherries card?

ONE LETTER LESS OR MORE

The word on the right side contains the letters of the word on the left side, plus or minus the letter in the middle. One letter is already in the right place.

MAGISTER +N _ T _ _ _ _ _ _ _

Spot the Differences

Find the nine differences in the image on the bottom right.

do you KNOW?

Once used as a currency, what are cowries?

_____

trivia

- Who created the cartoon cat Garfield?

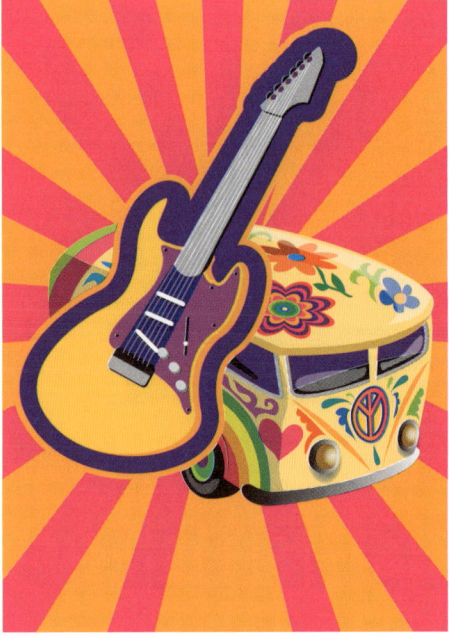

_____

CROSSWORD: An American in Paris

ACROSS

1 Presidency of 17 Across, in a sense
6 Ask for ID
10 Actress Turturro
14 Eckhart in *The Black Dahlia*
15 What Ali stung like
16 Sharing the secret
17 U.S. Minister to France (1784-89)
20 SW Arabian capital
21 Nobelist from Cape Town
22 Zeneca merger partner
23 It stands for something
25 Piquant
27 Trifling fuss
30 They may work with IVs
31 Shoot-from-the-hip comedy
34 Simpleton
36 Like Mozart's 18th Symphony
37 The eyes have it
39 Start of a quote by 17-Across
43 Fill to excess
44 German connective
45 "Long-Legged Fly" poet
46 Nelson was his VP
48 Opposite of WNW
50 Morse T
51 ___ sci (college major)
52 Part of DVD
54 Spy
57 Trot or canter
59 Russian range
63 More of quote
66 Peter Fonda role
67 Indigo plant
68 Timber rights, e.g.
69 Fit up
70 Lose gracefully
71 End of quote

DOWN

1 Makes antimacassars
2 Opposite of boo-hoo
3 Cold War curtain "material"
4 Trajan's empire
5 Courtroom evidence
6 Certain Louisianans
7 Obey the lawbreaker?
8 Taking care of gossip, maybe
9 Cool, to rappers
10 War correspondent's subject
11 The Smithsonian, e.g.
12 Way in
13 Actress Magnani
18 Stupefy
19 Holliday friend
24 Department of Normandy
26 Radio switch
27 Loan figs.
28 Hair-protecting kerchief
29 Hold the floor
32 Grotto nymph
33 Panorama
35 Vanquish
36 Neither Rep. or Dem.
38 Middle manager?
40 Cooling-off period
41 Autochthon
42 Roll-call calls
47 Japanese golfer Isao
48 Suitable for consumption
49 In ___ (in place)
53 Plant with arrow-shaped leaves
54 Cocksure
55 Part of VSOP
56 Four-F opposite
58 Short on originality
60 Word from the moon on 7/20/69
61 "Just take ___" ("Have a little drink")
62 "___ slip showing?"
64 USAF wing
65 Andy Capp's exclamation

Binairo

Complete the grid with zeros and ones until there are 5 zeros and 6 ones in every row and every column. No more than two of the same number can be next to or under each other. Rows or columns with exactly the same content are not allowed. There is only one valid solution.

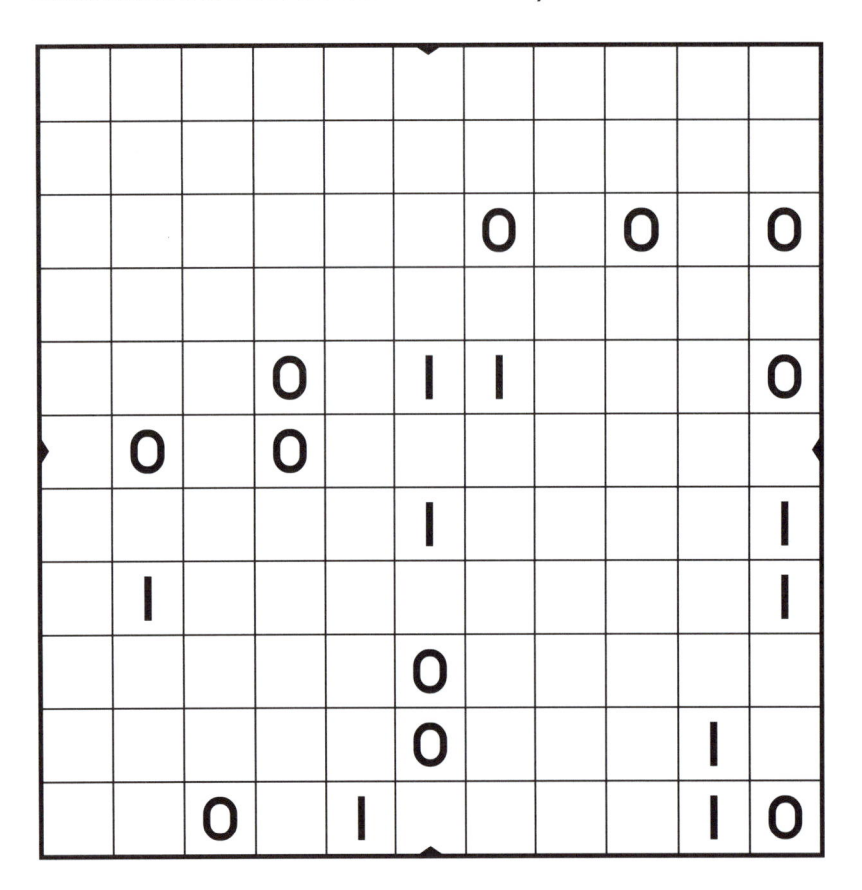

do you KNOW?

Where is the Queen's Plate horse race run?

_____

MISSING LETTER PROVERB

Fill in each missing letter, indicated by an X, to make a well-known proverb.

XN XXMX XARXXEX OX IXS XXOXAXH

Keep Going

Start on a blank square of your choice and connect as many blank squares as possible with one single continuous line. You can only connect squares along vertical and horizontal lines, not along diagonal lines. You must continue the connecting lineup until the next obstacle, i.e., the border of the box, a black square, or a square that already has been used. You can change direction at any obstacle you meet. Each square can only be used once. The number of blank squares that will be left unused is marked in the upper square. There is more than one solution. We only show one solution.

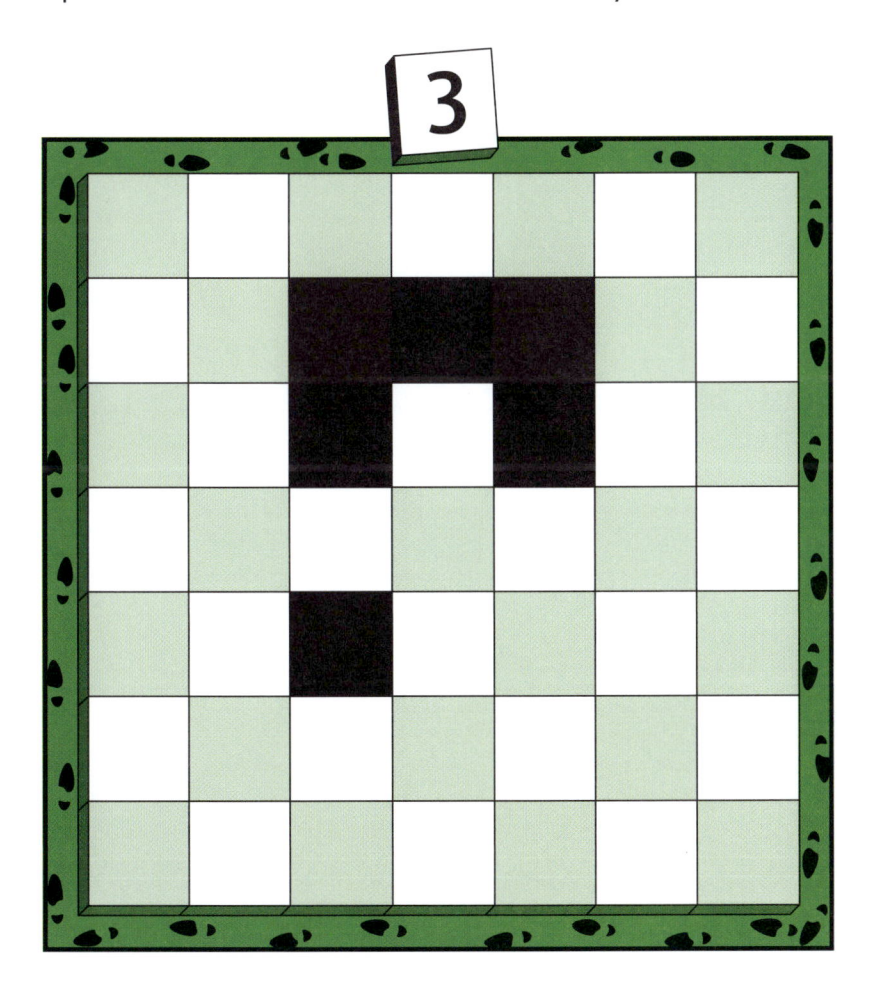

3

changeONE

Change one letter in each of these two words to form a common two-word phrase.

MOUSE DEER

TRIVIA QUIZ Take Your Partner

Dance around the dance floor—and around the world.
Check out these globetrotting questions about dance.

1. Which famous Scottish dance was originally performed by a warrior over his shield?
   a. The Highland Fling
   b. Reel of Tulloch
   c. The Cake Walk

2. Salsa evolved from Puerto Rican dance music and which other musical style?
   a. Western line dancing
   b. The Aboriginal didgeridoo
   c. Jazz

3. For which Pacific Islanders is Laka the goddess of dance?
   a. Hawaiians
   b. Samoans
   c. Fijians

4. Which athletic street dance was popular in the 1980s among urban teenagers in U.S. and U.K. cities?
   a. Electric bugaloo
   b. Break dancing
   c. Hip-hop dancing

5. Rangda the witch is the Queen of Evil in the dance-drama of which Indonesian island?
   a. Bali
   b. Java
   c. Borneo

6. In which African traditional religion are spirits called Orishas worshipped in dancing and drumming ceremonies?
   a. Yoruba
   b. Azande
   c. Santerìa

7. Arabic dancing is accompanied by music played on which stringed instrument, that is the forerunner of the lute and mandolin?
   a. The lyre
   b. The oud
   c. The sitar

8. What showman visited with entertainer Sammy Davis Jr. on his deathbed and then described Davis pretending to toss him a basketball?
   a. Jay Leno
   b. Bill Cosby
   c. Gregory Hines

9. How many positions are there in classical ballet?
   a. 15
   b. 10
   c. 5

10. In 1958 Bruce Lee won a championship in Hong Kong performing which dance style?
    a. Cha-cha
    b. Tap
    c. Salsa

CROSSWORD: Love Is...

ACROSS
1 1980s hairstyle
5 Peru's "City of the Kings"
9 Join spacecraft
13 *A God in Ruins* author
14 Nasal stimulus
15 Colorado River town
16 Part I of quote: "Love is ___"
19 Embarrassing occurrence
20 Away partner
21 "Make the ___ of it"
22 Part II of quote
26 Academic
29 "*Comme ci, comme ça*"
30 "No" from France
31 16th-century violin
32 *M*A*S*H* NCO
33 ___ polloi
34 Part III of quote
35 Weeks in a Roman calendar?
36 Part IV of quote
38 Tag players, at times
39 Part V of quote
40 Robot of Hebrew lore
41 Born
42 "Battle Hymn of the Republic" poet
44 "Look at Me, I'm ___ Dee"
45 "Still the One" band
47 English professor's deg.
48 "Ciao, Caesar"
49 Pricking punctures
53 Part VI of quote
56 Forbidden fruit locale
57 "And Still" singer McEntire
58 Beam
59 Multitude
60 Yankee number 13
61 Curtain hardware

DOWN
1 Apple variety
2 Make ___ for it
3 Frisbee
4 Approximation
5 At the bottom
6 "___ Wanna Play House": Wynette
7 *Bazooka Joe* character
8 Suffix for drunk
9 Ball of fire
10 Beyond the fringe
11 10th-century date
12 Penn of *House*
17 Persephone's love
18 "Blue Book" bogies
22 Not hollow
23 On the back burner
24 Midday nap
25 Mystery
26 Al in *Glengarry Glen Ross*
27 Melodramatic one
28 Camelot lass
29 Paperback back
32 Lobster features
36 "Queen of Crime" Christie
37 East Ender
42 Refuges
43 Binary digits
44 Singer O'Connor
46 Overhangs
47 Bar dance
49 Wing: Comb. form
50 VIP vehicle
51 Chisholm Trail town
52 Boot camp NCOs
53 Jewel
54 Mrs. McKinley
55 401(k) alternative

Sudoku Twin

Fill in the grid so that each row, each column, and each 3 x 3 frame contains every number from 1 to 9. A sudoku twin is two connected 9 x 9 sudokus.

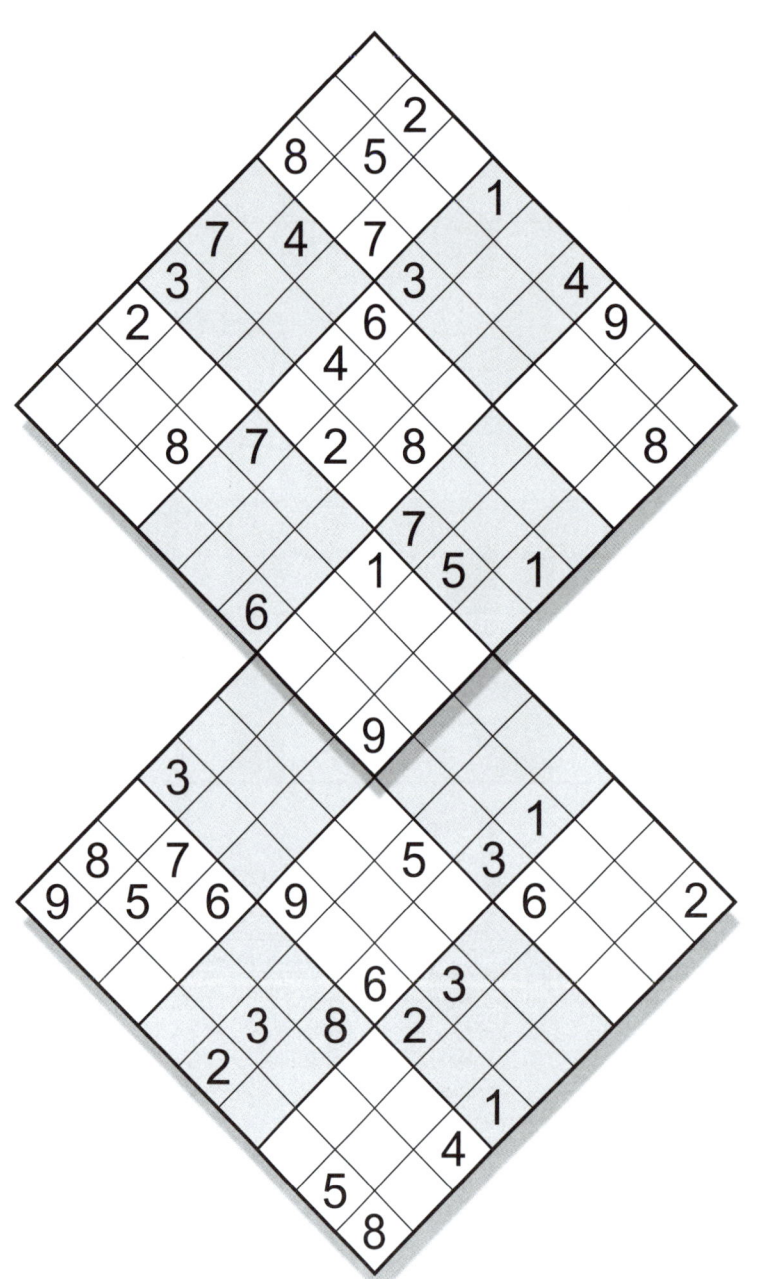

delete ONE

Delete one letter from each of these words, **SOON SUN TOIL**, and rearrange the rest to come up with the answer.

_____

BRAINSNACK® Vintage Barrels

Which date should replace the question mark?

SQUIRCLES

Place consonants in the squares and vowels in the circles and form words in each vertical column. The definitions of the words you are looking for are listed. (The grid will reveal the names of two flowers.)

1 Takes possession by force
2 Enrages
3 Territory
4 Many bees in flight
5 To have a high opinion of
6 A shaking
7 Gloomy and sad
8 A basket of fruit

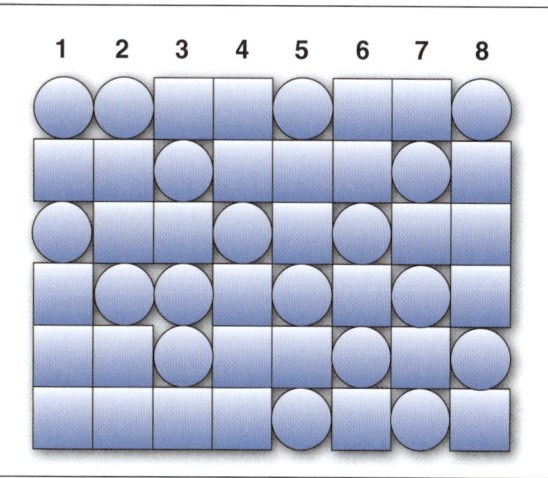

Kakuro

Each number in a black area is the sum of the numbers that you have to enter in the next empty boxes. The empty boxes that make up the sum are called a run. The sum of the across run is written above the diagonal in the black area, and the sum of the down run is written below the diagonal. Runs can only contain the numbers 1 through 9, and each number in a run can only be used once. The gray boxes only contain odd numbers and the white only even numbers.

do you KNOW?

What is the name of Amsterdam's main airport?

_____

ONE LETTER LESS OR MORE

The word on the right side contains the letters of the word on the left side, plus or minus the letter in the middle. One letter is already in the right place.

E A R D R O P S +T ☐ ☐ ☐ D ☐ ☐ ☐ ☐

Sport Maze

Draw the shortest way from the ball to the goal. You can only move along vertical and horizontal lines, not along diagonal lines. The figure on each square indicates the number of squares the ball must move in the same direction. You can change direction at each stop.

3	4	1	3	5	●
4	3	2	2	3	4
4	3	1	3	2	4
2	1	0	2	2	1
5	1	3	2	4	5
3	2	5	3	5	3

trivia

- Which policeman do you associate with Top Cat?

REPOSITION PREPOSITION

Unscramble **FOOD SUITE** and find a two-word preposition.

CROSSWORD: Monkey in the Middle

ACROSS

1 "Absolutely!"
5 "B.C." money
9 Third-stringer
14 *A Life for the ___* (Glinka opera)
15 Latvian capital
16 Culled
17 F1 neighbor
19 Revolting one
20 Acted as chair
21 Jacqueline in *Bullitt*
22 Long in *Boiler Room*
23 Rival of Adidas
24 Acclivity
28 Lake Huron tribe
32 Baby bug
33 Osso buco meat
34 *Big Bad John* actor Jack
35 "... dedicated to the ___ love"
36 Central position
37 Utah resort
38 *Fahrenheit 451* subject
39 "So that's it"
40 "Blue ___": Berlin
41 "Land of Opportunity"
43 Beef on the hoof
44 Oleo squares
45 Copyright symbol
46 Gun lock
49 "Cloudy and warm," e.g.
54 Maureen in *The Quiet Man*
55 Salsa peppers
56 Acknowledge
57 Rent-___ (1988)
58 *Bottled in Blonde* author Jaffe
59 Catkin
60 Glass designer Lalique
61 Companion of Ares

DOWN

1 Exercise aid
2 World power in 1990
3 Decathlon event
4 Chapters in history
5 Kind of union
6 Madonna's "___ Virgin"
7 Like fine wine
8 Merry time
9 Pinch pennies
10 Ohio railway partner
11 Steals
12 Certain plaintiff, at law
13 Single-gulp drink
18 Anatomical ear part
21 "... lived in the house that Jack ___"
23 Terrible twos, for one
24 Waikiki welcome
25 Better balanced
26 Haunted-house sound
27 1979 Patti LuPone stage role
28 Agrees not to keep
29 "Da Do Ron Ron" cowriter Greenwich
30 Dog soup, in diners
31 Accrue
33 Traveling papers
36 Johnny Mathis hit
40 Make tea
42 Afloat
43 Mexican shawl
45 Emoticon eyes
46 Alone, on the stage
47 "Attention please!"
48 The inevitable
49 Visage
50 Bill section
51 Presently
52 PlayStation parent
53 General on Chinese menus
55 Honey holder

CONCENTRATION # Eyes Closed

1. Place the tip of your pen on the red dot A and then on the white dot B.
   Do this ten times in a row.
2. Now place your pen on dot A and close your eyes.
   Try to indicate the middle of dot B as accurately as possible with your eyes closed.

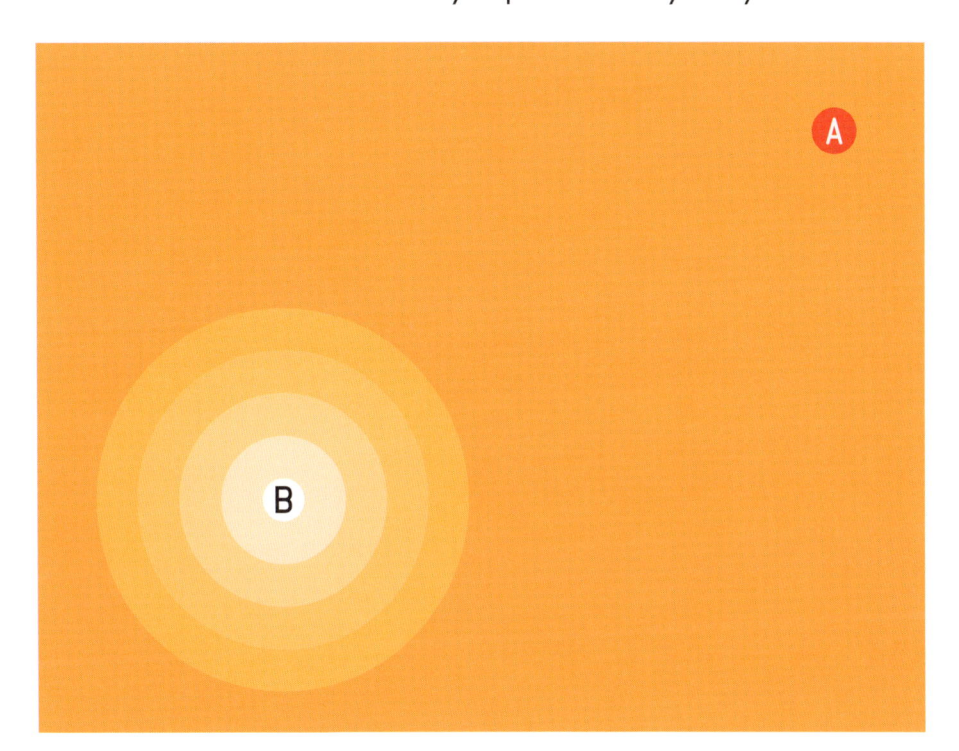

LETTER LINE

Put a letter in each of the squares below to make a word that means "to hold a second job." The number clues refer to other words that can be made from the whole.

8 2 1 6 4 7 PIGEON • 9 8 3 4 7 UNDERWEAR
7 5 2 3 1 DESPONDENCY • 7 6 5 9 EDGED

1	2	3	4	5	6	7	8	9

Cage the Animals

Draw lines to completely divide up the grid into small squares, with exactly one animal per square. The squares should not overlap.

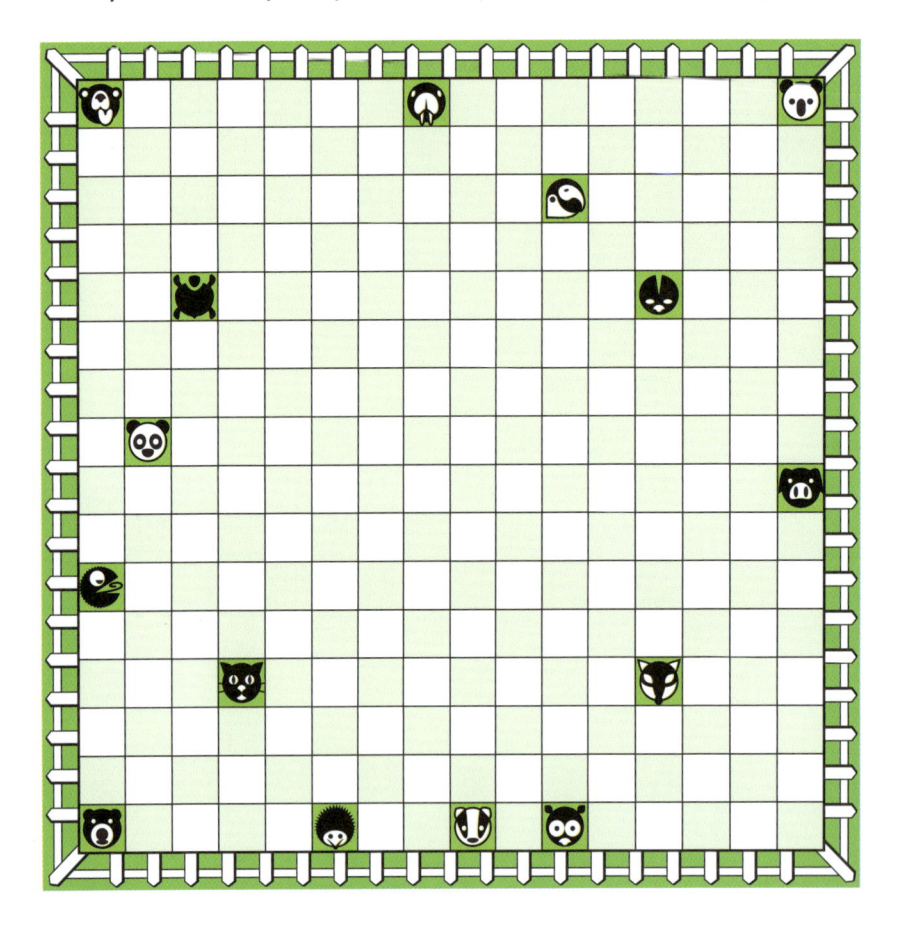

do you KNOW?

If cats are feline, what are sheep?

_____

DOODLE PUZZLE

A doodle puzzle is a combination of images, letters, and/or numbers that represent a word or a concept. If you cannot solve a doodle puzzle, do not look at the answer right away. Think hard—and outside the box.

$$\frac{SP}{SOR}$$

CROSSWORD: Surrounded

ACROSS

1. Pillow cover
5. "Norwegian Wood" instrument
10. "Welcome" sights
14. "Billy, Don't Be a ___" (1974 hit)
15. Mormon State city
16. Mormon State
17. "He was" in Caesar's time
18. BBs and bullets
19. All dried out
20. Vacation time surrounded by land?
23. Bemoans
24. "Addio!"
25. Careless
28. 2010 Jeff Bridges film
33. Chris in *The Losers*
34. *Get Smart* bad guys
35. Nuptial response
36. Canadian comedy duo surrounded by water?
40. Child-care author LeShan
41. Pythons
42. Scintillate
43. Canine specialists
46. Crinkled cotton
47. Starz! rival
48. Barbershop request
49. Stevie Wonder song surrounded by air?
57. Raise children
58. Overturn
59. Clef type
60. Occasional dummy
61. Backcomb
62. From ___ to stern
63. A bit pretentious
64. Cherbourg shes
65. Pipe tool

DOWN

1. Humorist Silverstein
2. Vengeful Olympian
3. Bedouin
4. Interstate sight
5. Deck suit
6. Madam Pince et al.
7. "Come ___ Window": Etheridge
8. Profess
9. Thorny shrub
10. Bog
11. To ___ (exactly)
12. Alpine lake
13. Yard structure
21. "Scherzo à la ___": Stravinsky
22. Spud sprout
25. Bonded again
26. Get around
27. *Apocalypto* character
28. "There you have it!" cries
29. *Glengarry Glen ___* (1992)
30. Acts of worship
31. Notions
32. *The Velvet Fog* singer
34. Clove hitch
37. Sheer
38. Jamaican fruits
39. Big name in diet shakes
44. Tennis point
45. "Son of" in Arabic
46. Leonine groups
48. Inflexible
49. Vicinity
50. *A Book of Nonsense* author
51. Final
52. German car
53. Cutlet meat
54. Canadian province: Abbr.
55. "Star" couple
56. Easy win

Curve Ball

A scientist does something to a ball and measures three things while the experiment is running. The measurements have been plotted on the graph below, which measures "height above ground," "speed," and "acceleration toward the ground."

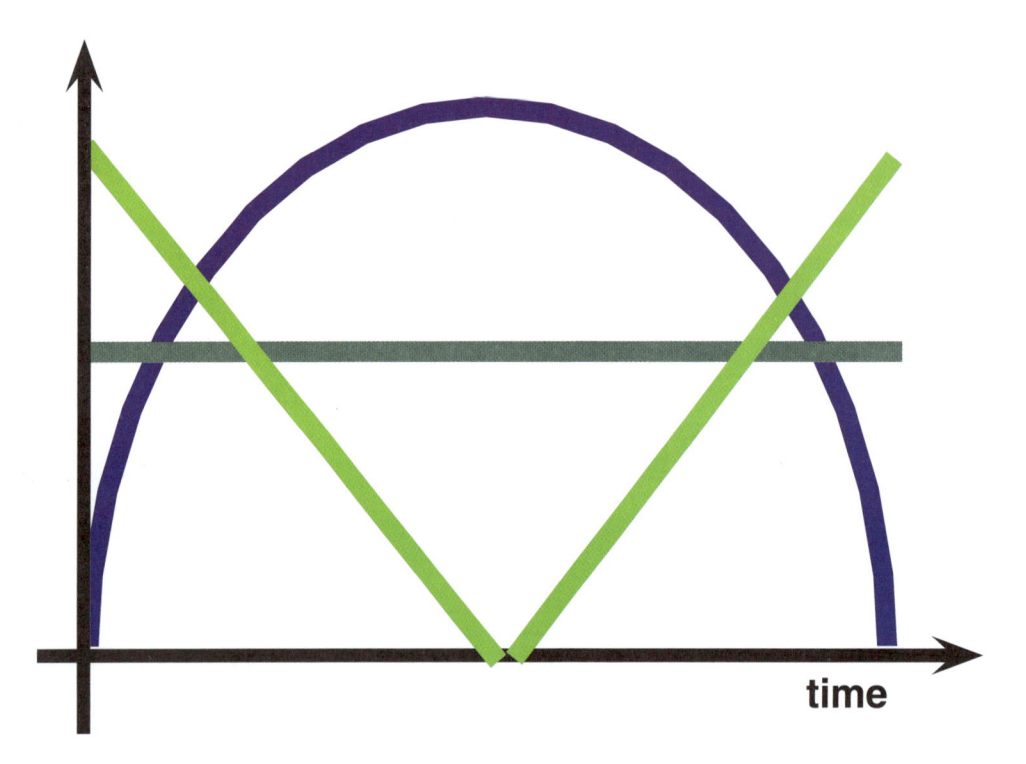

1. Explain what the scientist probably did to the ball.

   _____

2. Match the colored lines to the labels: "height above ground," "speed," and "acceleration toward the ground."

   _____

3. What name is given to the shape of the "height above ground" graph?

   _____

BRAINSNACK® Robot Romance

Robot B answers each of Robot A's statements according to an established pattern. What is its answer to LOVE YOU?

BIBOB OH
TATATI TATATA
HELLO HELLO
LOVE YOU

OBS
TIS
HOS
?

A

B

LETTER LINE

Put a letter in each of the squares below to make a word that means "precision tool." The number clues refer to other words that can be made from the whole.

7 1 4 4 8 9 3 GLOVES • 3 4 8 5 9 6 7 RIB CONNECTOR
7 1 2 8 5 EXTRACTOR • 2 1 9 8 IX

1	2	3	4	5	6	7	8	9	10

TRIVIA QUIZ **Legendary Lodgings**

The hotel business has always benefited from interesting stories, especially those that are impossible for people to forget. Do you remember enough to name all of these special spots?

1. Esther Williams starred in the 1949 movie *This Time for Keeps*, which was filmed at this Mackinac Island hotel.

2. Located at Fifth Avenue and Central Park South, this New York City hotel is also known as "The Home of Eloise" by Friends of Libraries, USA.

3. This Paradise Island resort, inspired by a lost city, features 50,000 marine animals swimming on site.

4. This swanky Park Avenue luxury spot was originally located on the site of the Empire State Building.

5. This boutique hotel just west of Los Angeles features Swan Lake in its picturesque front lawn.

6. Where was Robert Francis Kennedy shot?

7. What Memphis hotel features a daily parade of marching ducks?

8. Considered the tallest building in New York until 1899, this redbrick landmark played host to many notable artists, including Eugene O'Neill, William Burroughs, Arthur Miller, Jaspar Johns, Leonard Cohen, Janis Joplin, and Bob Dylan, among others.

9. There have been three hotels at the corner of State and Monroe streets in Chicago. Name the first, which burned down just 13 days after opening in 1871.

10. Originally called the Windsor Hotel, this Memphis sleeping spot is now home to the National Civil Rights Museum.

11. The Eagles won a Grammy for Record of the Year in 1977 for taking us all to this place with their music.

Keep Going

Start on a blank square of your choice and connect as many blank squares as possible with one single continuous line. You can only connect squares along vertical and horizontal lines, not along diagonal lines. You must continue the connecting lineup until the next obstacle, i.e., the border of the box, a black square, or a square that already has been used. You can change direction at any obstacle you meet. Each square can only be used once. The number of blank squares that will be left unused is marked in the upper square. There is more than one solution. We only show one solution.

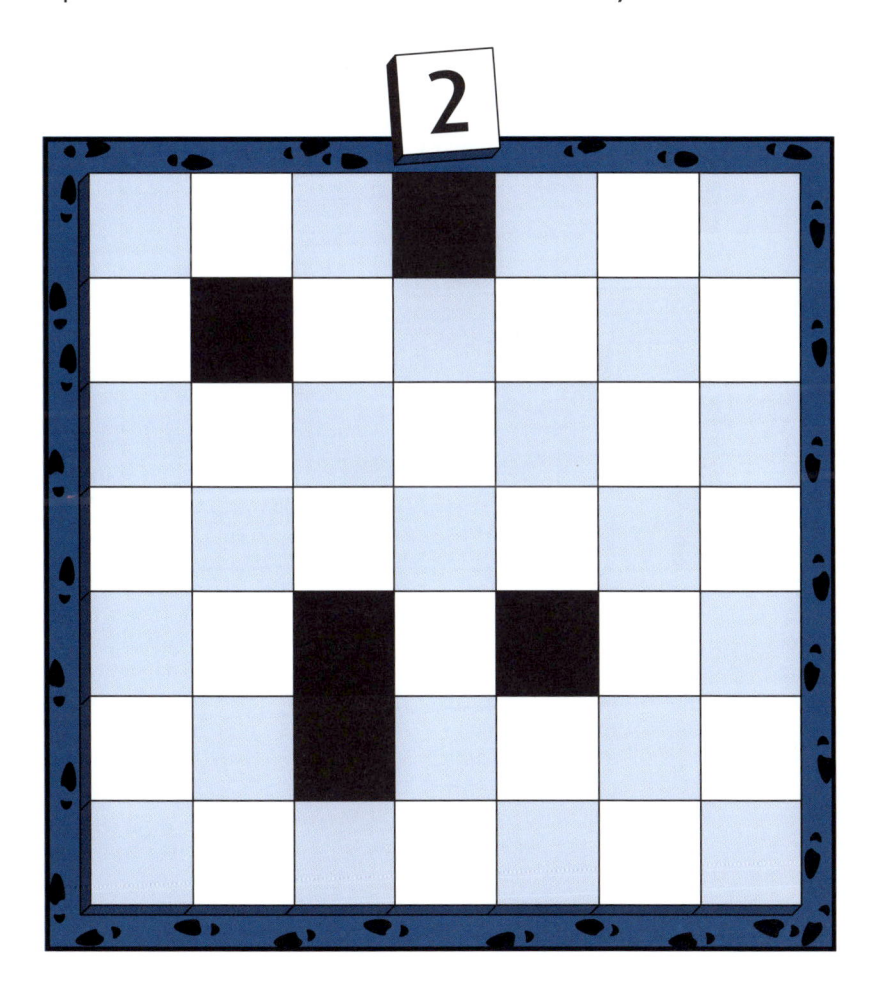

changeONE

Change one letter in each of these two words to form a common two-word phrase.

PRIME MEAL

CROSSWORD: The Simpsons

ACROSS

1. The *Kite Runner* boy
5. *The Limey* star Terence
10. "Pike's Peak or ___!"
14. "___ smile be your ..."
15. Martinique volcano
16. Filled cookie
17. Maggie Simpson's archenemy
19. S-shaped molding
20. 2009 Super Bowl champs
21. Phoenix nest
23. Mozart's *L'___ del Cairo*
24. Largest landmass
25. *Deep Impact* star Wood
29. Officer of the court
33. "Aw, shut up!"
34. Tequila of MTV
35. Icicle spot
36. Source of energy
37. Lobster eggs
38. *Gun Shy* actor Neeson
39. Almost-finished cigar
40. Cheers for the toreador
41. Clearing
42. Some protagonists
44. Dense
45. Witty remark
46. One to fight
47. Dragon that's a lizard
50. Ski race
55. Scottish actor Cumming
56. Homer Simpson's governor
58. *Little Man ___* (1991)
59. Sal in *Giant*
60. Boxer Benvenuti
61. Till slot
62. Atlanta university
63. James in *Giant*

DOWN

1. Clerical robes
2. Ravioli filling
3. "Wouldn't ___ Loverly?"
4. "If I Were You" singer Collin
5. Acceptance ___
6. ___ cotta
7. "Oi, vai!"
8. Karmazin of Sirius XM
9. Statue base
10. Springfield late-night monster movies host
11. Impulse
12. Clairvoyant
13. A rhea has six
18. Act self-satisfied
22. "O Sole ___"
24. Heavens holder
25. Digital dough
26. Starbucks order
27. "Peace ___ time": Chamberlain
28. Springfield Elementary bully
29. Buenos ___
30. Aquatic nymph
31. Duck the issue
32. Mideast land
34. "Apartment available"
37. Clear broth
41. Oscar winner Davis
43. Roadside bomb
44. Small dresser
46. Anteroom
47. Green Hornet's driver
48. *The Good Earth* heroine
49. Partner
50. 1962 James Bond film
51. Rearmost
52. "In a cowslip's bell ___": Shak.
53. Singer Horne
54. French cathedral city
57. "Fire!" preceder

WORD SEARCH: Sports

All the words are hidden vertically, horizontally, or diagonally—in both directions.

```
R L G N I C N E F A S P Y G O
A L S C I T E L H T A B E N R
W A T I N L O E S A G L K I P
F B H T O G L T Y U S L C W I
O Y R E H C R A R C A A O O D
G E L N T G A R B M E B H R O
U L O N A T R A A D M E E G W
T L E I R R E K O O N S C N N
N O B S A T A K L E S A I I H
C V X A M H E R C A C B H C I
P L I S S E T H G I A T S N L
W M I A E K P E L N R A L A L
Y I U M N C E O M P I C A D A
E Q O J B T S T R A D X L I B
S T D I I I O N B F O L O L F
O W U I N K N G C A E R M B R
T A J I N R S G N I L W O B O
U S S O R C O T O M L L E S K
```

- ARCHERY
- ATHLETICS
- BASEBALL
- BASKETBALL
- BOWLING
- BOXING
- CLIMBING
- CRICKET
- DANCING
- DARTS
- DOWNHILL
- DRESSAGE
- FENCING
- GOLF
- HANDBALL
- ICE HOCKEY
- JUDO
- KARATE
- KORFBALL
- MARATHON
- MOTOCROSS
- ROWING
- RUGBY
- SKI JUMP
- SLALOM
- SNOOKER
- SQUASH
- TENNIS
- TUG-OF-WAR
- VOLLEYBALL

WORD POWER: Extremes

Within the month of March, we greet the proverbial lion and lamb of weather. This quiz brings you other extremes and polar opposites.

1. **nethermost** ('neth-er-mohst) *adj.*—
   A: coldest. B: thinnest. C: lowest.

2. **extravagant** (ik-'stra-vi-gent) *adj.*—
   A: all gone. B: irate.
   C: over the top.

3. **acme** ('ak-mee) *n.*—
   A: verge. B: highest point.
   C: overflow.

4. **culminate** ('kul-mih-nayt) *v.*—
   A: fly into space. B: hit the bottom.
   C: reach a climax.

5. **acute** (uh-'kyoot) *adj.*—
   A: intense, urgent.
   B: tiny, insignificant.
   C: pretty, appealing.

6. **precipice** ('preh-sih-pis) *n.*—
   A: very steep side of a cliff.
   B: earliest moment.
   C: towering spire.

7. **superlative** (soo-'per-leh-tiv) *adj.*—
   A: outstanding. B: excessive. C: final.

8. **antithesis** (an-'ti-theh-sis) *n.*—
   A: exact opposite. B: end of time.
   C: extremely negative reaction.

9. **surfeit** ('sur-fet) *n.*—
   A: utter wreck. B: more than needed.
   C: intense heat.

10. **exorbitant** (ig-'zor-bih-tent) *adj.*—
    A: on a shore's edge.
    B: at a mountain's summit.
    C: far exceeding what is fair
    or reasonable.

11. **overweening** (oh-ver-'wee-ning)
    adj.— A: arrogant.
    B: too fond of food.
    C: severely strict.

12. **optimal** ('ahp-tih-mul) *adj.*—
    A: best. B: surplus.
    C: out of sight.

13. **radical** ('ra-di-kul) *n.*—
    A: supreme leader.
    B: extremist.
    C: middle-of-the-roader.

14. **penultimate** (peh-'nul-teh-mit)
    adj.— A: next to last.
    B: most recent.
    C: cream of the crop.

15. **maximal** ('mak-sih-mul) *adj.*—
    A: greatest possible.
    B: conflicting.
    C: most important.

16. **zealotry** ('ze-luh-tree) *n.*—
    A: extreme greed.
    B: overdone fervor.
    C: excess of noise.

CROSSWORD: Winning Spelling-Bee Words

ACROSS

1. No-___ mutual fund
5. Common name of Alpha Cygnus
10. Noncoms
14. Scopes Trial org.
15. Tomato swelling
16. Senior lobby
17. Twist in a bar
18. Improv joke
19. 5 Across is one
20. In an impertinent way
22. Chianti locale
24. Lock, stock and barrel
25. Fling to the mat
26. Planet visited by Flash Gordon
28. Winning word of 1940
31. "And now ..." sayer
34. ___ Romano (2001)
36. Victoria Island discoverer
37. Mr. Incredible Bob
38. Michigan Free Fair city
39. Cuban cow
40. Letters From ___ Jima (2006)
41. Join the club
42. "Old MacDonald" sounds
43. Green apple
45. Airbag, of a sort
47. Bluebird treat
48. Party punch?
52. Beatles' manager Brian
55. Changeling
56. 1980s pesticide
57. Ghana's largest city
59. Spare item
60. Big fish
61. Rabbit fur
62. Gull kin
63. Noncoms
64. Bar of sorts
65. Gulf of Aqaba city

DOWN

1. Memory gap
2. View from Coney Island
3. Aboriginal Alaskan
4. Winning word of 1949
5. Cleveland Plain ___"
6. Whirlpool
7. ___ blu dipinto di blu
8. Beam
9. Headscarf
10. NEXTEL Cup org.
11. Winning word of 1959
12. Algerian seaport
13. Chipper
21. "Dies ___" (funeral hymn)
23. Loom part
27. Jeer at
28. Sing like a bird
29. 52 cards
30. "For" votes
31. Sweeping story
32. Bryn ___
33. Winning word of 1970
35. "No, No, No" singer
38. Winning word of 1941
39. Winning word of 1952
41. "En garde" weapon
42. "Step ___!"
44. Hindu precepts
46. High ground
49. Mexican film award
50. Earth, in sci-fi films
51. "You ___ serious!"
52. Café sign
53. Free ad
54. "March Madness" org.
55. Domingo solo
58. Radar's rank: Abbr.

Sudoku X

Fill in the grid so that each row, each column, and each 3 x 3 frame contains every number from 1 to 9. The two main diagonals of the grid also contain every number from 1 to 9.

do you KNOW?

What is the capital of the Italian island of Sardinia?

___

IMPORTANT CAPITAL

There is one word that changes from a noun or verb to a nationality when its first letter is capitalized. What is it?

___

BRAINSNACK® Art of Numbers

Which number should replace the question mark?

LEONARDO DA VINCI

470231
59368?

CHANGELINGS

Each of the three lines of letters below should spell the names of breeds of dogs. Some of the letters have been mixed up. Four letters from the first breed are now in the third line, four letters from the third breed are in the second line, and four letters from the second breed are in the first line. The remaining letters are in their original places. What are the breeds?

B P O M D H O R N A
T O W E L A N I R N
R O T T L O E I U E D

Kakuro

Each number in a black area is the sum of the numbers that you have to enter in the next empty boxes. The empty boxes that make up the sum are called a run. The sum of the across run is written above the diagonal in the black area, and the sum of the down run is written below the diagonal. Runs can only contain the numbers 1 through 9, and each number in a run can only be used once. The gray boxes only contain odd numbers and the white only even numbers.

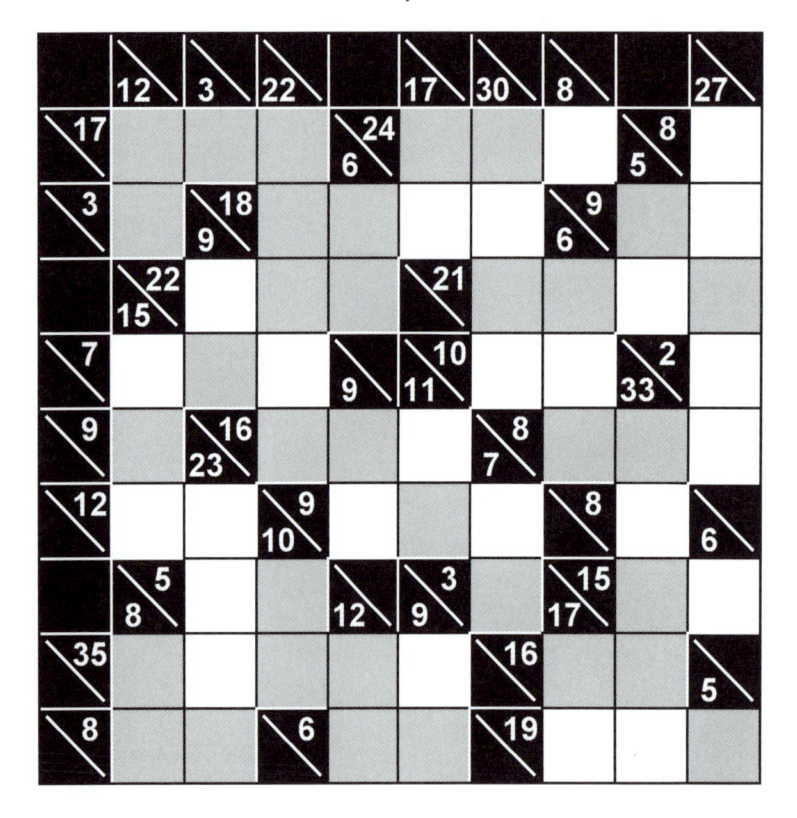

do you KNOW?

What is added to gin to make it "pink"?

SANDWICH

What five-letter word belongs between the word at left and the word at right, so that the first and second word, and the second and third word, each form a common compound word or phrase?

TIME _ _ _ _ _ WORK

Spot the Differences

Find the nine differences in the image on the bottom right.

do you KNOW?
What is entomology?

trivia
- What was the largest of Christopher Columbus's expeditionary vessels to sail from Spain across the Atlantic Ocean?

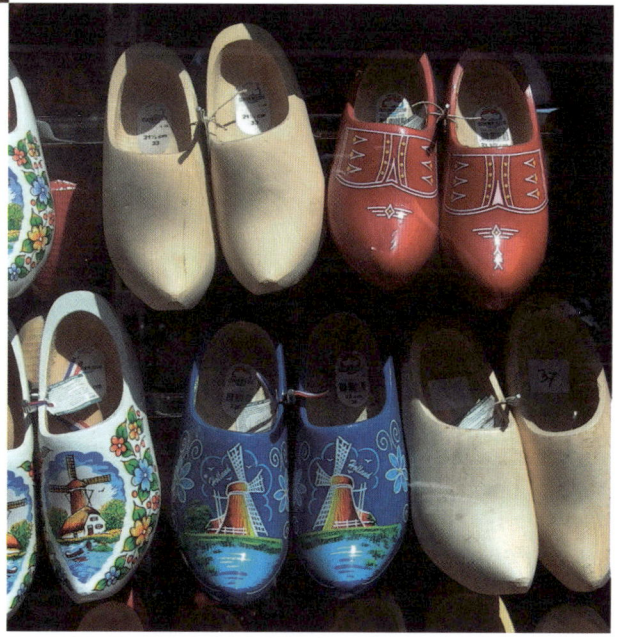

CROSSWORD: Bond Bad Guys

ACROSS
1. Bond opponent, 2 words
3. Vicious fish in *Live and Let Die*
8. Villain whose last name is the title of a Bond film, 2 words
10. In a 1964 film, Bond discovers the _____ of Jill Masterson covered in gold paint
11. First name of the evil colonel in *From Russia with Love*
13. Trucker's radio
17. Graphic showing data
20. Loud noise
21. *Thunderball* villain, Emilio _____ (pictured)
22. _____ Affair to Remember
24. Pair
25. Tatiana _____ in *From Russia with Love* is bait to lure Bond to his death
28. First name of the villain in *The Living Daylights*
30. Hang loosely
32. Former Russian space station
33. Shark-biting henchman in *The Spy Who Loved Me*
34. Villain from the Spangled Mob in *Diamonds are Forever*, 2 words
36. Charles _____ Reilly
38. Villain in *A View to a Kill*, Max _____
39. Soldier
41. Follower
42. Youngest March girl
43. Villain in *Live and Let Die*, 2 words
44. Evening gown

DOWN
1. Bond villain in *Moonraker,* named after one of Ian Fleming's friends
2. Drug pusher
3. Villain in *You Only Live Twice* who liked to pet white cats
4. Assassin in *From Russia With Love*, 2 words
5. The greatest boxer
6. Implore
7. What we breathe
9. Crime buster
12. *The Man From Uncle*'s Napoleon _____
14. Evidence of foul play, 2 words
15. Villain in *The Man with the Golden Gun*
16. Hospital trauma center
18. M's character was based on _____ John Godfrey, Ian Fleming's spy boss
19. Bond often gets one in the sunny islands he visits
23. Nickname for The Big Easy
26. Promises
27. Capp, Pacino and others
29. Police search
31. Partner of 34 across, 2 words
35. The _____ Show, hosted by Chuck Barris
37. Electrical unit
39. In Bond films, it's usually poisonous
40. Lung disease, abbr.
41. Santa ___

Pixel Fun

Color the correct squares black and discover the pixel image. The numbers on the outer border against the black or the white background indicate the total number of black or white squares on a column or row. The numbers on the inner border indicate the largest group of adjacent black or white squares to be found anywhere on that column or row. For instance, if there is a six on the outer ring and a two on the inner ring against a white background, then there are six white blocks in that row, and the biggest group or groups consist of a maximum of two adjacent white blocks.

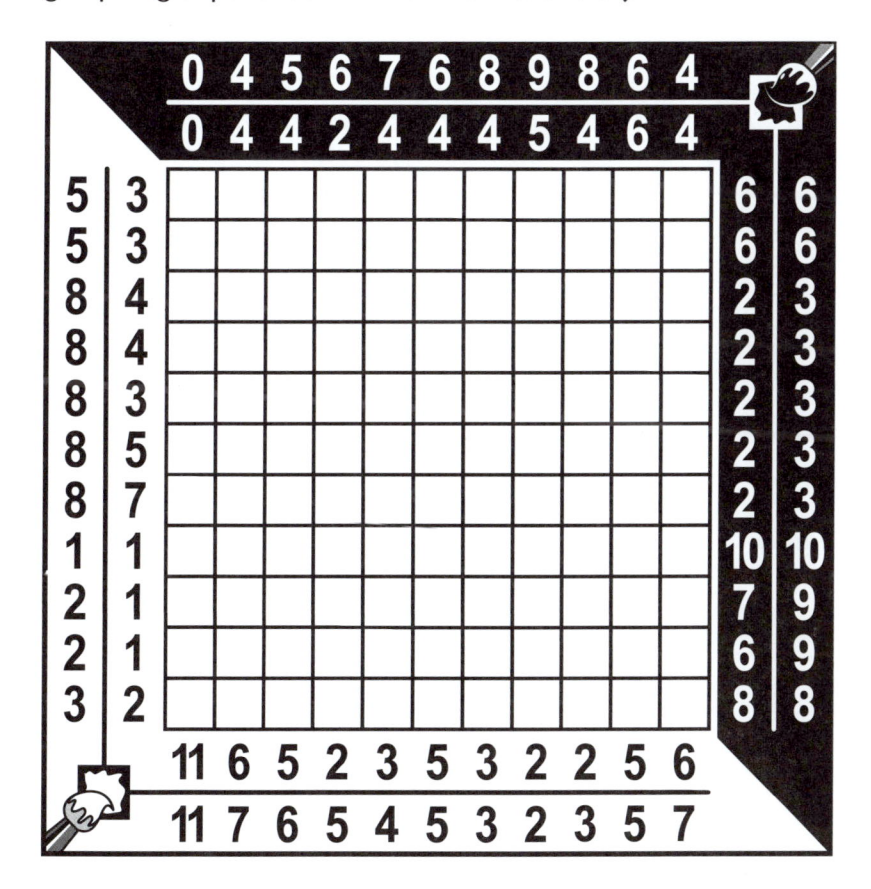

change ONE

Change one letter in each of these two words to form a common two-word phrase.

GRAIN TRAIN

_____

TRIVIA QUIZ **Beliefs from Other Lands**

Many cultures have myths describing the origin of their customs, rituals, and identity. See how well you know the gods, symbols, and heroes from these lands.

1. In Russian myth, what was Bannik the spirit of?
   a. The bakery
   b. The brewery
   c. The bathhouse
   d. The belfry

2. In Norse mythology, what form does the bridge called Bifrost take?
   a. A rainbow
   b. A giant snake
   c. A golden sword
   d. A cloud

3. What is a *havhest*?
   a. A magic Viking helmet
   b. A sea monster
   c. A Swedish pixie
   d. A Danish festival

4. Where, according to the ancient Greeks, does a dryad reside?
   a. In an animal
   b. In a lake
   c. In a rock
   d. In a tree

5. Which Polynesian god is said to have fished up the islands with a fish hook and given fire to mankind?
   a. Maui
   b. Rangi
   c. Papa
   d. Tane

6. The trickster god known as Anansi Spider in the West Indies originated on what continent?
   a. South America
   b. Australia
   c. North America
   d. Africa

7. Thoth, the Egyptian god of learning, was often depicted as what animal?
   a. A wolf
   b. A baboon
   c. An owl
   d. A monkey

8. What mythical Chinese animal was said to have the horns of a deer, the head of a camel, the claws of an eagle, and the feet of a tiger?
   a. The phoenix
   b. The sphinx
   c. The dragon
   d. The griffin

9. What, in Irish myth, is the Fianna?
   a. A screaming witch
   b. A royal bodyguard
   c. An enchanted sword
   d. A festival

10. Which Egyptian god presides over funeral rites and has the head of a jackal?
    a. Anubis
    b. Seth
    c. Isis
    d. Toth

CROSSWORD: The Simpsons 2

ACROSS
1 *Pâté de foie* ___
5 Flip a lid off
10 Cook Cajun-style
14 Meth lab buster
15 Veranda
16 *And Still* singer McEntire
17 Pilaster
18 Clio's sister Muse
19 A pop
20 Personal assistant to Monty Burns
23 Stow cargo
24 Caveman Alley
25 Deserve
28 *Little ___ Sunshine* (2006)
30 Nero's 300
33 "Milk's favorite cookie"
34 *Agnes Grey* author
36 Pizarro's gold
37 Springfield exotic dancer
40 1,000,000,000 years
41 Be an angel?
42 Paula Cole album
43 *ER* extras
44 Red carpet group
45 *Sanford and Son* spinoff
46 Jazz job
47 Askew
49 Springfield Elementary cafeteria chef
56 Aries or Taurus
57 Eternal City river
58 "Ack!!!!"
59 Neeson in *Ethan Frome*
60 *Dirty Dancing* director Ardolino
61 Broadway beacon
62 *Days of Grace* memoirist
63 Venetian magistrates
64 Balanced

DOWN
1 Waste away
2 Frog genus
3 A bit pretentious
4 Leek or shallot
5 Knock over
6 Icelandic speakers
7 Hit the books
8 *Hamlet* starter
9 Old copy
10 Pussyfoot around
11 Lend an ear
12 *Sesame Street* lesson
13 Arena shout
21 Straw grass
22 *Backdraft* gear
25 Vespa
26 Misstep
27 Jockey straps
28 Grandma of art
29 Signs
30 Pause sign
31 Shouted
32 Cliché-ridden
34 Unenlightened
35 "Answer, please"
38 Municipal
39 Pequod's missiles
45 The Omnipotent
46 Aphorism
47 "Chasing Pavements" singer
48 Greek harps
49 *Los Olvidados* director Buñuel
50 Normandy beach
51 Exec's wheels
52 "Nine, ten, ___ fat hen"
53 *Cheers* actress Perlman
54 Part of the loop
55 40-decibel unit
56 "Au" alternative

WEATHER CHART **Cloudy**

Where will the clouds appear? With the knowledge that each arrow points to a place where a symbol should be, can you locate the cloudy spots? The symbols cannot be next to each other vertically, horizontally, or diagonally. A symbol cannot be placed on top of an arrow. We show one symbol.

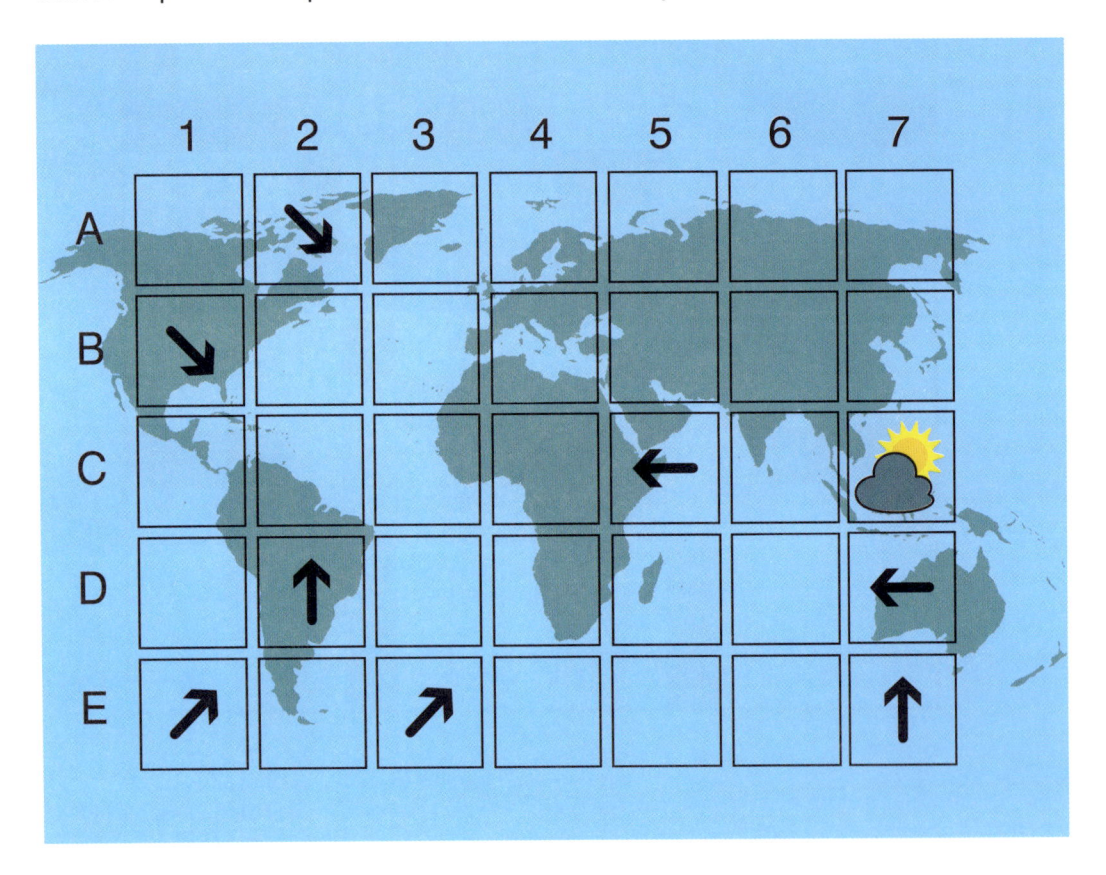

DOUBLETALK

What three-letter word will need you to bend at the waist or tie with a ribbon?

Sudoku

Fill in the grid so that each row, each column, and each 3 × 3 frame contains every number from 1 to 9.

		2			4		5	1
1	7		5			4		8
				3	1			
							2	5
	6		9					3
8		5			3			
		8				7	4	
5					2			
				1				

do you KNOW?

What is the average life expectancy of a camel?

HIDDEN WORDS

Think of the three separate words that, when grouped into one, mean exactly that.

_ _   _ _ _   _ _ _

Binairo

Complete the grid with zeros and ones until there are 6 zeros and 6 ones in every row and every column. No more than two of the same number can be next to or under each other. Rows or columns with exactly the same content are not allowed. There is only one valid solution.

trivia
- Where was Leonardo da Vinci born?

MISSING LETTER PROVERB

Fill in each missing letter, indicated by an X, to make a well-known proverb.

TXE XXRXX XIRX XAXCXEX TXE XOXM

Number Cluster

Cubes showing numbers have been placed on the grid below, with some spaces left empty. Can you complete the grid by creating runs of the same number and of the same length as the number? So, where a cube with number 5 has been included on the grid, you need to create a run of five number 5's, including the cube already shown. The run can be horizontal, vertical, or both horizontal and vertical.

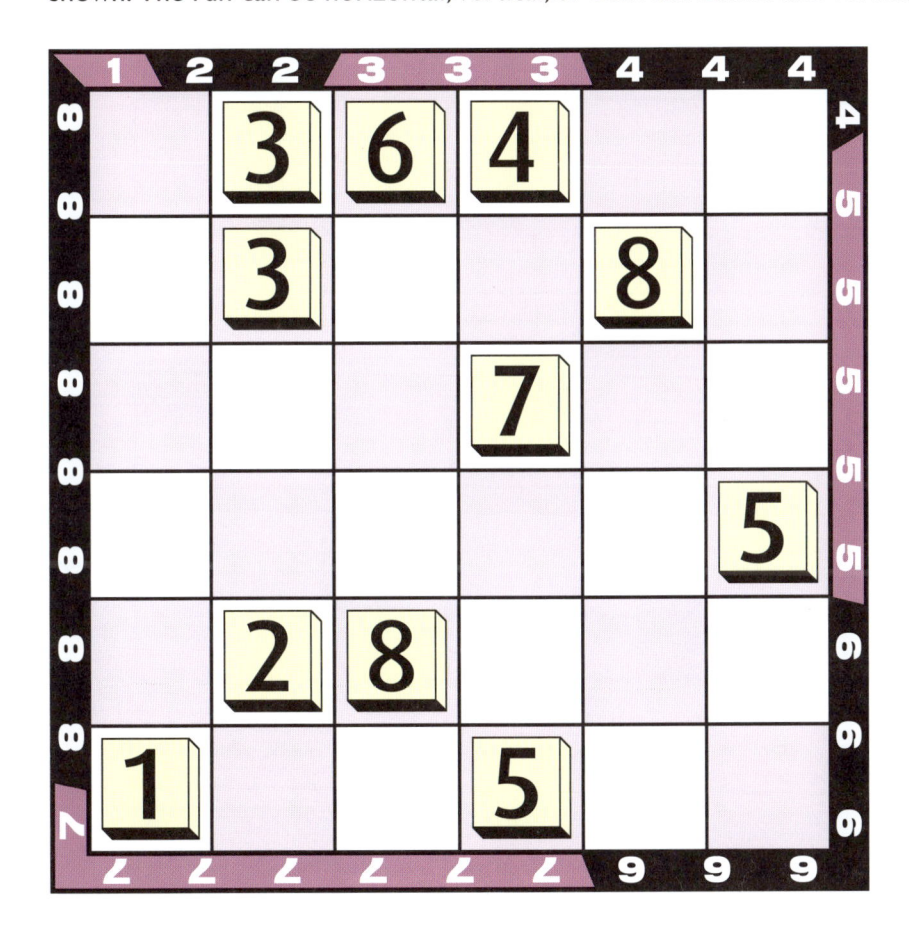

do you KNOW?

What is "aqua fortis" better known as?

_____

WORKPLACES

Rearrange the letters in the words below to spell out the names of different workers.

LAMENESS DRIVE INTERIMS CHEATER TERRAIN

CROSSWORD: Dig Deep

ACROSS
1 Police officer
4 Ali ___ and the Forty Thieves
8 Requirement
12 Actress Gardner
13 Spring flower
14 Desire
15 ___ Miserables
16 Spring is time to replace the ___ in the garden
18 Start planting in spring after the last ___
20 Sea lion kin
21 "Roses ___ red..."
23 Had nighttime visions
27 Use this decayed organic material for fertilizer
31 "Dwelt a miner, forty-___"
32 Spanish gold
33 Female pig
35 ___ chi (type of exercise)
36 Genius group
39 Gardeners spend time ___ the soil in spring
42 One-celled organism
44 Former GM brand
45 Jeans maker Strauss
47 Early spring bloomer
51 Garden sprouts
55 Before mark or lobe
56 ___ the Wild
57 Excited
58 The ___ of Innocence
59 Quantity of paper
60 International military alliance (abbr.)
61 Snappy dresser

DOWN
1 Baby cow
2 "The bear went ___ the mountain"
3 Texas city, El ___
4 Cafe
5 Rainbow shape
6 Prejudice
7 ___ as a beet (2 words)
8 The center of atoms
9 Goof
10 Feeling of importance
11 It's found on the grass in the morning
17 Merit
19 It leaks from a tree
22 Road curve
24 Against, prefix
25 Not nice
26 Math subject (abbr.)
27 Unconscious state
28 Utah city
29 One, prefix
30 Youngster
34 Hairpiece
37 Rare
38 Cain's brother
40 Releases (2 words)
41 CNN's Dobbs
43 Relating to birds
46 Actress Swenson
48 Part of a tree
49 Villain in Othello
50 Spring planting involves bed ___
51 British title
52 Kentucky to West Virginia direction (abbr.)
53 Airport abbr.
54 Have

WORD SEARCH: Half-Baked

All the words are hidden vertically, horizontally, or diagonally—in both directions.

```
K R Q F P E C I U J B J H Y F H C S P
C S P J U V H R E K O O C I I F T D O
O S U S A N Z U C C H I N I V E L R H
R S G U O R N U E K S N E C E E R G F
C Y T X V L S E C K P J H B C E U M Z
U Q R R Q B I J L M Q I N J L P C U K
G A C W A L J D M C S I Q E Z A I L W
Z P I J X I D V S G T C E K R C M D X
Y M M Z S B N L R C J P E R Y W E R F
W H M N L A F E E O P T O S D O C T V
A Y A H V W B P R O C T S T Z N U U Z
A E M D W T U G P H S H H J Z J A A A
B Q E O T O U G U I P E A C H E S R H
E O C D J N G P L P C S D D B V E K K
C L E N T G I C C R W K W H C B L J T
J K W W S S W A S L A S L O E H P S W
A A S E O T A M O T J I R E E J P A Y
M Q E R Z N G I V F D N J T S Z A U R
K G Q C I A V C G R E M I T Y L K G W
```

- APPLESAUCE
- BEANS
- BEETS
- CARROTS
- COOKER
- CORN
- CROCK
- FUNNEL
- JAM
- JARS
- JUICE
- KETCHUP
- KRAUT
- LIDS
- PEACHES
- PECTIN
- PEELER
- PICKLES
- SALSA
- STRAINER
- TIMER
- TOMATOES
- TONGS
- ZUCCHINI

NAME THAT CAR — Heir to the Farm Car

When the weather got hot, one could mount an old-time swamp cooler on the side window, of this full-sized automobile produced by the American manufacturer Plymouth. But usually the cowl vent kept passengers comfortable. Can you name the year and model?

tips

1. The car hood has an image of the Mayflower.
2. The automaker switched to working for the war effort in this model year.
3. The model carried the chassis code P-14C.
4. This model year was the last to use a hand crank to start the engine.
5. For wartime production, some of the maker's cars this year had less metal trim, nicknamed blackout models.

CHANGELINGS

Each of the three lines of letters below spell the names of islands, but some of the letters have been mixed up. Four letters from the first name are now in the third line, four letters from the third name are in the second line, and four letters from the second name are in the first line. The remaining letters are in their original places. What are the names of the islands?

A	A	T	A	Q	A	S	U	A	R
M	C	R	N	I	N	I	S	A	E
M	I	M	R	O	D	E	G	I	E

CROSSWORD: Dancing with Fred

ACROSS
1 Harry Potter's Hedwig
4 Woodard in *Mandela*
9 Lobster trap
12 Competed
14 Sniggled
15 Compos mentis
16 Ballerina Pavlova
17 "The Highwayman" poet
18 Steamed
19 Pewter component
20 Oklahoma city
21 Beseech
22 Empty
24 Probable
25 City SE of Paris
28 Smiles
30 Hunter in *Crash*
31 Fall guy
32 Going into overtime
36 Notion: Comb. form
37 "Operator" singer Jim
38 Jim Davis dog
39 Broadway sign
40 Inventor Elias
41 Scrat's *Ice Age* quest
42 Scott in *Secretariat*
44 Big name in sunglasses
45 *Barbary Shore* author
48 Country singer Clark
50 Messed up
51 Bewail
52 Convent members
56 Dancing shoe
57 Twain's "Ah Sin" collaborator
58 Biting fly
59 Scams
60 Wicker wood
61 Corn Belt tower
62 Sancho's mount
63 Mountebank
64 *This Is Spinal ___* (1984)

DOWN
1 Ford's logo
2 Coq au vin ingredient
3 *Victory* heroine
4 Trojan War hero
5 Téa in *Spanglish*
6 Where Fred first danced with Ginger
7 Panpipe
8 Asner and O'Neill
9 "After they've seen ___ ..."
10 Shaq of the NBA
11 Nursery bear
13 Where Fred danced with Leslie
15 Where Fred danced with Cyd
21 Flagstick
23 Marina del ___
24 Vitamin-C source
25 Bony
26 Was a passenger
27 Stick in the fridge
29 Hare loss
31 Ralston of *127 Hours*
33 Pedestal figure
34 Hibernia
35 Disavow
37 *Burlesque* star
41 Bern river
43 Headed up
44 Cantankerous
45 Gene Pitney hit
46 Guthry and Eisenberg
47 Callaway clubs
49 Polished off
51 Pulpy mixture
53 Module
54 *Lion King's* queen
55 Give it a rest
57 Hip partner

Word Sudoku

Complete the grid so that each row, each column, and each 3 x 3 frame contains the nine letters from the black box below. The hidden nine-letter word is in the diagonal from top left to bottom right.

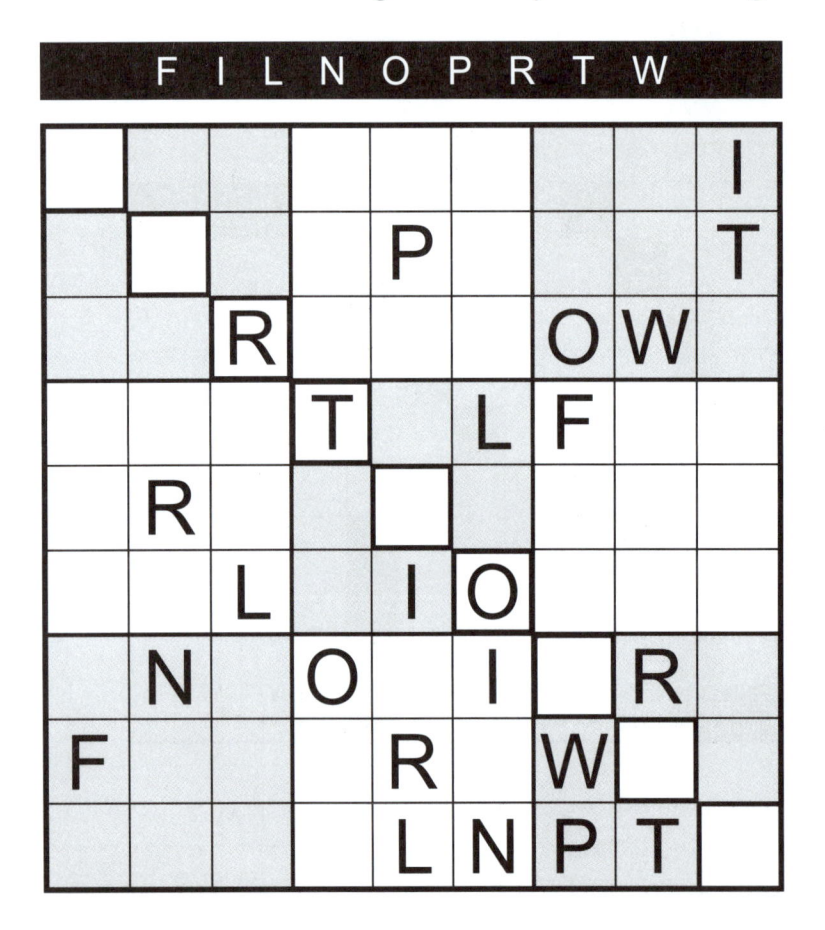

F I L N O P R T W

								I
				P				T
		R					O	W
			T		L	F		
	R							
		L		I	O			
	N		O		I		R	
F				R		W		
			L	N	P	T		

trivia
- What is "agerasia"?

_____

ONE LETTER LESS OR MORE

The word on the right side contains the letters of the word on the left side, plus or minus the letter in the middle. One letter is already in the right place.

C A N C E L E D +O ☐ ☐ ☐ C ☐ ☐ ☐ ☐

BRAINSNACK® Parking Spaces

Which cars (1–6) belong in parking spaces A to G?

DOUBLETALK

What five-letter word can either mean part of a tree or to stab?

_____

Sport Maze

Draw the shortest way from the ball to the goal. You can only move along vertical and horizontal lines, not along diagonal lines. The figure on each square indicates the number of squares the ball must move in the same direction. You can change direction at each stop.

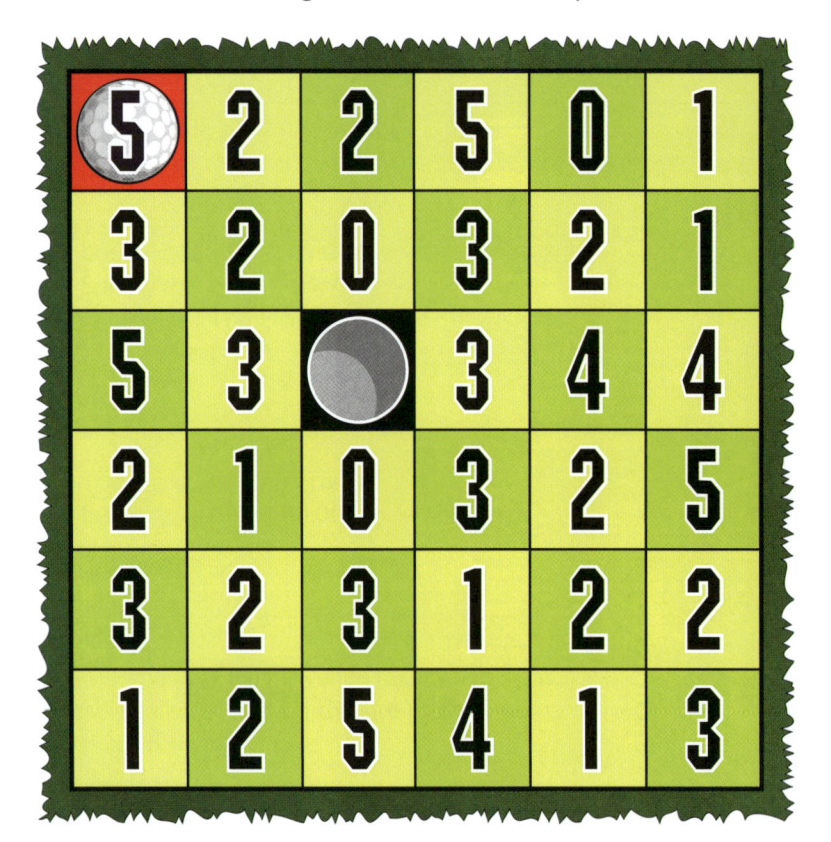

do you KNOW?

What city in India was once called Madras?

_____

RUNNING REPAIRS
Adding the same letters front and back puts this word back together.
__ __ __ to __ __ __

TRIVIAL PURSUIT Liverpool Lads

Last names quickly were superfluous for John, Paul, George and Ringo, who had a blockbuster year in 1964.

HOW MANY OTHER BEATLES' FAB FIRSTS DO YOU REMEMBER?

1 These two albums issued 10 days apart by different record companies are the first Beatles' albums with a U.S. release.

2 This No. 1 hit is the band's first in the U.S.

3 A jaw-dropping 73 million people first see them live on this TV show.

4 The Fab Four play their first American concert here.

5 The Beatles were one of only a few groups to occupy multiple top spots on Billboard's Top 100 simultaneously. How many songs were in the top five?

6 The Beatles' first film premieres in London on July 6. Its name?

7 The Beatles meet this folk singer for the first time at the Delmonico hotel in New York.

8 This 1978 Robert Zemeckis comedy about Beatlemania depicts the group's first appearance on American TV.

9 Who brought the Beatles to the United States?

10 What age were the Beatles when they landed in New York in 1964?

CROSSWORD: Holiday Treats

ACROSS

1. ___ the Man Down
5. ___ and pans
9. Cable internet alternative
12. Ursa Major animal
13. Westerner Wyatt
14. Airport abbr.
15. Holiday baked good: fruit___
16. Holiday candy with caramel and nuts
18. "___, Captain!"
20. Positive attribute
21. Lessen
24. ___ Day (June holiday)
26. Teens who like to wear black
27. Delivery service
28. Holiday candy: buck___
29. Much ___ About Nothing
30. Common bird
34. Hairpiece
35. Billy Joel's instrument
36. Evaluate one to another
40. Finished
41. Tests
42. Person honored on 24 Across
43. Holiday candy, also called seafoam
46. Smell
50. Lemon drink
51. Garfield's roommate
52. Had on
53. Cartoon characters ___ and Stimpy
54. Gets some sun
55. Flower's base

DOWN

1. English TV channel
2. Meadow
3. Grand tree
4. Holiday treat: cornflake ___
5. Cartoon character ___ Le Pew
6. Canoe need
7. ___ la la
8. Makes an impact like a water balloon
9. Thick
10. Bull
11. Survives a long time
17. Kind of (suffix)
19. 18 Across synonym
21. An ___-old truth
22. Little guy
23. Had breakfast
24. Holiday candy usually made of chocolate
25. GI's address
29. What you breathe
30. Holiday cookies: stained glass ___
31. Awesome
32. Direction opposite WSW
33. ___ off to sleep
34. "Rome ___ built in a day" (2 words)
35. Tiny green veggie
36. Fragrant wood
37. Iron ___ (rust)
38. Whiz
39. Extra fee for house payments (abbr.)
42. Colors fabric
44. Ore-___ french fries
45. Old material for roofs
47. Nickname for Dorothy
48. Mineral such as iron
49. Stage of sleep

Binairo

Complete the grid with zeros and ones until there are 5 zeros and 6 ones in every row and every column. No more than two of the same number can be next to or under each other. Rows or columns with exactly the same content are not allowed. There is only one valid solution.

triVia

- What did Burt Lancaster do in the circus?

MISSING LETTER PROVERB

Fill in each missing letter, indicated by an X, to make a well-known proverb.

XEXNX XIXE PXXNX FXXLXSX

TRIVIA QUIZ **Taking a Leaf from Literature**

Authors often draw on the natural world in their creations.
Can you tell what happens when nature and these written works collide?

1. What plant of the primrose family was the code name of Baroness Orczy's spy character?
   a. The Fushia Fandango
   b. The Clarkia Rubicunda
   c. The Scarlet Pimpernel

2. What is the only insectivorous mammal to appear in the title of a Shakespeare play?
   a. The bat
   b. The badger
   c. The shrew

3. The title of what John Steinbeck novel includes the name of a rodent and a primate?
   a. *King Rat*
   b. *The Organ Grinder's Monkey*
   c. *Of Mice and Men*

4. What group of insects appears in the title of William Golding's reworking of *The Coral Island*?
   a. Flies, in *Lord of the Flies*
   b. Locusts, in *Day of the Locusts*
   c. Ants, in *King of the Ant Hill*

5. In the *Ingoldsby Legends*, what thieving bird was cursed by the Cardinal Lord Archbishop?
   a. The Jackdaw of Rheims
   b. The Altar Boy's Macaw
   c. The Bishop's Canary

6. Who wrote *The Scarlet Letter*?
   a. Nathaniel Hawthorne
   b. Henry David Thoreau
   c. Washington Irving

7. In a movie about Henry II and his wife Eleanor of Aquitaine (based on a Broadway play), Henry was referred to as what large carnivore at what time of year?
   a. The bear in springtime
   b. The lion in winter
   c. The vulture in November

8. What type of whale was the subject of the novel *Moby Dick*?
   a. A killer whale
   b. A humpback whale
   c. A sperm whale

9. Which tree appears in the title of a wintry novel by David Gutterson?
   a. Aspen *(The Aspens of Vail)*
   b. Cedar *(Snow Falling on Cedars)*
   c. Maple *(Maple Syrup, New Hampshire Hotcakes)*
   d. Apple *(Apple House Rules)*

10. Which bird appears in a poem by Edgar Allen Poe, where it says repeatedly, "Nevermore"?
    a. Mockingbird
    b. Raven
    c. Parrot

BRAINSNACK® Letter Logic

Underlined words below satisfy a certain logic. Which word—not underlined—also follows that same logic?

> Odio dignixim qui blandit praesent luptatum zzril delenit augue duix dolore te feugait nulxa facilisi. Loro ixsum dolor sit amex, consectetuer adixcinang elit, sed diam nonummy nibh euismod tincidunt ux laxoreet dolorex magna aliquam erat volutpat.

FIVES AND FOURS

Each line contains a five-letter and four-letter word that have been mixed together (the order of the letters in each word has not been changed). Unmix the two words on each line and write them in the spaces provided. When you're done, find a two-part answer to the clue by reading down the letter columns in the answers.

CLUE: Top of the bill?

S S P W O I R D T _ _ _ _ _ + _ _ _ _
Z T A U B L L E U _ _ _ _ _ + _ _ _ _
A S O A B O R V E _ _ _ _ _ + _ _ _ _
M R O A D O N A R _ _ _ _ _ + _ _ _ _

Cage the Animals

Draw lines to completely divide up the grid into small squares, with exactly one animal per square. The squares should not overlap.

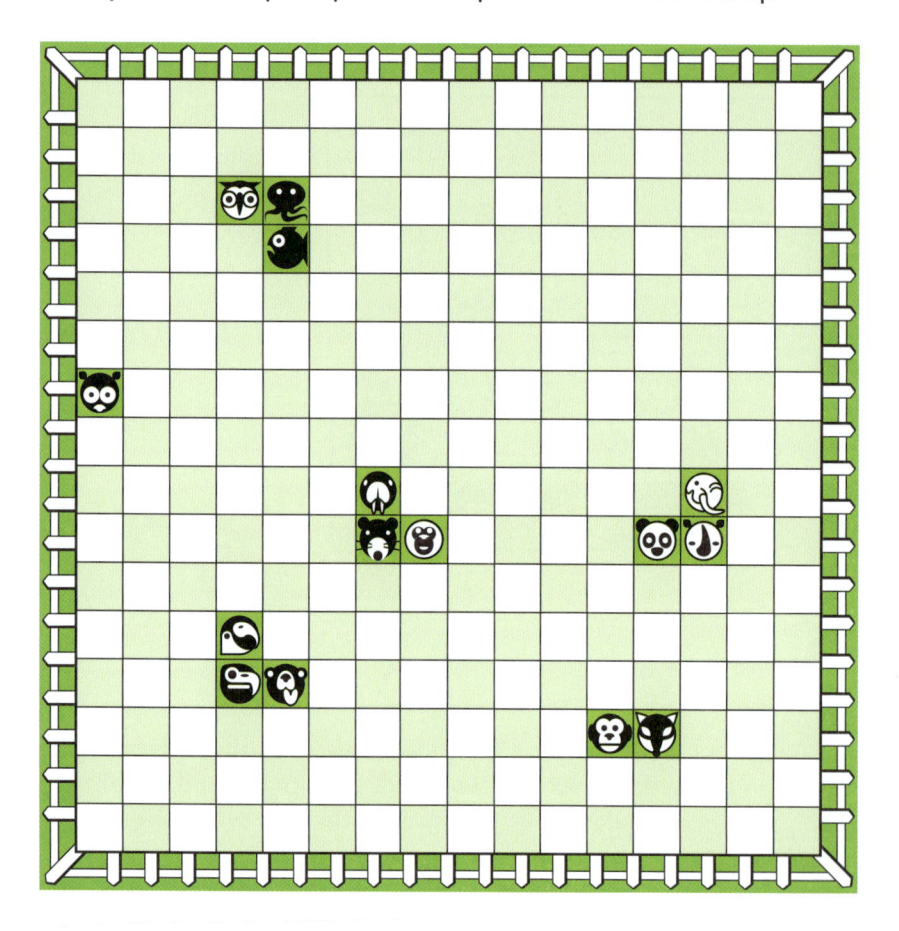

do you KNOW?

What is hummus made of?

ODD CAP OUT

Which baseball cap (1-6) does not belong?

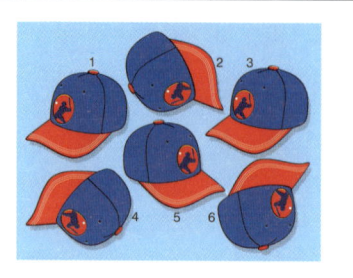

CROSSWORD: Eclectic Mix

ACROSS
1. Sink or swim, e.g.
5. Hennessy and Ireland
10. A hole in the wall?
14. "En garde" weapon
15. "Arrivederci!"
16. Nuncupative
17. Ocean motion
18. Athletic competitions
19. A faux fur
20. Edinburgh daily, with "The"
22. 1/3 a James Brown hit
24. "Follow me, Fido"
25. Visionary
26. Honda model
29. Minacious
33. Dry Italian wine
34. Big bins
35. Place for an icicle
36. Sheet of stamps
37. Sexy Beatles girl
38. Fairway obstacle
39. Mouse target
40. Richard in *Pollyanna*
41. Change a bill
42. "___ Trees in Flower": van Gogh
44. Like 76 trombones?
45. Amazon.com, for one
46. Diner's card
47. Clue in
50. Diana Ross film
54. Bamboozle
55. Watts in *The International*
57. Boxer Oscar De La ___
58. Once, formerly
59. Neckwear item
60. "___ Day Has Come": Celine Dion
61. Bit of folklore
62. Abated
63. Citi Field team

DOWN
1. Cat scanners?
2. *Aeneid*, for one
3. Alter the appearance of
4. Pastoral Symphony
5. Filled to capacity
6. "In an ___ world ..."
7. Creditor's claim
8. Nadal's reserve?
9. Hitchcock specialty
10. *Of Human Bondage* author
11. *The Magic Flute* solo
12. Groupies
13. *A Shot in the Dark* actress Sommer
21. All dried up
23. Aloha Day wear
25. 1960s protest
26. Base for food glazes
27. Athletic advisor
28. Tippy craft
29. President of Egypt (1970–81)
30. Weight deductions
31. Smoothes out
32. Bassoon-like
34. Amorphous
37. Send up the river
41. Florentine river
43. "My country, ___ ..."
44. After
46. "Crazy Blues" singer Smith
47. "Beg pardon"
48. Blue fish in *Finding Nemo*
49. All-encompassing
50. Extinct ostrich cousins
51. Primo
52. "No way, Sergei!"
53. Course deviations
56. Epiphanic cry

Kakuro

Each number in a black area is the sum of the numbers that you have to enter in the next empty boxes. The empty boxes that make up the sum are called a run. The sum of the across run is written above the diagonal in the black area, and the sum of the down run is written below the diagonal. Runs can only contain the numbers 1 through 9, and each number in a run can only be used once. The gray boxes only contain odd numbers and the white only even numbers.

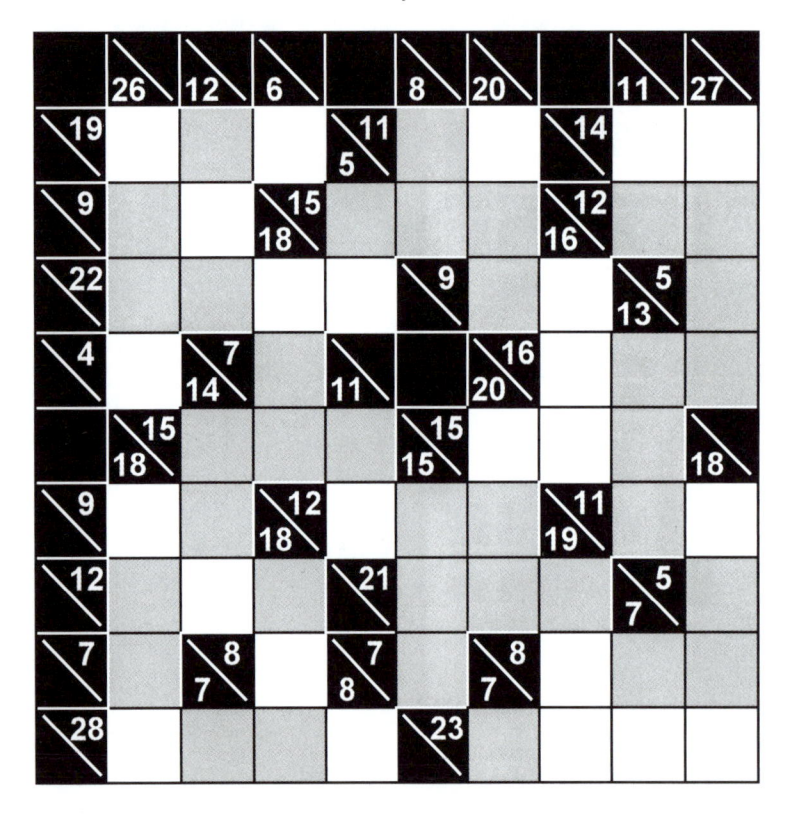

do you KNOW?

Who discovered chloroform?

_____

ONE LETTER LESS OR MORE

The word on the right side contains the letters of the word on the left side, plus or minus the letter in the middle. One letter is already in the right place.

DECIPHER -H- ☐☐ E ☐☐☐☐

Keep Going

Start on a blank square of your choice and connect as many blank squares as possible with one single continuous line. You can only connect squares along vertical and horizontal lines, not along diagonal lines. You must continue the connecting lineup until the next obstacle, i.e., the border of the box, a black square, or a square that already has been used. You can change direction at any obstacle you meet. Each square can only be used once. The number of blank squares that will be left unused is marked in the upper square. There is more than one solution. We only show one solution.

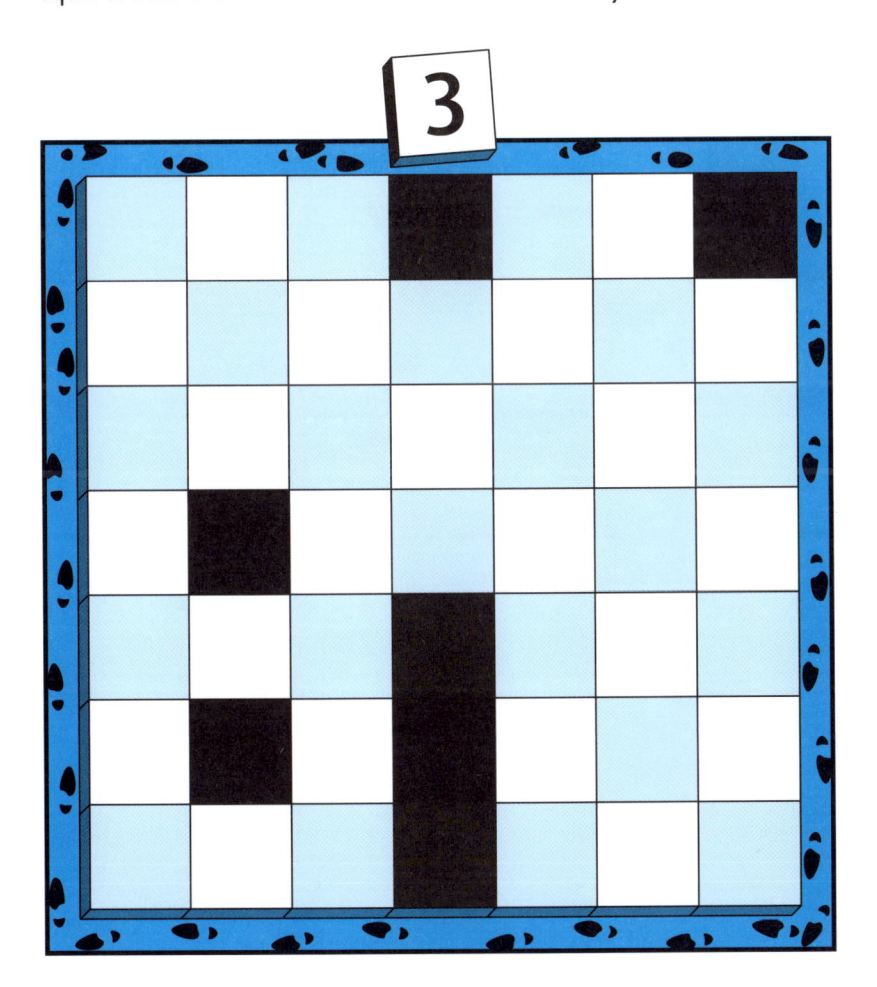

3

change ONE

Change one letter in each of these two words to form a common two-word phrase.
WINE PUNCH

MIND MAZE **Weights**

Make the set of scales balance by placing all the supplied weights in the pans — one weight per pan. The weight of the rods and pans can be ignored, and the stripes on each rod are of exactly the same length. To get you started, the one-pound weight has already been placed.

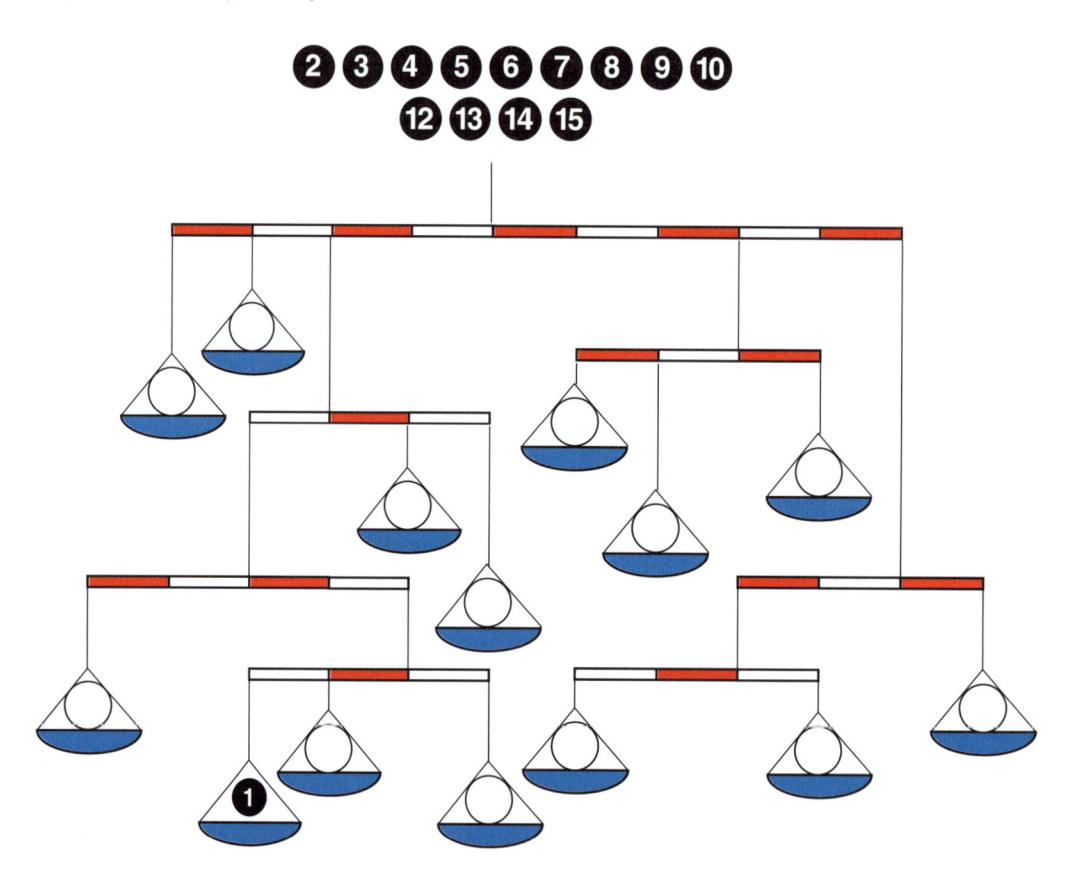

2 3 4 5 6 7 8 9 10
12 13 14 15

SOUND ALIKE

Homophones or homonyms are pairs of words that sound the same but are spelled differently. One of such a pair means to hit or strike; the other is a vegetable. What are they?

_____

WORD SEARCH: Thriller

All the words are hidden vertically, horizontally, or diagonally—in both directions.

```
E C L A N C Y T O M M H T N R
R A I C L L E G A E R I P W E
U R S T T H I H N T E N I O S
T R A O M T S D L E O F R R A
N I D R R I E U A E F W C B H
E E I E R S A C M T L I S I C
V O V G T S V N H E N T A L G
D E N J S E I S E T M N T R E
A I U A A S C D H V Y E W A E
L R R L A I T T E O E S N S B
Y T E E T H I E I N R S R T N
A M L I C E M O F V T R T O O
H E L C A T F A M O E I O U F
C O I S L R O B B E R Y T R S
P O K T I I R R E C O R D Y D
B Y U O B M M U L D U L I C A
H A E R I N I A L L I V L J R
A C K Y T S O N X M U S I C K
```

- ACTOR
- ADVENTURE
- ALIBI
- ASSAULT
- BATTLE
- BROWN
- CARRIE
- CHASE
- CLANCY
- CLIMAX
- COURT
- DARK
- DETECTIVE
- DIRECTOR
- FORSYTH
- GRISHAM
- HORROR
- IDENTITY
- JURY
- KILLER
- LUDLUM
- MEMENTO
- MENDES
- MUSIC
- POLITICS
- ROBBERY
- SCRIPT
- SEVEN
- STORY
- VERTIGO
- VICTIM
- VILLAIN
- WITNESS

WORD POWER: Verbal Misuse

Combat conversation miscues with our quiz, which tackles some frequent examples of verbal misuse (and abuse!). How sure are you about these troublemaking morphemes? Let's see!

1. **noisome** ('noy-sum) *adj.*—
   A: loud. B: stinky. C: crowded.

2. **enervated** ('eh-ner-vayt-ed) *adj.*—
   A: lacking energy. B: refreshed.
   C: feeling anxiety.

3. **proscribe** (proh-'skriyb) *v.*—
   A: encourage.
   B: dispense a medicine. C: forbid.

4. **nonplussed** (non-'pluhst) *adj.*—
   A: baffled. B: cool under pressure.
   C: subtracted.

5. **principle** ('prin-seh-pul) *n.*—
   A: interest-earning money.
   B: basic rule. C: school head.

6. **flout** ('flowt) *v.*—
   A: display proudly. B: scorn.
   C: defeat decisively.

7. **discrete** (dis-'kreet) *adj.*—
   A: separate and distinct.
   B: showing good manners.
   C: whole and \undamaged.

8. **ingenuous** (in-'jen-yew-us) *adj.*—
   A: showing innocence or simplicity.
   B: extremely clever.
   C: one-of-a-kind.

9. **cachet** (ka-'shay) *n.*—
   A: secret stockpile.
   B: perfumed bag.
   C: prestige.

10. **allusion** (uh-'lew-zhun) *n.*—
    A: misleading image or perception.
    B: crazy idea.
    C: indirect reference.

11. **reticent** ('reh-tuh-sent) *adj.*—
    A: inclined to keep silent.
    B: reluctant. C: backward.

12. **bemused** (bih-'myuzd) *adj.*—
    A: entertained. B: puzzled.
    C: inspired.

13. **diffuse** (di-'fyuz) *v.*—
    A: make less dangerous.
    B: come together.
    C: spread or pour out freely.

14. **eminent** ('eh-muh-nent) *adj.*—
    A: prominent. B: about to happen.
    C: inherent.

15. **apprise** (uh-'priyz) *v.*—
    A: estimate a value.
    B: promote.
    C: inform of or give notice.

CROSSWORD: Classic Magazines

ACROSS

1. Classic women's magazine, goes with 6 down, 3 words
6. Magazine that led coverage of civil rights in the 1950s and 1960s
9. Sit for
10. Magazine known for its Norman Rockwell covers, goes with 37 across, 3 words
11. Fashionable women's magazine that started in 1892
14. Damage
15. Refinement
19. Coffee alternative
20. Basketball org.
22. Magazine revenue sources
24. Back
26. Part of an hr.
28. Magazine launched in 1954 (with swimsuit issues since 1964), goes with 49 across
32. Actor Guinness
34. Martinique, for one
35. Apple state (abbr.)
36. Borden mascot Elsie
37. See 10 across
39. Masterpiece
40. On the job, 2 words
41. Magazine known for science and technology, goes with 26 down
47. Classic card game
48. "I Like ___" (old campaign slogan)
49. See 28 across
50. Wall ___ (abbr.)
51. It was *Sports Cars Illustrated* in 1955, 3 words

DOWN

1. Hungarian pianist Franz
2. Romantic meetings
3. ___, nose and throat
4. "Young at ___"
5. Everest, e.g. (abbr.)
6. See 1 across
7. Ending for Japan and Senegal
8. Lawrence of Arabia's first two initials
9. Golf tour
12. Actor Sharif
13. Magazine magnate Conde
16. "What Kind of Fool ___?" 2 words
17. College helper (abbr.)
18. Magazine bosses, abbr.
21. Makes beer
23. Fashionable criminal (British slang)
25. O.K. Corral's Wyatt
26. See 41 across
27. *Time* competitor founded in 1933
29. Jackie Kennedy's designer Cassini
30. *Tin Cup* actress Russo
31. Break a commandment
33. 1942 horror movie, ___ *People*
37. Make a mistake
38. Was a burden, with on
42. More refined
43. A or an, in Spain
44. Auction unit
45. Golf event first played in 1927
46. *The Man from U.N.C.L.E.'s* ___ Kuryakin (alt. spelling)
49. Actress Lupino, who directed *The Hitch-Hiker* (1953)

CROSSWORD: Where the Buck Stops

ACROSS

1. Run when wet
6. C&W singer Tillis
9. Bremerhaven "but"
13. Networking giant
14. Role for Cruise
16. Ovid's family name
17. Start of a quotation by Bertrand Russell
20. Benz attachment
21. ___ supra (where mentioned)
22. Indian elephant
23. "___ Different World": Four Tops
25. Like some drugs
26. More of a quotation by Bertrand Russell
32. Figurine material
33. Wine prefix
34. Slap on
36. Wee hrs.
37. Russell in *Black Widow*
41. Rd.
42. Seriously hurt
44. Mutt's morsel
45. Building plans
47. More of a quotation by Bertrand Russell
51. ___ *Kapital*
52. Darlings
53. Shows the ropes to
57. Marg Helgenberger series
58. NYC hrs.
61. End of a quotation by Bertrand Russell
64. Like some causes
65. Wander
66. Handled, in a way
67. MTA stops
68. Hostilities
69. Memorable Las Vegas casino

DOWN

1. A following
2. Creditor's claim
3. Model Marshall
4. *Foucault's Pendulum* author
5. Substantiate
6. Carter's birthplace
7. Truman's nuclear agcy.
8. Chichen Itza dweller
9. Rolaids, e.g.
10. Bangkok buck
11. Morales in *Paid in Full*
12. Campus cadet org.
15. Turns one's back on
18. Rockies' stats
19. Jedi foe
23. Here, in Paris
24. Halted the launch
26. Hyde Park buggy
27. Plan a new route
28. Davis in *The Hill*
29. "___-haw!"
30. Hall-of-Fame Angel
31. Starsky's partner
35. Cancun kiss
38. Pistol case
39. Cockney's location locution?
40. Gave credit to
43. Cars of 1909
46. Qt. duo
48. Hunger pain
49. Satyr
50. Rest
53. Nocturnal hunters
54. Urban uprising
55. "Play it, Sam" source
56. Pack
58. Deserve
59. Neverland pirate
60. Knight and Danson
62. Dam-commissioning org.
63. Batting coach Charlie

Number Towers

The fourth tower (D) is about to topple because a number is missing from its foundations. The key is to uncover the logic of the sequence.

A	B	C	D
7½	15	22½	30
15	22½	30	37½
22½	30	37½	45
30	37½	45	52½
37½	45	52½	60
45	52½	60	x

trivia

- Who sang the theme song "Rawhide"?

_____

Answers *(Do You Know? and Trivia answers are on page 224)*

PAGE 8
Familiar Address

PAGE 9
Cage the Animals

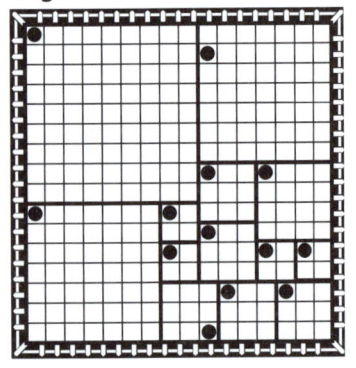

DOODLE PUZZLE • BinD

PAGE 10
Word Pyramid
(1) RE
(2) EAR
(3) DEAR
(4) GRADE
(5) DANGER
(6) READING
(7) DREAMING

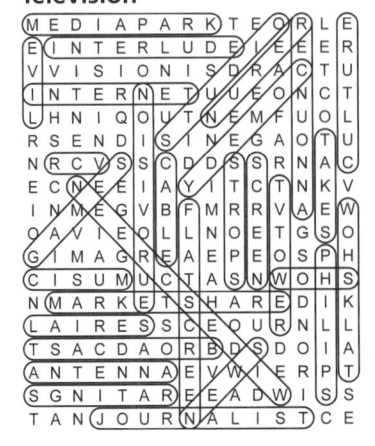

PAGE 11
Television

PAGE 12
The Cold Stuff
1. A "99"
2. *Kulfi*
3. A *gelateria*
4. The United States—the European-sounding name was intended as a marketing tool
5. Margaret Thatcher
6. *Dulce de leche*
7. Finland, at nearly 14 liters per person (though U.S. residents eat an average of 23 liters per person)
8. Lower—despite the rich flavor, gelato typically has 7 percent to 8 percent fat, compared to the average 10 percent fat in American ice cream
9. Powdered green tea
10. Goat's milk
11. 50
12. Ben & Jerry's
13. July
14. Vanilla, chocolate and strawberry

PAGE 13
Director's Chair

PAGE 14
Sudoku

BLOCK ANAGRAM • STREET MAP

PAGE 15
Dominoes
Domino 7. All other black dominoes have only odd numbers on each end and all white dominoes have only even numbers.

THE NUMBER IS THE QUESTION • **20.** EGG WHITE = 10. YOLK = +1. YOLK OUTSIDE THE EGG WHITE = -1.

PAGE 16
Sunny
A2, A5, A7, C3, C7, E1, E4, E7

DOUBLETALK • BASS

PAGE 17
Summer Pleasures

S	W	A	B		D	A	N	K		N	A	M
H	O	P	E		E	T	O	N		A	D	O
E	W	E	R		B	A	R	E	F	O	O	T
		R	A	T		L	I	M	B	O		
S	O	L	I	D		S	A	L	T	I	E	R
A	R	I	E	S		T	I	S				
G	E	E	S		H	A	M		I	T	E	M
				M	A	R		A	C	U	T	E
A	B	S	C	E	S	S		L	E	G	A	L
N	A	T	A	L		O	L	D				
G	R	I	L	L	I	N	G		T	U	T	U
L	O	N		O	M	A	R		E	R	O	S
E	N	G		W	A	G	E		A	N	N	E

PAGE 18
Spot the Differences

PAGE 19
Binairo

I	O	I	O	O	I	O	O	I	O	I	I
O	I	O	I	I	O	O	I	I	O	O	I
I	I	O	I	O	O	I	I	O	I	O	O
I	O	I	O	O	I	I	O	I	O	I	O
O	O	I	O	I	I	O	O	I	I	O	I
I	I	O	I	O	O	I	I	O	O	I	I
O	O	I	O	I	I	O	I	O	I	O	I
O	I	O	I	I	O	I	O	I	O	I	O
I	O	I	I	O	O	I	O	O	I	I	O
O	I	O	O	I	I	O	I	O	I	O	I
I	O	I	I	O	I	O	O	I	I	O	I
O	I	O	O	I	O	I	I	O	I	O	I

LETTERBLOCKS • TEACHER / DENTIST

PAGE 20
A-List

1. **banal**—[C] trite. Whenever the teacher says something too banal, Dorothy rolls her eyes.

2. **annals**—[B] chronicles. In the annals of sports idiocy, that was the biggest bonehead play I've ever seen!

3. **arcana**—[A] mysterious or specialized knowledge. I'd rather not know all the deep arcana of your arachnid research.

4. **masala**—[B] Indian spice blend. Easy on the masala—Sarah doesn't have the stomach for spicy dishes.

5. **llama**—[a] beast of burden. The llama is a domesticated South American camelid that has been used as a pack animal since the Pre-Columbian era.

6. **bazaar**—[B] marketplace. During her hunt at the bazaar, Sally found a turn-of-the-century compass that had belonged to her great-grandfather.

7. **paschal**—[C] relating to Easter. Terri spent hours on her Paschal bonnet—it started as a flowerpot!

8. **amalgam**—[A] mixture. Our team is a strong amalgam of raw youth and seasoned leadership.

9. **plantar**—[C] of the sole of the foot. "What do these plantar prints tell us, Holmes?" asked Watson.

10. **catamaran**—[C] boat with two hulls. Jack thinks he's Admiral Nelson now that he has won the marina's annual catamaran race.

11. **balaclava**—[A] knit cap. Hang your balaclava in the foyer and grab some stew.

12. **avatar**—[B] incarnation of a god. In Hindu mythology, Rama is the seventh avatar of the god Vishnu. (And yes, James Cameron, an avatar is also a being representing and controlled by a human.)

13. **spartan**—[B] marked by simplicity and lack of luxury. We didn't expect such spartan conditions in the honeymoon suite.

14. **allay**—[C] calm. Yesterday's board meeting did more than just allay our fears—it gave us an uptick of hope!

15. **lambda**—[A] Greek letter. Invert a V, and you've got a Greek lambda—or Bob's mustache.

VOCABULARY RATINGS
9 and below: A-
10–12: A
13–15: A+

PAGE 21
This and That

S	T	I	R		Z	E	R	O	S		D	A	H	S
T	O	D	O		E	T	A	P	E		A	M	A	S
E	R	I	S		N	O	L	A	N		N	E	W	T
M	A	G	A	Z	I	N	E		T	H	I	N	K	S
			N	A	T	S		C	R	E	E			
B	L	A	N	C	H		H	A	I	R	L	E	S	S
A	L	L	A	H		C	E	R	E	B	R	A	T	E
S	A	L	A		T	H	A	T	S		A	G	E	E
I	N	A	R	R	E	A	R	S		A	D	L	E	R
C	O	N	Q	U	E	R	S		R	A	C	E	R	S
			U	N	T	O		G	I	R	L			
J	O	B	E	T	H		D	E	C	E	I	V	E	D
A	D	I	T		I	R	I	S	H		F	A	R	E
D	O	L	T		N	O	L	T	E		F	I	N	E
E	R	L	E		G	I	L	E	S		E	N	O	S

PAGE 22
Sudoku X

9	6	5	4	7	2	1	3	8
3	1	4	9	8	6	5	7	2
8	2	7	5	3	1	6	9	4
1	8	6	2	9	4	7	5	3
4	9	3	8	5	7	2	6	1
5	7	2	1	6	3	4	8	9
6	4	9	3	1	5	8	2	7
7	3	1	6	2	8	9	4	5
2	5	8	7	4	9	3	1	6

FIRST THINGS FIRST • TIME WAITS FOR NO MAN

Answers

PAGE 23
Insect Out

4. The other insects have 2 white + 1 black spot on the left wing and 1 black and two white spots on the right wing.

SPEAKING VOLUMES • A BIBLIOPOLE

PAGE 24
Legends of the Game

D	U	A	L		P	R	I	G	S		B	O	N	D
E	R	G	O		R	I	L	E	Y		A	L	A	I
E	S	A	U		I	C	I	E	R		C	A	P	E
M	A	R	I	A	S	H	A	R	A	P	O	V	A	
			S	L	O				C	A	N			
S	T	E	V	E	N		F	O	U	L		A	P	R
T	U	N	I	C		E	R	G	S		A	S	E	A
A	N	N	I	K	A	S	O	R	E	N	S	T	A	M
M	A	U	I		R	A	S	E		O	H	A	R	E
P	S	I		S	K	I	T		A	V	E	R	S	E
		B	E	A				L	E	V				
	S	E	R	E	N	A	W	I	L	L	I	A	M	S
A	L	D	A		S	L	I	G	O		L	E	I	A
L	O	I	S		A	G	L	O	W		L	O	R	D
A	P	E	S		S	A	L	T	S		E	N	Y	A

PAGE 25
Kakuro

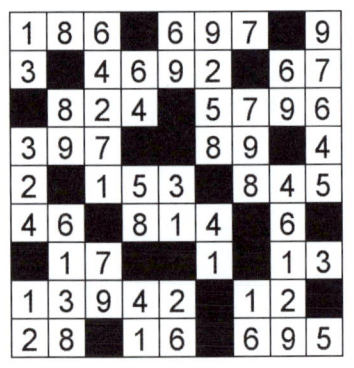

1	8	6		6	9	7		9
3		4	6	9	2		6	7
	8	2	4		5	7	9	6
3	9	7		8	9		4	
2		1	5	3		8	4	5
4	6		8	1	4		6	
	1	7		1		1	3	
1	3	9	4	2		1	2	
2	8		1	6		6	9	5

SANDWICH • HEART

PAGE 26
Keep Going

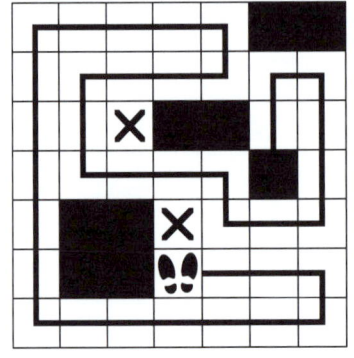

DELETE ONE • DELETE A AND FIND THE TEN COMMANDMENTS

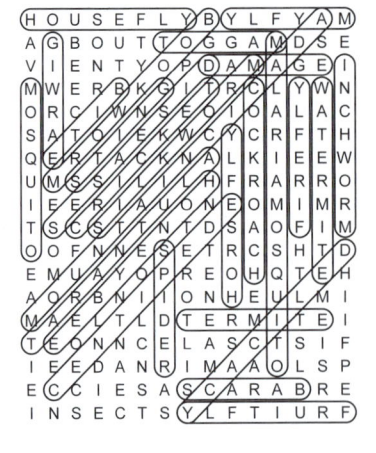

PAGE 27
Insects

PAGE 28
The National Pastime

1. Two acres
2. Nine
3. National League
4. Toronto Blue Jays
5. Boston Red Sox
6. Yankee Stadium
7. Joe DiMaggio
8. A home run
9. 1994
10. Five
11. Red Sox's Roger Clemens
12. 108
13. "Mr. October", Reggie Jackson of the New York Yankees.
14. Slugging percentage represents the total number of bases a player records per at-bat. $(1B + 2B \times 2 + 3B \times 3 + HR \times 4) \div AB$.

PAGE 29
Comedy Teams

F	O	R	T		D	E	B	I	T		E	T	O	N
O	P	I	E		E	P	O	C	H		I	O	L	E
N	A	D	A		G	O	M	E	R		G	L	O	W
T	H	E	M	A	R	X	B	R	O	T	H	E	R	S
			S	L	E	Y		W	E	T				
G	E	N	T	L	E		F	A	I	T	H	F	U	L
A	L	O	E	S		P	A	I	N	E		A	L	E
L	A	I	R		C	L	U	N	G		D	I	N	A
E	T	S		B	L	U	N	T		H	A	S	T	E
N	E	E	D	L	E	S	S		I	A	N	S		
			A	A	A		I	A	N	S				
T	H	E	T	H	R	E	E	S	T	O	O	G	E	S
R	U	T	S		I	N	T	E	R		L	E	D	A
I	G	L	U		N	O	T	R	E		V	E	N	T
M	E	A	N		G	L	U	E	D		E	R	A	S

PAGE 30
Sudoku

1	8	9	5	6	4	2	3	7
7	6	3	2	1	8	4	9	5
5	4	2	3	9	7	6	8	1
8	7	5	9	2	1	3	6	4
9	1	6	4	8	3	5	7	2
2	3	4	6	7	5	9	1	8
4	9	8	1	5	6	7	2	3
3	2	7	8	4	9	1	5	6
6	5	1	7	3	2	8	4	9

BLOCK ANAGRAM • ROOM SERVICE

PAGE 31
Tulip Teaser

Tulip 4. All the other tulips have a stem.

DAIRY NOTE • ALL OF THEM

PAGE 32
Divas

O	V	U	M		L	A	M	P	S		A	D	A	M
P	I	S	A		I	B	E	R	T		N	I	N	A
A	V	E	R		T	I	G	E	R		G	O	N	G
L	A	D	Y	G	A	G	A		A	R	E	N	A	S
			J	A	N		N	A	T	A	L			
R	O	S	A	L	Y	N		B	E	Y	O	N	C	E
O	Z	O	N	E		O	S	A	G	E		A	I	L
R	A	L	E		P	U	T	T	Y		L	O	D	E
E	W	E		S	E	G	U	E		R	A	M	E	N
M	A	D	O	N	N	A		S	H	A	K	I	R	A
			P	O	E	T	S		O	N	E			
S	C	R	A	W	L		A	G	U	I	L	E	R	A
I	R	A	Q		O	L	L	A	S		A	T	O	M
M	E	N	U		P	E	E	V	E		N	U	D	E
P	E	T	E		E	A	M	E	S		D	I	E	S

PAGE 33
Number Cluster

FRIENDS • EACH CAN HAVE THE PREFIX UNDER- TO FORM A NEW WORD.

PAGE 34
Match Game

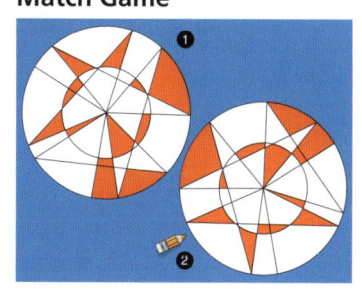

LETTER LINE • BLOODHOUND; DUO, BOND, HOOD, UNDO

PAGE 35
Binairo

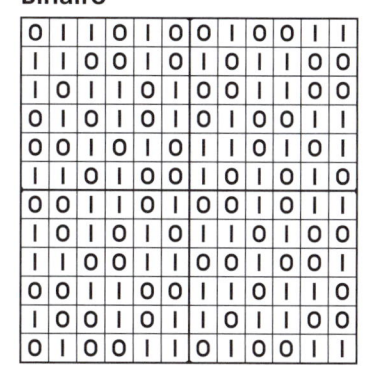

0	I	I	0	I	0	0	I	0	0	I	I
I	I	0	0	I	0	I	0	I	I	0	0
I	0	I	I	0	I	0	0	I	I	0	0
0	I	0	I	0	I	0	I	0	0	I	I
0	0	I	0	I	0	I	I	0	I	0	I
I	I	0	I	0	0	I	0	I	0	I	0
0	0	I	I	0	I	0	0	I	0	I	I
I	0	I	0	I	0	I	I	0	I	0	0
I	I	0	0	I	I	0	0	I	0	0	I
0	0	I	I	0	0	I	I	0	I	I	0
I	0	0	I	0	I	I	0	I	I	0	0
0	I	0	0	I	I	0	I	0	0	I	I

LETTERBLOCKS • BROTHER/HUSBAND

PAGE 36
Pick the Biggest

1. b. Asia
2. a. Sardinia
3. c. Pacific Ocean
4. c. Ukraine
5. a. Nigeria
6. d. Tokyo
7. d. Lake Victoria
8. d. Poland
9. a. Cumbria
10. c. Alaska

PAGE 37
Gray-Scale Extremes

G	M	A	C		H	O	O	P	S		E	L	M	O
R	A	S	H		A	L	G	A	E		R	E	A	D
A	R	C	O		B	E	R	R	A		N	I	N	E
B	L	A	C	K	E	Y	E	D	S	U	S	A	N	S
S	O	N	O	R	A			H	A	T				
			L	O	S		M	O	O	R		B	A	D
S	O	L	A	N		H	O	U	R		S	O	L	E
W	H	I	T	E	H	O	U	S	E	S	T	A	F	F
A	I	D	E		I	S	N	T		A	R	R	A	Y
N	O	S		E	A	S	T		C	U	E			
			S	E	W			O	D	E	S	S	A	
B	L	A	C	K	A	N	D	W	H	I	T	E	T	V
E	U	R	O		T	O	O	N	E		C	R	E	E
L	I	E	U		H	O	V	E	R		A	V	E	R
T	S	A	R		A	R	E	T	E		R	E	N	T

PAGE 38
Word Sudoku

H	A	R	N	W	J	Z	O	I
I	O	J	Z	A	R	H	N	W
Z	W	N	I	O	H	J	A	R
W	J	A	O	H	N	I	R	Z
O	H	Z	J	R	I	A	W	N
N	R	I	W	Z	A	O	J	H
A	I	W	H	N	O	R	Z	J
R	N	H	A	J	Z	W	I	O
J	Z	O	R	I	W	N	H	A

UNCANNY TURN • VIOLENCE

PAGE 39
A Texas Native
1959 Buick Electra 225

CHANGELINGS • WASHINGTON / COPENHAGEN / ALEXANDRIA

PAGE 40
Traffic Light

B	U	S	H		B	U	R	S	T		L	I	E	U
A	N	T	E		U	T	I	L	E		E	R	A	T
R	I	L	L		T	A	T	A	R		S	A	V	E
S	T	O	P	S	T	H	E	P	R	E	S	S	E	S
			L	O	O	N			A	T	E			
A	S	T	E	R	N		E	S	P	R	E	S	S	O
T	H	O	S	E		A	N	N	I	E		N	P	R
T	A	T	S		C	L	E	A	N		M	O	U	E
I	D	A		B	L	I	M	P		K	A	R	M	A
C	E	L	E	B	R	I	T	Y		U	N	I	T	E	D
			L	I	P			O	P	E	N			
G	O	J	U	M	P	I	N	T	H	E	L	A	K	E
A	V	I	D		E	R	A	T	O		A	R	I	A
B	A	B	E		R	A	V	E	L		N	E	W	T
S	L	E	D		S	N	E	R	D		D	A	I	S

Answers

PAGE 41
Cage the Animals

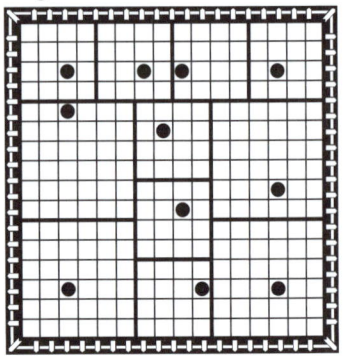

DOODLE PUZZLE • AirLine

PAGE 42
Sport Maze

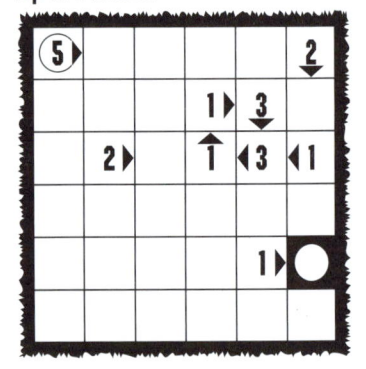

REPOSITION PREPOSITION • BY MEANS OF

PAGE 43
Europe

PAGE 44
Country Comes to Broadway

1. Oscar Hammerstein II
2. Agnes de Mille
3. "Oh, What a Beautiful Mornin'"
4. Celeste Holm (Ado Annie)
5. "Surrey with the Fringe on Top"
6. Alfred Drake
7. "Farmer and the Cowman"
8. "People Will Say We're in Love"
9. "Pore Jud is Daid"
10. Green Grow the Lilacs
11. St. James Theater
12. I Cain't Say No"

PAGE 45
'60s' Rock

PAGE 46
Sudoku

8	3	4	1	6	9	5	7	2
6	7	5	3	4	2	1	8	9
1	2	9	8	5	7	4	6	3
3	9	7	4	1	5	8	2	6
4	8	6	2	9	3	7	1	5
5	1	2	7	8	6	9	3	4
2	5	8	6	7	4	3	9	1
7	4	3	9	2	1	6	5	8
9	6	1	5	3	8	2	4	7

BLOCK ANAGRAM • SUITCASES

PAGE 47
Skewered

Kebab 2. The meatball in the middle of this kebab was made by a different butcher.

TRANSADDITION •
CONSTITUTION

PAGE 48
Down Under

PAGE 49
Pixel Fun

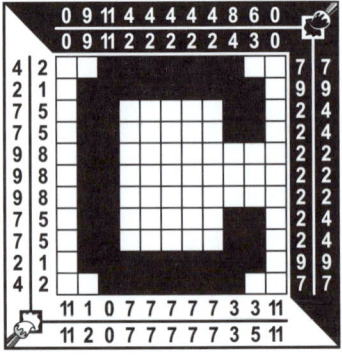

CHANGE ONE • SPRAY ON

204

PAGE 50
Keep Going

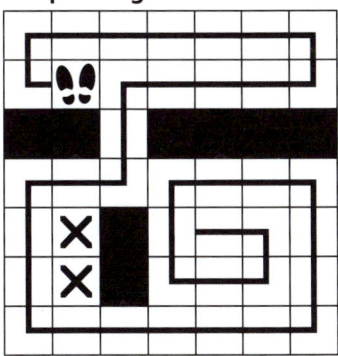

DELETE ONE • DELETE S AND FIND ELECTION RESULT

PAGE 51
Binairo

0	0	1	1	0	0	1	0	1	1	0	1
1	0	0	1	0	1	0	1	1	0	1	0
0	1	1	0	1	0	0	1	0	1	0	1
0	1	0	0	1	0	1	0	1	0	1	1
1	0	1	1	0	1	0	0	1	1	0	0
0	0	1	0	1	0	1	1	0	0	1	1
0	1	0	1	0	1	0	1	0	1	0	1
1	0	1	0	0	1	1	0	1	0	1	0
1	1	0	0	1	1	0	1	0	1	1	0
0	0	1	1	0	1	1	0	1	0	0	1
1	1	0	0	1	1	0	1	0	0	1	0
1	1	0	1	1	0	1	0	0	1	0	0

LETTERBLOCKS • LIBRARY / STORAGE

PAGE 52
Magic

1. **levitate**—[A] defy gravity. Before dunking the basketball, Michael *levitates* long enough to polish the backboard and rim.
2. **clairvoyant**—[C] seeing beyond ordinary perception. As a bookie, I find being *clairvoyant* really helps me call the races.
3. **planchette**—[B] Ouija board pointer. My *planchette* just spelled out "You're too gullible."
4. **mojo**—[B] magical spell. I've got my *mojo* working, but I still can't charm Angelina.
5. **telekinetic**—[C] using mind over matter. Chloe employs her *telekinetic* powers to make the trash empty itself.
6. **voilà**—[B] "There it is!" As he threw back the curtain, Houdini cried, "*Voilà!*"
7. **whammy**—[C] hex or curse. After the gypsy placed a *whammy* on Tex, he fell into the duck pond three times.
8. **soothsaying**—[A] prophecy. If Joe is so good at *soothsaying*, why does he always lose in Vegas?
9. **mesmerized**—[B] hypnotized. Since meeting Jenny, Paul has been stumbling around as though *mesmerized*.
10. **augur**—[A] serve as an omen. A flat tire on the first day surely *augurs* ill for our vacation.
11. **shaman**—[B] healer using magic. The local *shaman* recited a few incantations to heal my broken nose.
12. **occult**—[C] secret. At midnight, I was poring over an *occult* black-magic text.
13. **invoke**—[C] summon up, as spirits. While studying ancient Rome, I tried to *invoke* the ghost of Caesar to appear before me.
14. **sibyl**—[B] fortune-teller. My apprehension grew as the *sibyl* looked into her crystal ball and winced.
15. **pentagram**—[B] five-pointed star. David said his spells don't work unless he traces a *pentagram* with his wand.

VOCABULARY RATINGS

9 & below: Sorcerer's apprentice
10–12: Skilled conjurer
13–15: Wonder-worker

PAGE 53
From B to B

B	O	O	B		D	E	L	A		A	B	A	S	E
E	L	L	A		E	L	A	L		M	U	S	E	S
B	I	L	L	Y	C	L	U	B		O	F	T	E	N
E	N	A	M	O	R	E	D		D	E	F	I	N	E
			G	E	N		T	U	B	A				
H	E	R	B	I	E		P	A	R	A	L	L	E	L
O	N	E	R	S		E	L	L	E		O	I	S	E
L	O	S	E		A	D	A	I	R		B	E	T	A
E	L	I	A		R	I	T	A		L	O	G	E	S
S	A	N	D	W	I	C	H		R	O	B	E	R	T
			C	H	E	T		G	O	P				
S	T	A	R	E	S		R	E	L	E	V	A	N	T
A	U	G	U	R		B	E	E	L	Z	E	B	U	B
C	R	I	M	E		A	N	N	E		A	I	D	A
K	N	O	B	S		T	O	A	D		L	E	E	R

PAGE 54
Sudoku Twin

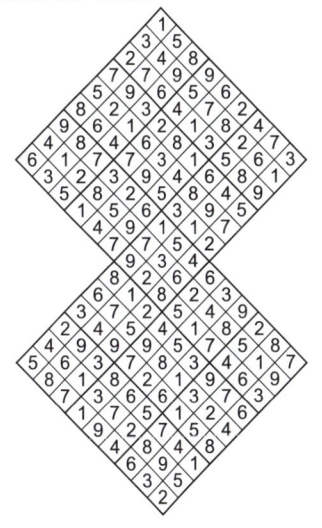

DELETE ONE • REBATE

PAGE 55
Sign Language

1015. Every group of signs contains two multiples of the smallest number: 1-2-3, 5-10-15, 3-6-9, 2-4-6, 4-8-12.

TRANSADDITION • IVANHOE BY SIR WALTER SCOTT

Answers

PAGE 56–57
Train Your Brain
1. Lock in Place

   D

2. Patchwork
   Sequence B

PAGE 58
Number Cluster

FRIENDS • EACH CAN HAVE A PREFIX BREAK- TO FORM A NEW WORD.

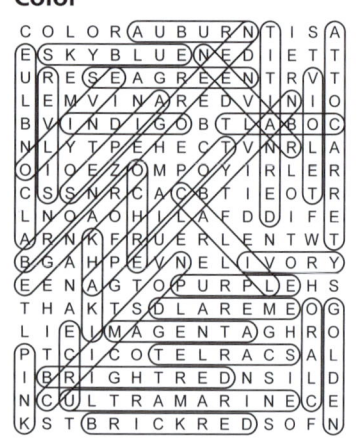

PAGE 59
Color

PAGE 60
Mostly Magazines
1. *Time*
2. *Playboy*
3. Mia Farrow
4. Canada
5. Tina Brown
6. Annie Liebovitz
7. Jann Wenner
8. *Cosmopolitan*
9. Bonnie Fuller
10. *George*

PAGE 61
Hidden Gems

PAGE 62
Sudoku

9	1	8	3	6	4	2	7	5
7	4	5	2	8	9	3	1	6
3	2	6	7	1	5	8	9	4
4	6	1	9	7	8	5	2	3
8	7	2	5	3	6	1	4	9
5	3	9	4	2	1	6	8	7
2	8	7	6	9	3	4	5	1
6	9	4	1	5	2	7	3	8
1	5	3	8	4	7	9	6	2

BLOCK ANAGRAM • BUNGEE JUMP

PAGE 63
Gear Up
Direction A, counterclockwise.

TRANSADDITION • ADD I AND T AND FIND THE TITANIC DISASTER

PAGE 64
High Cards

PAGE 65
Kakuro

SANDWICH • HOUSE

PAGE 66
Sport Maze

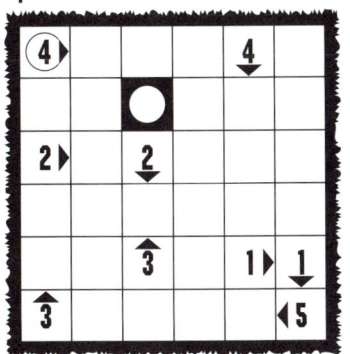

REPOSITION PREPOSITION • PURSUANT TO

PAGE 67
Binairo

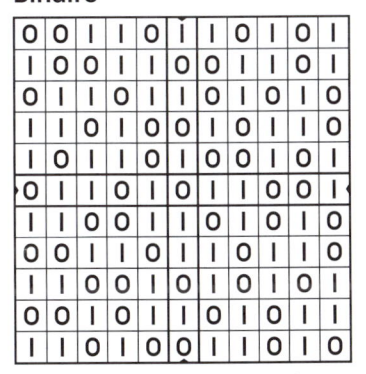

0	0	1	1	0	1	1	0	1	0
1	0	0	1	1	0	0	1	1	0
0	1	1	0	1	1	0	1	0	0
1	1	0	1	0	0	1	0	1	0
1	0	1	0	1	0	1	0	0	1
0	1	0	1	0	1	1	0	0	1
1	1	0	0	1	1	0	1	0	0
0	0	1	1	0	1	1	0	1	1
1	1	0	0	1	0	1	0	1	1
0	0	1	0	1	1	0	1	0	1
1	1	0	1	0	0	1	1	0	1
1	1	0	1	0	0	1	1	0	1

LETTERBLOCKS • PARTNER / WEDDING

PAGE 68
All Iced Up

1. Ice Age
2. Iceland
3. Ice shelf
4. Iceberg
5. Icefall
6. Iceblink
7. Icebreaker
8. Ice sheet
9. Ice jam
10. Ice needles
11. Icebound
12. Ice cap

PAGE 69
Seeing Double

E	M	U	S		R	O	W	A	N		B	A	C	H
L	E	N	T		O	R	I	B	I		A	L	E	E
B	A	D	E	N	B	A	D	E	N		N	U	D	E
A	D	O	R	A	B	L	E		E	D	D	I	E	D
			D	E	S		S	T	A	Y				
M	E	A	G	E	R		S	A	I	L	B	O	A	T
A	R	B	O	R		D	U	N	E		A	R	G	O
G	I	N	O		P	E	P	E	S		N	L	E	R
I	C	E	D		O	N	E	R		I	D	O	N	T
C	H	R	Y	S	L	E	R		C	R	Y	P	T	S
			G	L	I	B		D	O	I				
I	G	L	O	O	S		H	O	R	S	E	M	E	N
A	R	E	O		H	U	B	B	A	H	U	B	B	A
M	E	N	D		E	M	A	I	L		L	E	A	P
A	W	A	Y		D	A	R	E	S		A	S	Y	E

PAGE 70
Word Sudoku

C	A	W	I	F	N	T	O	H
N	H	F	O	T	A	I	C	W
T	O	I	H	C	W	N	F	A
F	I	A	N	H	C	W	T	O
O	W	T	F	A	I	H	N	C
H	N	C	W	O	T	A	I	F
I	C	N	A	W	F	O	H	T
A	T	H	C	N	O	F	W	I
W	F	O	T	I	H	C	A	N

UNCANNY TURN • SILENT

PAGE 71
Getting Hot

129. Always x2 and -1.

WORD POWER • CRASH

PAGE 72
Superstars

A	L	E	X		M	E	D	O	C		F	R	A	Y
L	A	D	E		E	L	I	N	A		L	O	R	E
A	N	I	N		R	I	S	E	R		Y	U	M	A
	G	E	O	R	G	E	C	L	O	O	N	E	Y	
			P	E	E	L		L	O	N				
R	A	S	H	A	D		A	T	I	P		P	A	M
O	T	T	O	I		A	S	A	N		O	E	N	O
B	A	R	B	R	A	S	T	R	E	I	S	A	N	D
B	R	I	E		N	E	A	T		S	C	R	E	E
Y	I	P		A	J	A	R		S	T	I	L	E	S
			E	Y	E		S	T	O	L				
	A	N	G	E	L	I	N	A	J	O	L	I	E	
C	H	E	R		I	C	O	N	O		A	D	A	M
P	A	N	E		C	O	U	T	H		T	O	R	E
A	B	E	T		A	N	S	O	N		E	L	L	A

PAGE 73
Cage the Animals

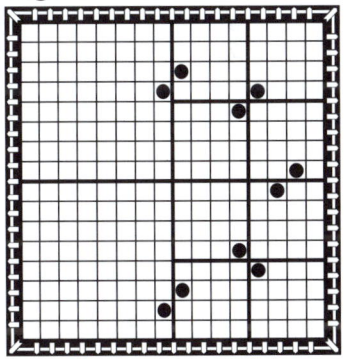

DOODLE PUZZLE • SURROUNDED

PAGE 74
Keep Going

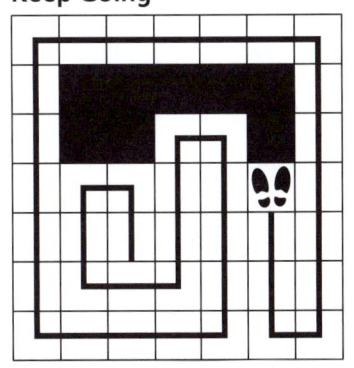

DELETE ONE • GUITARISTS

PAGE 75
The Rolling Stones

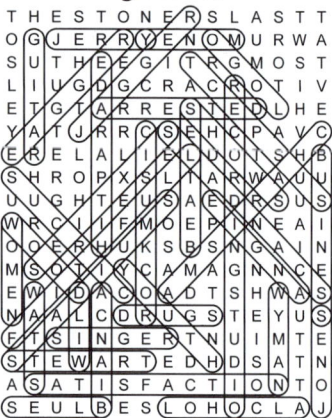

PAGE 76
News

1. amnesty—[B] pardon. President Obama's deportation *amnesty* is a key controversy across the nation.

2. harridan—[C] haggard, old woman. During trial, former Virginia governor Bob McDonnell portrayed his wife as a *harridan*, said the *New York Times*.

3. repudiate—[B] refuse to accept or support. After the midterm elections, Senator Paul said, "Tonight is a *repudiation* of Barack Obama's policies."

4. indict—[B] charge with a crime. Darren Wilson was not *indicted* for the killing of Michael Brown.

5. gentrification—[C] displacement of the poor by the affluent. Spike Lee has denounced the *gentrification* in neighborhoods such as Fort Greene.

6. sovereignty—[B] supreme power. Ukraine will not settle its conflicts with Russia until it regains full *sovereignty* over Crimea.

7. conflate—[C] confuse or combine into a whole. Newsman Brian Williams doesn't know what caused him to "*conflate* one aircraft with another."

8. solipsistic—[A] highly egocentric. Some view Facebook as a simply *solipsistic* forum.

9. intransigence—[A] stubbornness. The government shutdown was a display of *intransigence*, said the *Los Angeles Times*.

10. subterfuge—[A] deceptive stratagem. Democratic Leader Nancy Pelosi said the Republicans' intent to sue the president was a "*subterfuge*."

11. inherent—[A] inborn. When the Declaration of Independence refers to "unalienable" rights, it is describing the *inherent* privileges people are entitled to.

12. eponymous—[C] named for a person. Who was the original Oscar behind the *eponymous* statuette?

13. intrepid—[C] fearless. After "stealing" a block while playing, Prince George was called "very *intrepid*."

14. sectarian—[B] of religious factions. The UN has warned of "further *sectarian* violence" in Iraq.

15. culpable—[A] blameworthy. Oscar Pistorius was found guilty of *culpable* homicide in South Africa.

VOCABULARY RATINGS
9 & below: Up-to-date
10–12: In the know
13–15: Newshound

PAGE 77
Take It Easy

PAGE 78
Sudoku

9	6	1	4	8	2	3	5	7
3	4	5	1	6	7	8	2	9
8	2	7	5	9	3	1	6	4
7	9	3	2	5	6	4	1	8
2	8	4	3	1	9	5	7	6
5	1	6	8	7	4	9	3	2
4	7	2	9	3	5	6	8	1
1	3	9	6	2	8	7	4	5
6	5	8	7	4	1	2	9	3

BLOCK ANAGRAM • MORPHINE

PAGE 79
Ages Apart

32. The key to the puzzle is to realize that, in the circumstances given, the age difference must be equal to the time elapsed. Sixteen years ago, we can see that the difference between Peter and Gail's age was 16 years. Obviously, this never changes. But now Peter is 48 the difference only accounts for one-third of his age rather than half.

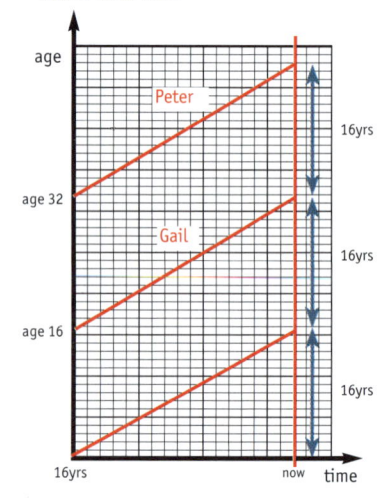

PAGE 80
Tree-Huggers

A	C	L	U		H	A	I	L		A	M	A	S	S
L	O	I	S		E	D	D	S		G	A	S	P	E
E	L	M	S	T	R	E	E	T		A	P	I	A	N
A	D	O	R	A	B	L	E		I	S	L	A	N	D
			L	I	E		A	N	S	E				
M	A	R	C	I	E		A	N	T	I	L	L	E	S
A	L	O	H	A		E	M	I	R		E	A	S	T
I	L	S	E		E	R	I	C	A		A	S	T	A
N	O	I	R		D	A	T	E		O	F	T	E	N
E	T	E	R	N	I	T	Y		B	U	S	S	E	D
			Y	O	N	O		N	O	T				
P	H	O	B	I	A		P	O	I	T	I	E	R	S
E	U	R	O	S		W	I	L	L	O	W	B	A	Y
C	R	E	M	E		E	T	T	E		A	R	U	N
S	L	O	B	S		E	Y	E	D		S	O	L	E

PAGE 81
Cheese Escape

Three cheese cubes in the lower right corner.

LETTER LINE • PRODUCED
OUR / DUPED / CUP

PAGE 82
Spot the Differences

PAGE 83
Binairo

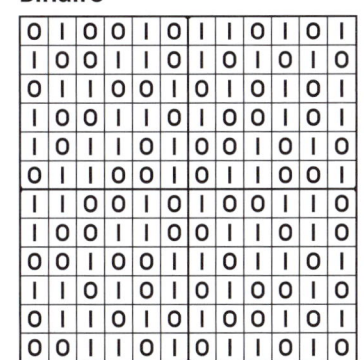

0	1	0	0	1	0	1	1	0	1	0	1
1	0	0	1	1	0	1	0	1	0	1	0
0	1	1	0	0	1	0	1	0	1	0	1
1	0	0	1	1	0	1	0	0	1	0	1
1	0	1	1	0	1	0	0	1	0	1	0
0	1	1	0	0	1	0	1	1	0	0	1
1	1	0	0	1	0	1	0	0	1	1	0
1	0	0	1	1	0	0	1	1	0	1	0
0	0	1	0	0	1	1	0	1	1	0	1
1	1	0	1	0	1	0	1	0	0	1	0
0	1	1	0	1	0	1	0	0	1	0	1
0	0	1	1	0	1	0	1	1	0	1	0

LETTERBLOCKS • CALYPSO / LAMBADA

PAGE 84
Short for…

1. File Transfer Protocol
2. Criminal Investigation Department
3. First-day cover
4. Paris
5. Royal Mail Steamer
6. Search and rescue
7. Unique selling proposition
8. Federal Bureau of Investigation
9. Air traffic control
10. Committee of State Security
11. Videocassette recorder
12. By the way
13. China
14. Digital
15. London Heathrow
16. Special Air Service

PAGE 85
School Clubs

|C|H|E|S|S|C|L|U|B| |M|A|T|H|
|H| |V| |E| |A| |O|E| |R|I|B|
|E|L|E|M|E|N|T|S| |D|E|B|A|T|E|
|E| |R| |T| |I| |C|A|T| |C| |T|
R	E	T	R	O		N	O	O	N		S	K	I	S
L			E	I	N			U		E		A		Y
E	L	E	C	T		Y	E	N		D	U	N	E	
A		V		E	C	G		D			G			
	D	R	A	M	A		A	N	I	M	A	L		O	R
E			L		R		L	R		A			E
R	E	F		D	E	B	I		L		G	L	E	E
S		I	A		O		C	E	E		U		T
B	E	E		M	O	N	O	G	R	A	M		I
T	I	L		M	K		P	I		N		N
O	D	D	J	O	B		M	A	R	C	H	I	N	G

PAGE 86
Word Sudoku

D	C	I	T	W	P	Q	E	V
V	E	Q	C	D	I	W	T	P
P	W	T	V	E	Q	D	C	I
W	D	C	E	Q	V	P	I	T
E	T	P	I	C	D	V	Q	W
Q	I	V	W	P	T	E	D	C
C	V	E	D	T	W	I	P	Q
T	Q	W	P	I	E	C	V	D
I	P	D	Q	V	C	T	W	E

UNCANNY TURN • THE MORSE CODE

PAGE 87
Cubed

Piece 4. Only the pieces 2, 4 and 6 consist of the 10 blocks that you need to complete the cube. Only piece 4 has the right shape and the right colors.

INHERITANCE TEST •

PAGE 88
Wet Set

P	A	R	R		A	R	O	S	E		J	O	G
O	D	I	U	M		S	O	P	H	S		O	R	O
M	U	D	D	Y	W	A	T	E	R	S		A	A	R
P	E	S	E	T	A		E	R	E		A	N	T	E
			S	H	I	M		A	D	J	U	R	E	D
S	U	B	T	O	T	A	L		S	A	R	I		
P	S	I		S	O	L	A	N		R	A	V	E	N
I	D	L	E		N	A	B	O	B		L	E	D	A
T	A	L	L	Y		Y	E	T	I	S		R	I	M
			Y	O	U	R		L	I	C	E	N	S	E	E
D	R	O	P	L	E	T		N	A	N	O			
R	A	C	E		P	O	I		R	O	B	R	O	Y
U	K	E		G	A	R	T	H	B	R	O	O	K	S
B	E	A		A	S	T	H	E		A	D	D	L	E
S	S	N		S	T	E	E	P		Y	E	A	R	

Answers

PAGE 89
Sunny
A1, A7, B3, C1, C7, D5, E1, E7.

DOUBLETALK • CONTENT

PAGE 90
Sport Maze

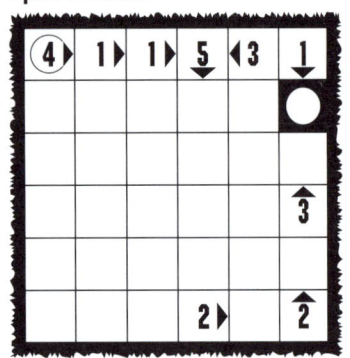

REPOSITION PREPOSITION • AS WELL AS

PAGE 91
Reptiles

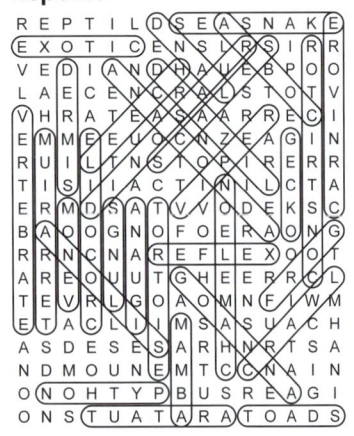

PAGE 92
Gotta Dance!
1. *Brigadoon*
2. Gene Kelly

3. *A Star Is Born*
4. *Seven Brides for Seven Brothers*
5. "White Christmas"
6. Danny Kaye
7. Carmen Jones
8. "There's No Business Like Show Business"

PAGE 93
U.S. History

PAGE 94
Sudoku X

2	3	7	9	5	8	4	6	1
1	5	4	3	6	2	9	7	8
8	9	6	1	7	4	3	5	2
7	2	1	8	9	5	6	4	3
3	8	5	6	4	7	2	1	9
6	4	9	2	1	3	7	8	5
4	7	8	5	2	9	1	3	6
5	6	2	7	3	1	8	9	4
9	1	3	4	8	6	5	2	7

GREEDY LETTER • W

PAGE 95
Party Time
Dice on 3.

LONELY WORDS • MONTH / ORANGE / SILVER / PURPLE.

PAGE 96
Oscar Winners

PAGE 97
Cage the Animals

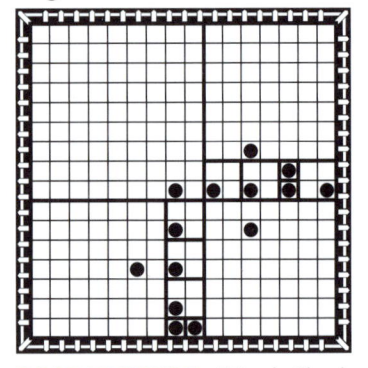

DOODLE PUZZLE • THunderCloud

PAGE 98
Number Cluster

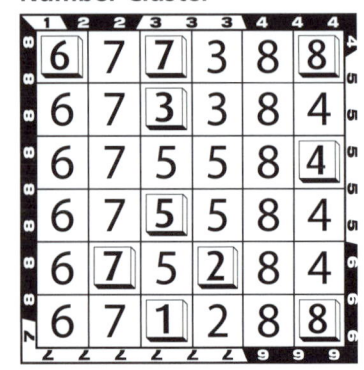

FRIENDS • EACH CAN ADD THE PREFIX HYDRO- TO FORM A NEW WORD.

PAGE 99
Binairo

1	0	1	1	0	1	0	1	0	0
0	1	1	0	0	1	0	1	1	0
1	0	0	1	1	0	1	0	1	0
0	1	1	0	1	0	1	1	0	1
1	1	0	1	0	1	0	0	1	0
0	0	1	0	1	1	0	1	0	1
0	1	0	1	1	0	1	1	0	1
1	0	1	1	0	0	1	0	1	0
1	1	0	0	1	1	0	1	1	0
0	1	1	0	0	1	1	0	0	1
1	0	0	1	0	1	0	1	1	0

LETTERBLOCKS • CUMULUS / SUNRISE

PAGE 100
Getting the Runaround

1. John Walker
2. Maurice Greene
3. Starting blocks
4. 10
5. Ed Moses
6. One
7. Eric Henry Liddell
8. 1928
9. 800 meters
10. Eight
11. Carl Lewis
12. Dick Fosbury
13. Wilma Rudolph
14. Nike

PAGE 101
Presidential Runners

Crossword answers include: BACH, RAMS, OCALA, LILA, OLAN, NADAL, ODER, BARA, EMAIL, GEORGEMCGOVERN, INRO, BOO, COMSAT, WHET, HCG, IDIOT, HOUSEBILL, PENN, EERIE, ITOO, ROOSEVELT, BLESS, ONS, COLD, COLMES, UKR, DOOM, MICHAELDUKAKIS, TESLA, LEAR, HYDE, SALAR, LAYS, ELLA, PLANT, ELSE, REEL

PAGE 102
Sudoku

4	3	7	6	2	5	9	8	1
9	5	1	3	7	8	2	6	4
6	8	2	4	1	9	5	7	3
2	1	9	5	8	4	7	3	6
3	7	4	9	6	2	8	1	5
8	6	5	1	3	7	4	9	2
5	4	6	8	9	1	3	2	7
7	9	3	2	5	6	1	4	8
1	2	8	7	4	3	6	5	9

BLOCK ANAGRAM • HORMONES

PAGE 103
Ping-Pong

Pass F. Starting with the player on the right, this is the order of all passes: CHIBAGFED. The player on the right hit the ball incorrectly on his own half during pass F.

DOODLE PUZZLE • MonKey

PAGE 104
Hizzoner

Crossword answers include: LABS, TIBIAS, JAG, BLAH, OVERDO, OLE, JIMMYWALKER, HAN, OPENS, CENSE, BEGORRA, SWELL, AMAZES, NEARMISS, LIVES, DALLY, NEA, SLID, PAGET, ADDS, AIN, DAVIS, MESAS, MANDOLIN, BERATE, EELED, ARRAYED, JEWEL, ALERT, EDS, ANDREWYOUNG, ENO, REVIVE, RABE, PAM, SPIDER, SWAM

PAGE 105
Umbrella Trouble

1. **X = 31.** Start at the lowest number (6) and work clockwise, adding progressive odd numbers each time and jumping two segments at a time to unravel the sequence: 6 (+ 1) 7 (+ 3) 10 (+ 5) 15 (+ 7) 22 (+ 9) 31 (+ 11) 42.

2. **X = 24.** Start at the 1 in the top right position and, working clockwise, jump to alternate segments, multiplying by 1, 2, 3, 4, 5, 6 in turn to unravel the sequence 1, 1, 2, 6, 24, 120, 720.

PAGE 106
Keep Going

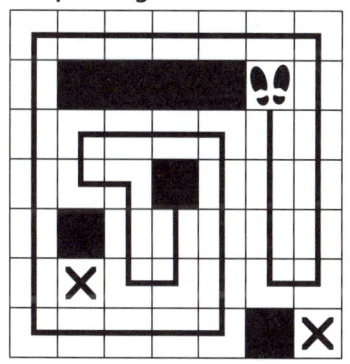

DELETE ONE • DELETE A AND FIND TENDONITIS

PAGE 107
Airplanes

Word search containing: SUITCASE, DROCNOC, TROPRIA, HOCEEU, SIEOFSEA, NRR, PRL, RAANUDKETASHA, IA, ETSBISKRSOMDEF, M, TURLCHOHGRAVITY, SIGDILFSCRUSPIS, AEANTONOVDNEAPG, SATOSTEWARDESSR, IVWRUNWAYTIDSVR, DEAEACOCTNNOEOA, RLVBSVAEOAQUNEN, IOIUOTEELNCGGGS, APAEEMSLIONLEAP, WUTROLBTPHEARGO, ILITEENSVIRSOGR, NNONMUCUSTOMSUT, GRNENFTAIRFIELD

Words found: SUITCASE, CONCORD, TROPICAL, AIR, SEA, ANTONOV, STEWARDESS, RUNWAY, GRAVITY, CUSTOMS, AIRFIELD

Answers

PAGE 108
On the Job

1. oeuvre—[B] body of work. *Annie Hall* is my favorite movie in Woody Allen's *oeuvre*.

2. arduous—[C] difficult. Rounding up all 400 guests proved a tad *arduous* for the groom.

3. bum's rush—[C] forcible eviction or firing. Whoever built these wobbly chairs should be given the *bum's rush*.

4. functionary—[C] one who works in a specified capacity or as a government official. A local *functionary* for 20 years, Tyler plans to run for a federal post in 2014.

5. remunerate—[A] pay for work. Which office *remunerates* us for these long-distance deliveries?

6. proletariat—[A] working class. Claire is clearly too aristocratic for the rank-and-file *proletariat*.

7. indolent—[B] averse to work, lazy. Santa is furious with this new generation of *indolent* elves.

8. Luddite—[A] one who opposes technological change. Etymology note: *Luddite* refers originally to 19th-century workmen who destroyed machinery as a protest (they took their name from folkloric rebel Ned Ludd).

9. on spec—[A] with no assurance of payment. Despite the lousy market, we agreed to build the house *on spec*.

10. trouper—[A] traveling theater actor. Darla's first paid gig was as a *trouper* with the national cast of *Annie*.

11. sinecure—[C] cushy job. Carol's uncle is the boss, so she's got a *sinecure* as a paper shuffler.

12. métier—[C] area of expertise. They pay her to sing, but Margot's true *métier* is astrophysics.

13. sedentary—[C] not physically active. Studies warn that your body was not meant to be *sedentary* all day.

14. garnishment—[B] withholding of wages. Half of Troy's salary is in *garnishment* for alimony.

15. indentured—[B] bound to work. Hey, I'm not your *indentured* servant—I quit!

VOCABULARY RATINGS
9 and below: Underemployed
10–12: Worked wonders
13–15: All in day's work

PAGE 109
Men of Letters

(crossword solution)

PAGE 110
Sudoku Twin

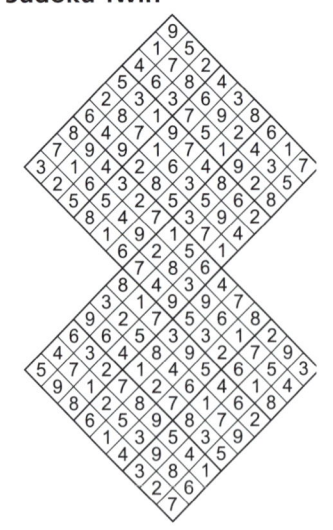

(sudoku solution)

DELETE ONE • MINISTRY

PAGE 111
Memorable Model

1937 DeSoto Business Coupe S3.

CHANGELINGS • LONGFELLOW / WORDSWORTH / FITZGERALD

PAGE 112
State Mottoes

(crossword solution)

PAGE 113
Kakuro

(kakuro solution)

SANDWICH • LIGHT

PAGE 114
Word Pyramid

(1) RI
(2) AIR
(3) RAIN
(4) IRENA
(5) AIRMEN
(6) CARMINE
(7) AMERICAN

PAGE 115
Binairo

1	1	0	0	1	0	1	0	1	0	0	1
0	0	1	0	1	1	0	1	0	1	1	0
1	1	0	1	0	0	1	1	0	0	1	0
0	0	1	0	1	0	1	0	1	1	0	1
1	1	0	1	0	1	0	0	1	0	1	0
1	0	1	1	0	1	0	1	0	1	0	0
0	0	1	0	1	0	1	1	0	0	1	1
0	1	0	1	0	1	0	0	1	1	0	1
1	0	0	1	1	0	1	0	0	1	1	0
0	0	1	0	0	1	0	1	1	0	1	1
0	1	1	0	0	1	1	0	1	0	0	1
1	1	0	1	1	0	0	1	0	1	0	0

LETTERBLOCKS • ASSAULT / PURSUIT

PAGE 116
Myths of the Americas

1. Pontiac
2. Toltecs
3. North America
4. The Aztecs
5. The Incas
6. The Inuit
7. A hallucinogenic drug
8. Shaman
9. The Maya
10. The pipe of peace
11. Xolotl
12. The Milky Way
13. The Incas
14. The llama; white ones were sacrificed to ask for blessings; black ones to bring rain

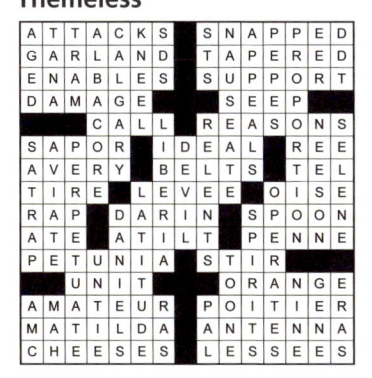

PAGE 117
Themeless

A	T	T	A	C	K	S	■	S	N	A	P	P	E	D
G	A	R	L	A	N	D	■	T	A	P	E	R	E	D
E	N	A	B	L	E	S	■	S	U	P	P	O	R	T
D	A	M	A	G	E	■	S	E	E	P	■	■	■	■
■	■	■	C	A	L	L	■	R	E	A	S	O	N	S
S	A	P	O	R	■	I	D	E	A	L	■	R	E	E
A	V	E	R	Y	■	B	E	L	T	S	■	T	E	L
T	I	R	E	■	L	E	V	E	E	■	O	I	S	E
R	A	P	■	D	A	R	I	N	■	S	P	O	O	N
A	T	E	■	A	T	I	L	T	■	P	E	N	N	E
P	E	T	U	N	I	A	■	S	T	I	R	■	■	■
■	■	■	■	U	N	I	T	■	O	R	A	N	G	E
A	M	A	T	E	U	R	■	P	O	I	T	I	E	R
M	A	T	I	L	D	A	■	A	N	T	E	N	N	A
C	H	E	E	S	E	S	■	L	E	S	S	E	E	S

PAGE 118
Word Sudoku

B	P	S	D	R	I	V	E	A
I	E	V	A	S	P	B	D	R
R	A	D	B	E	V	S	I	P
P	D	E	S	B	A	I	R	V
V	I	R	E	P	D	A	S	B
A	S	B	V	I	R	D	P	E
D	B	P	R	A	S	E	V	I
E	V	I	P	D	B	R	A	S
S	R	A	I	V	E	P	B	D

UNCANNY TURN • DIRTY ROOM

PAGE 119
Golf Holes

B7. All holes are one square further from each other diagonally.

LETTER LINE • **UNEMPLOYED;** MEDLEY / DEPLOY / MONEY / LEMON

PAGE 120
A+ Novels

R	S	V	P	■	R	I	A	T	A	■	M	E	S	A
I	T	E	R	■	E	M	B	E	R	■	A	N	A	S
P	E	R	U	■	S	A	L	E	M	■	D	I	K	E
A	P	A	S	S	A	G	E	T	O	I	N	D	I	A
■	■	■	S	O	L	O	■	O	I	S	E	■	■	■
R	E	S	I	D	E	■	S	T	R	I	P	P	E	D
O	R	C	A	S	■	B	L	U	E	S	■	E	E	R
R	A	I	N	■	B	R	I	M	S	■	B	A	R	E
E	T	O	■	R	O	A	D	S	■	D	O	R	I	A
M	O	N	G	O	O	S	E	■	H	A	R	L	E	M
■	■	■	A	S	K	S	■	A	O	N	E	■	■	■
A	F	A	R	E	W	E	L	L	T	O	A	R	M	S
Y	A	R	N	■	O	R	A	L	E	■	N	Y	E	T
E	L	I	E	■	R	I	V	A	L	■	A	N	I	L
S	L	A	T	■	M	E	A	N	S	■	Z	E	R	O

PAGE 121
Duel on the Green

Chris hasn't lost a single hole so far. Neither has he drawn any matches. Therefore, he must have played only one match, which he won by 5 holes to zero. Notice that Archie has lost only three holes so far. This means that Chris has not played Archie yet, hence Chris's 5–0 game must have been against Bernard. The only remaining possible match is Bernard against Archie. The three holes lost by Archie must have been holes won by Bernard in their match. Of the six holes lost by Bernard, five have already been accounted for in his match with Chris. Therefore, Archie must have won one hole in the match with Bernard. **The two matches were: Bernard beat Archie by 3 holes to 1, Chris beat Bernard by 5 holes to 0.**

Final table:

	Played	Matches Won	Matches Lost	Matches drawn	Holes Won	Holes Lost
Archie	1	0	1	0	1	3
Bernard	2	1	1	0	3	6
Chris	1	1	0	0	5	0

Answers

PAGE 122
Sport Maze

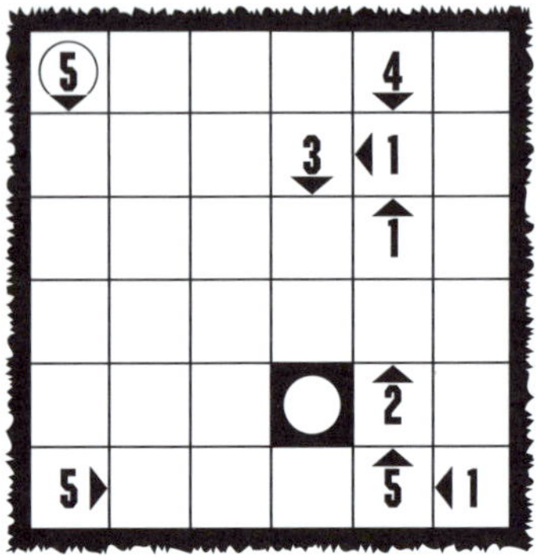

REPOSITION PRESPOSITION • ALONG WITH

PAGE 123
Fruit Salad

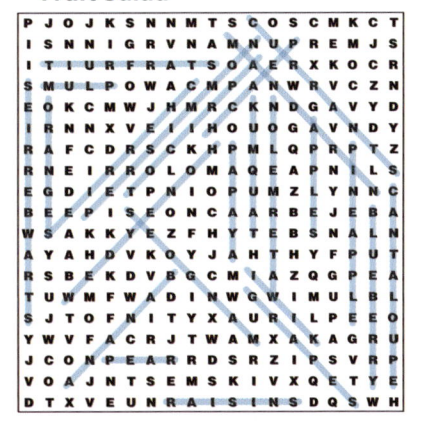

PAGE 124
Who Said It?
1. Nathan Hale
2. Franklin D. Roosevelt
3. F. Scott Fitzgerald
4. H. L. Mencken
5. Thomas Paine
6. Lloyd Bentsen
7. John Wilkes Booth
8. Paul Revere
9. Yogi Berra
10. Thomas Edison
11. Cary Grant
12. Benjamin Franklin
13. Abraham Lincoln
14. Mark Twain
15. Henny Youngman
16. Neil Armstrong

PAGE 125
National Parks

PAGE 126
Sudoku

1	7	3	8	6	2	9	5	4
6	8	4	9	5	1	7	3	2
9	5	2	3	7	4	8	1	6
4	3	6	2	1	7	5	9	8
5	2	9	4	3	8	1	6	7
7	1	8	5	9	6	2	4	3
8	9	1	6	2	3	4	7	5
3	4	5	7	8	9	6	2	1
2	6	7	1	4	5	3	8	9

BLOCK ANAGRAM • TELEPATHY

PAGE 127
Web of Intrigue

Zone 2. Starting at the triangle with all 3 zones controlled, the spider leaves one more zone unmonitored in each succeeding triangle.

ECONOMICAL • DEEDED

PAGE 128
Shipwrecks

PAGE 129
Cage the Animals

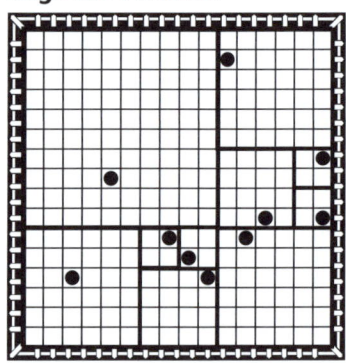

DOODLE PUZZLE • Red EYES

PAGE 130
Keep Going

DELETE TWO • CARTHORSE

PAGE 131

Binairo

I	O	I	I	O	I	I	O	O	I	O	O
I	I	O	O	I	I	O	I	O	I	O	O
O	I	O	I	O	O	I	O	I	O	I	I
O	O	I	I	O	I	O	I	I	O	I	O
I	I	O	O	I	O	I	I	O	I	O	O
I	O	I	I	O	I	O	O	I	O	O	I
O	I	I	O	I	O	I	O	I	O	I	O
I	O	O	I	I	O	O	I	O	I	O	I
O	O	I	O	O	I	I	O	I	O	I	I
O	I	O	I	O	I	O	I	O	I	I	O
I	O	I	O	I	O	I	O	O	I	O	I
O	I	O	O	I	O	O	I	I	O	I	I

MISSING LETTER PROVERB • NEITHER A BORROWER NOR A LENDER BE

PAGE 132

Favorite Words

1. plangent—[B] very loud. My nephew blasts *plangent*, sad music in his room. (director Wes Craven)

2. ruckus—[B] melee. There was quite a *ruckus* when the fire alarm went off. (Penn Jillette of Penn & Teller)

3. vermilion—[C] bright red. The theater had eye-catching *vermilion* walls. (writer A. S. Byatt)

4. chthonic—[A] of the underworld. I love the story of Orpheus's *chthonic* journey. (Margaret Atwood)

5. gormless—[C] stupid. The writer dismissed his critics as *gormless* twits. (author Barbara Taylor Bradford)

6. interstitial—[B] in the spaces between. The film's action sequences were thrilling; I found the *interstitial* scenes rather dull. (Al Gore)

7. unilateral—[A] one-sided. The volleyball squad had a *unilateral* advantage in height. (editor Helen Gurley Brown)

8. palimpsest—[C] written-over document. My address book is a *palimpsest*—I keep erasing names and adding new ones. (Joyce Carol Oates)

9. beguiling—[C] cleverly deceptive. Those *beguiling* ads persuaded me to buy a phone I didn't really need. (playwright Wendy Wasserstein)

10. lambent—[C] luminous. Sofia loved hiking by the *lambent* moonlight. (activist Andrea Dworkin)

11. incarnadine—[A] flesh-colored. Mia chose a pretty *incarnadine* dress for the wedding. (Arthur C. Clarke)

12. phosphorescent—[B] glittering. The *phosphorescent* firefly flew right into the jar. (John Updike)

13. ramshackle—[B] rickety-looking. Jack carefully stepped onto the *ramshackle* bridge. (Ray Bradbury)

14. pixilated—[C] mentally unbalanced. Dad's *pixilated* behavior has us worried. (Mark Hamill)

15. qua—[A] in the capacity of. Forget the painter's political views—can we enjoy her art *qua* art? (Dave Barry)

VOCABULARY RATINGS

9 & below: almost famous
10–12: famous
13–15: infamous

PAGE 133

Fall Fun

C	I	D	E	R		T	E	N		A	L	S
A	T	O	N	E		A	G	O		C	A	T
P	A	N	D	A		B	O	N	F	I	R	E
			E	L	M			F	U	D	G	E
C	A	R	A	M	E	L		A	N	S	E	L
O	V	E	R		T	A	C	T				
B	E	D	S		E	Y	E		R	A	T	S
				B	R	U	T		E	C	R	U
A	G	A	T	E		P	U	M	P	K	I	N
C	U	B	A	N			S	A	L			
H	A	Y	R	I	D	E		D	I	N	E	S
E	R	S		G	A	S		A	C	E	R	S
D	D	S		N	Y	C		M	A	Z	E	S

PAGE 134

Sudoku

9	3	4	1	6	8	7	2	5
2	8	6	7	5	3	4	1	9
7	5	1	2	9	4	8	6	3
1	7	5	8	2	6	9	3	4
3	2	9	4	7	1	5	8	6
6	4	8	9	3	5	1	7	2
8	1	2	3	4	9	6	5	7
5	9	3	6	1	7	2	4	8
4	6	7	5	8	2	3	9	1

ANAGRAM • ARREST / STOP / BAR / END

PAGE 135

Mismatched Cards

5 5 (diamonds)	4 spades	3 hearts	2 clubs
3 clubs	2 hearts	5 spades	4 4 (diamonds)
2 spades	3 diamonds	4 clubs	5 hearts
4 4 (hearts)	5 clubs	2 diamonds	3 3 (hearts)

Answers

PAGE 136
Flying Colors
The anagram is Mother Teresa.

PAGE 137
American History

PAGE 138
Number Cluster

FRIENDS • EACH CAN ADD THE SUFFIX -MENT TO FORM A NEW WORD.

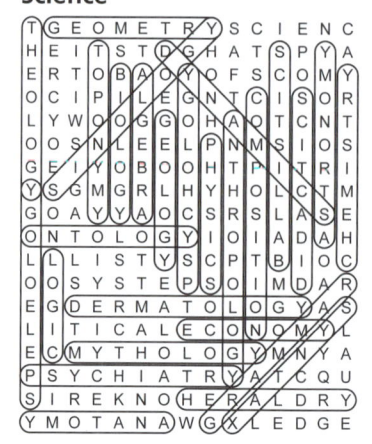

PAGE 139
Science

PAGE 140
But Cerealously
1. Alpha-Bits Discontinued in 2011
2. Raisin Bran
3. Cocoa Puffs
4. Bran Flakes
5. Cocoa Krispies renamed Cocoa Rice Krispies in 2003
6. Trix
7. Sugar Smacks or Honey Smacks
8. Frosted Flakes

PAGE 141
End Rhyme

PAGE 142
Word Sudoku

UNCANNY TURN • FUNERAL

PAGE 143
Cherry-picking
Card 6. Identical cards are always as far away from each other as the number of elements on the card. There are 5 cherries on the card so the other cherries card is 5 steps further.

ONE LETTER LESS OR MORE • STREAMING

PAGE 144
Spot the Differences

216

PAGE 145
An American in Paris

T	H	I	R	D		C	A	R	D		A	I	D	A
A	A	R	O	N		A	B	E	E		I	N	O	N
T	H	O	M	A	S	J	E	F	F	E	R	S	O	N
S	A	N	A		T	U	T	U		A	S	T	R	A
			N	O	U	N		T	A	R	T			
A	D	O		R	N	S		I	M	P	R	O	V	
M	O	R	O	N		I	N	F		I	R	I	S	
T	R	A	V	E	L	I	N	G	M	A	K	E	S	A
S	A	T	E		U	N	D		Y	E	A	T	S	
	G	E	R	A	L	D		E	S	E		D	A	H
		P	O	L	I		D	I	S	C				
S	P	O	O	K		G	A	I	T		A	L	A	I
M	A	N	W	I	S	E	R	B	U	T	L	E	S	S
U	L	E	E		A	N	I	L		C	L	A	I	M
G	E	A	R		C	E	D	E		H	A	P	P	Y

PAGE 146
Binairo

0	1	0	1	1	0	1	0	1	0	1
0	0	1	1	0	1	1	0	1	0	1
1	0	1	0	1	1	0	1	0	1	0
1	1	0	1	1	0	0	1	0	0	1
0	1	1	0	0	1	1	0	1	1	0
1	0	1	0	1	0	1	1	0	1	0
1	0	0	1	0	1	0	1	1	0	1
0	1	1	0	0	1	1	0	0	1	1
1	1	0	1	1	0	0	1	1	0	0
0	0	1	1	0	0	1	1	0	1	1
1	1	0	0	1	1	0	0	1	1	0

MISSING LETTER PROVERB • AN ARMY MARCHES ON ITS STOMACH.

PAGE 147
Keep Going

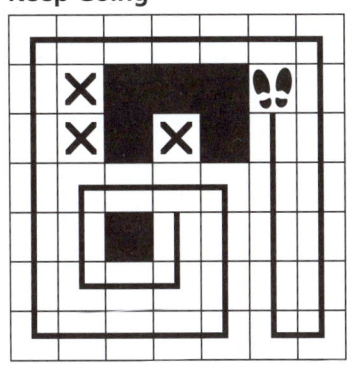

CHANGE ONE • HOUSE DEED

PAGE 148
Take Your Partner

1. **a.** The Highland Fling
2. **c.** Jazz
3. **a.** Hawaiians
4. **b.** Break dancing
5. **a.** Bali
6. **a.** Yoruba
7. **b.** The oud
8. **c.** Gregory Hines
9. **c.** (5 positions)
10. **a.** Cha-Cha

PAGE 149
Love Is…

F	A	D	E		L	I	M	A		D	O	C	K
U	R	I	S		O	D	O	R		Y	U	M	A
J	U	S	T	A	W	O	R	D	U	N	T	I	L
I	N	C	I	D	E	N	T		F	A	R		
			M	O	S	T		S	O	M	E	O	N	E
P	E	D	A	N	T		S	O	S	O		N	O	N
A	M	A	T	I		C	P	L		H	O	I	
C	O	M	E	S		L	I	I		A	L	O	N	G
I	T	S			A	N	D		G	O	L	E	M
N	E	E		H	O	W	E		S	A	N	D	R	A
O	R	L	E	A	N	S		L	I	T	D		
			A	V	E		P	I	N	H	O	L	E	S
G	I	V	E	S	I	T	M	E	A	N	I	N	G
E	D	E	N		R	E	B	A		E	M	I	T
M	A	S	S		A	R	O	D		R	O	D	S

PAGE 150
Sudoku Twin

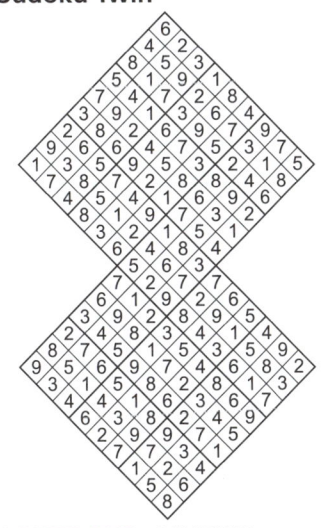

DELETE ONE • SOLUTION

PAGE 151
Vintage Barrels

1995. From left to right the next year always equals the previous plus the sum of the decennium. The last barrel is therefore 1979+7+9= 1995.

SQUIRCLES •

u a d s a t m a
S N O W D R O P
u g m a m e r p
r e a r i m o l
P R I M R O S E
s s n s e r e s

PAGE 152
Kakuro

5	6	8		7	4	2
	4	9		8	1	
8	9	6	1		9	3
6			3	2	8	
		9	8	6		
3	6	1		3	9	2
2	1				6	1

ONE LETTER LESS OR MORE • PREDATORS

PAGE 153
Sport Maze

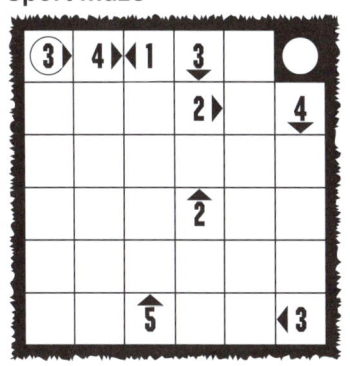

REPOSITION PREPOSITION • OUTSIDE OF

Answers

PAGE 154
Monkey in the Middle

S	U	R	E		C	L	A	M		S	C	R	U	B
T	S	A	R		R	I	G	A		C	H	O	S	E
E	S	C	A	P	E	K	E	Y		R	E	B	E	L
P	R	E	S	I	D	E	D		B	I	S	S	E	T
			N	I	A		P	U	M	A				
A	S	C	E	N	T		C	H	I	P	P	E	W	A
L	A	R	V	A		V	E	A	L		E	L	A	M
O	N	E	I		M	I	D	S	T		A	L	T	A
H	E	A	T		I	S	E	E		S	K	I	E	S
A	R	K	A	N	S	A	S		S	T	E	E	R	S
			P	A	T	S		C	E	E				
S	A	F	E	T	Y		F	O	R	E	C	A	S	T
O	H	A	R	A		J	A	L	A	P	E	N	O	S
L	E	T	O	N		A	C	O	P		R	O	N	A
A	M	E	N	T		R	E	N	E		E	N	Y	O

PAGE 155
LETTER LINE • MOONLIGHT;
HOMING / THONG / GLOOM / GILT

PAGE 156
Cage the Animals

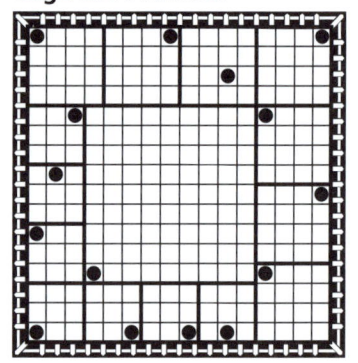

DOODLE PUZZLE • SpONsor

PAGE 157
Surrounded

S	H	A	M		S	I	T	A	R		M	A	T	S
H	E	R	O		P	R	O	V	O		U	T	A	H
E	R	A	T		A	M	M	O	S		S	E	R	E
L	A	B	O	R	D	A	Y	W	E	E	K	E	N	D
			R	U	E	S				B	Y	E		
R	E	M	I	S	S		T	R	U	E	G	R	I	T
E	V	A	N	S		K	A	O	S		I	D	O	
W	A	Y	N	E	A	N	D	S	H	U	S	T	E	R
E	D	A		B	O	A	S		G	L	E	A	M	
D	E	N	T	I	S	T	S		P	L	I	S	S	E
			H	B	O		T	R	I	M				
A	L	L	I	N	L	O	V	E	I	S	F	A	I	R
R	E	A	R		U	P	E	N	D		A	L	T	O
E	A	S	T		T	E	A	S	E		S	T	E	M
A	R	T	Y		E	L	L	E	S		T	A	M	P

PAGE 158
Curve Ball

1. The simplest explanation is that the scientist threw the ball up in the air.
2. The blue line is the 'height above ground' – this is the natural shape that projectiles make (unless there is significant wind resistance). The red line is the speed – this slows down to zero when the ball reaches its peak. The acceleration line is green – it is constant because the gravitational force is effectively constant (unless the ball is fired high up into the atmosphere, at which point the Earth's gravitational pull becomes weaker).
3. The shape of the 'height above ground' graph is called a parabola.

PAGE 159
Robot Romance

YES. Robot B's answer is composed of the first letter of robot A's last word + the last letter of its first word + an S.

LETTER LINE • INSTRUMENT;
MITTENS / STERNUM / MINER / NINE

PAGE 160
Legendary Lodgings

1. Grand Hotel
2. The Plaza
3. Atlantis
4. Waldorf Astoria
5. Hotel Bel Air
6. Ambassador Hotel, Los Angeles
7. The Peabody
8. The Chelsea Hotel
9. The Palmer
10. Lorraine Motel
11. Hotel California

PAGE 161
Keep Going

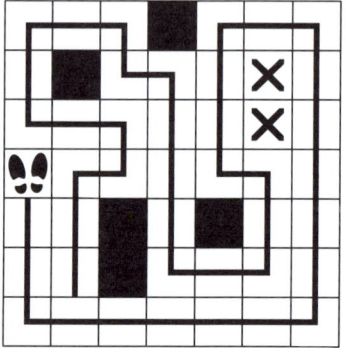

CHANGE ONE • PRICE DEAL

PAGE 162
The Simpsons

A	M	I	R		S	T	A	M	P		B	U	S	T
L	E	T	A		P	E	L	E	E		O	R	E	O
B	A	B	Y	G	E	R	A	L	D		O	G	E	E
S	T	E	E	L	E	R	S		E	M	B	E	R	S
			O	C	A		A	S	I	A				
E	L	I	J	A	H		A	T	T	O	R	N	E	Y
C	A	N	I	T		T	I	L	A		E	A	V	E
A	T	O	M		C	O	R	A	L		L	I	A	M
S	T	U	B		O	L	E	S		G	L	A	D	E
H	E	R	O	I	N	E	S		L	E	A	D	E	N
			J	E	S	T		F	O	E				
K	O	M	O	D	O		D	O	W	N	H	I	L	L
A	L	A	N		M	A	R	Y	B	A	I	L	E	Y
T	A	T	E		M	I	N	E	O		N	I	N	O
O	N	E	S		E	M	O	R	Y		D	E	A	N

PAGE 163

Sports

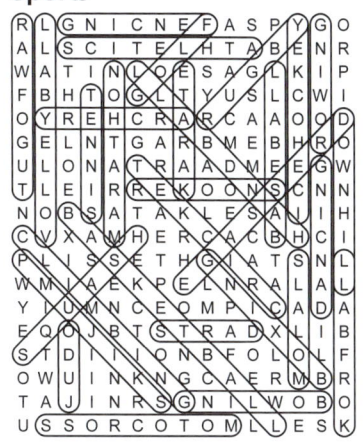

(word search grid)

PAGE 164

Extremes

1. nethermost—[C] lowest. No one dares explore the *nethermost* dungeons of this castle.

2. extravagant—[C] over the top. How can Monty afford to throw such *extravagant* parties?

3. acme—[B] highest point. Going to the top of the Empire State Building was literally the *acme* of our trip.

4. culminate—[C] reach a climax. Nearly every scene with the Stooges in a cafeteria *culminates* in a pie fight.

5. acute—[A] intense, urgent. Joey has an *acute* hankering for chocolate.

6. precipice—[A] very steep side of a cliff. As Alex peered over the *precipice*, he developed a sudden case of acrophobia.

7. superlative—[A] outstanding. Despite Willie's *superlative* effort to catch the ball, it landed in the bleachers.

8. antithesis—[A] exact opposite. Slovenly Oscar is the *antithesis* of a neatnik.

9. surfeit—[B] more than needed. We have a *surfeit* of nachos but absolutely no salsa!

10. exorbitant—[C] far exceeding what is fair or reasonable. I nearly fainted from sticker shock when I saw the *exorbitant* price.

11. overweening—[A] arrogant. I enjoy the art class, but not Professor Prigg's *overweening* attitude.

12. optimal—[A] best. Now is not the *optimal* time to pester the boss about a raise. [Note: The synonym optimum is best used as a noun.]

13. radical—[B] extremist. We knew Carey loved her pup, but we didn't realize what a *radical* she was until she tattooed its face on her arm.

14. penultimate—[A] next to last. My *penultimate* finish in the marathon was my best showing ever.

15. maximal—[A] greatest possible. "OK" is *maximal* praise from that old curmudgeon. [Like optimum, the synonym maximum is best used as a noun.]

16. zealotry—[B] overdone fervor. *Zealotry* gets TV attention, but it rarely brings compromise.

VOCABULARY RATINGS

10 & below: In the middle
11–13: On the rise
14–16: At the apex

PAGE 165

Winning Spelling-Bee Words

L	O	A	D		D	E	N	E	B		N	C	O	S
A	C	L	U		E	D	E	M	A		A	A	R	P
P	E	E	L		A	D	L	I	B		S	T	A	R
S	A	U	C	I	L	Y		T	U	S	C	A	N	Y
E	N	T	I	R	E			S	L	A	M			
			M	A	R	S		T	H	E	R	A	P	Y
E	M	C	E	E		C	O	R	K	Y		R	A	E
P	A	R	R		I	O	N	I	A		V	A	C	A
I	W	O		E	N	R	O	L		O	I	N	K	S
C	R	I	S	P	I	N		L	U	N	G			
			S	U	E	T			P	I	N	A	T	A
E	P	S	T	E	I	N		A	L	T	E	R	E	R
A	L	A	R		A	C	C	R	A		T	I	R	E
T	U	N	A		L	A	P	I	N		T	E	R	N
S	G	T	S		S	A	L	A	D		E	L	A	T

PAGE 166

Sudoku X

(solved 9×9 grid)

IMPORTANT CAPITAL • POLISH

PAGE 167

Art of Numbers

7. The difference between the number on the top and bottom row forms an ascending series from 1 to 6: 123456.

CHANGELINGS • BLOODHOUND / POMERANIAN / ROTTWEILER

PAGE 168

Kakuro

(solved grid)

SANDWICH • FRAME

Answers

PAGE 169
Spot the Differences

PAGE 170
Bond Bad Guys

PAGE 171
Pixel Fun

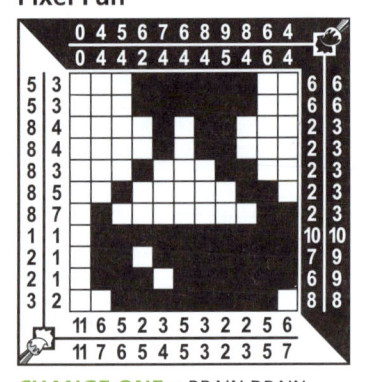

CHANGE ONE • BRAIN DRAIN

PAGE 172
Beliefs from Other Lands

1. **c.** The bathhouse
2. **a.** A rainbow
3. **b.** A sea monster
4. **d.** In a tree
5. **a.** Maui
6. **d.** Africa
7. **b.** A baboon
8. **c.** The dragon
9. **b.** A royal bodyguard
10. **a.** Anubis

PAGE 173
The Simpsons 2

PAGE 174
Cloudy
A5, A7, B2, C4, C7, D1, E4, E6.

DOUBLETALK • BOW

PAGE 175
Sudoku

HIDDEN WORDS • TO GET HER (TOGETHER)

PAGE 176
Binairo

MISSING LETTER PROVERB
• THE EARLY BIRD CATCHES THE WORM

PAGE 177
Number Cluster

WORKPLACES • SALESMEN / DIVER / MINISTER / TEACHER / TRAINER

PAGE 178
Dig Deep

C	O	P		B	A	B	A		N	E	E	D
A	V	A		I	R	I	S		U	R	G	E
L	E	S		S	C	A	R	E	C	R	O	W
F	R	O	S	T		S	E	A	L			
			A	R	E		D	R	E	A	M	T
C	O	M	P	O	S	T		N	I	N	E	R
O	R	O			S	O	W			T	A	I
M	E	N	S	A		T	I	L	L	I	N	G
A	M	O	E	B	A		G	E	O			
			L	E	V	I		T	U	L	I	P
S	E	E	D	L	I	N	G	S		E	A	R
I	N	T	O		A	G	O	G		A	G	E
R	E	A	M		N	A	T	O		F	O	P

PAGE 179
Half-Baked

```
K R Q T P E C I U J B J H Y F H C S P
C S P J U V H R E K O O C I I F T D O
O S U S A N Z U C C H I N I V E L R H
R G U O R N U E K S N E C E E R G F
C Y T X V L S E C K P J H B C E U M Z
U Q R R Q B I J L M Q I N J L P C U K
G A C W A L J D M C S Q E Z A I L W
Z P I J X I D V S G T C E K R C M D X
Y M M Z S B N L R C J P E Y W E R F
W H M N L A F E E O P T O S D O C T V
A Y A H V W B P R O C T S T Z N U U Z
A E M D W T U G P H S H H J Z J A A A
B Q E O T O U G U I P E A C H E T R H
E O C D J N G F L P C S D D B V L E K
C L E N T G I C C R W K W H C B L J T
I K W W S S W A S L A S L O E H P S W
A A S E O T A M O T J I R E J P A Y
M Q E R Z N G I V F D N J T S Z A U R
K G Q C I A V C G R E M I T Y L K G W
```

PAGE 180
Heir to the Farm Car

1942 Plymouth Special De Luxe.

CHANGELINGS • MADAGASCAR / MARTINIQUE / MICRONESIA

PAGE 181
Dancing with Fred

O	W	L		A	L	F	R	E		P	O	T
V	I	E	D		E	E	L	E	D		S	A	N	E
A	N	N	A		N	O	Y	E	S		I	R	E	D
L	E	A	D		E	N	I	D		P	L	E	A	D
			D	R	A	I	N		L	I	K	E	L	Y
T	R	O	Y	E	S		G	R	I	N	S			
H	O	L	L	Y		A	D	A	M		T	I	E	D
I	D	E	O		C	R	O	C	E		O	D	I	E
N	E	O	N		H	O	W	E		A	C	O	R	N
			G	L	E	N	N		O	A	K	L	E	Y
M	A	I	L	E	R		T	E	R	R	I			
E	R	R	E	D		M	O	A	N		N	U	N	S
C	L	O	G		H	A	R	T	E		G	N	A	T
O	N	S		O	S	I	E	R		S	I	L	O	
A	S	S		P	H	O	N	Y		T	A	P		

PAGE 182
Word Sudoku

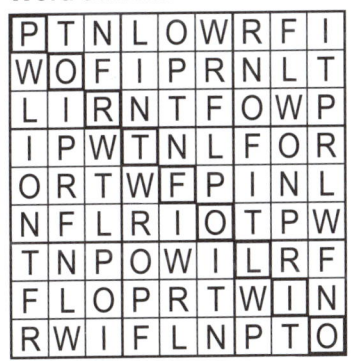

P	T	N	L	O	W	R	F	I
W	O	F	I	P	R	N	L	T
L	I	R	N	T	F	O	W	P
I	P	W	T	N	L	F	O	R
O	R	T	W	F	P	I	N	L
N	F	L	R	I	O	T	P	W
T	N	P	O	W	I	L	R	F
F	L	O	P	R	T	W	I	N
R	W	I	F	L	N	P	T	O

ONE LETTER LESS OR MORE • CONCEALED

PAGE 183
Parking Spaces

6565656. Starting in the upper left corner, per type of car, there is always one car more, and the cars alternate being parked nose inward and outward.

DOUBLETALK • STICK

PAGE 184
Sport Maze

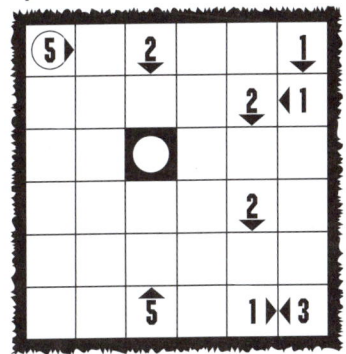

RUNNING REPAIRS • RESTORES

PAGE 185
Liverpool Lads

1. *Introducing the Beatles* and *Meet the Beatles*
2. *I Want to Hold Your Hand*
3. *The Ed Sullivan Show*
4. Washington Coliseum in Washington, D.C.
5. Five
6. *A Hard Day's Night*
7. Bob Dylan
8. *I Wanna Hold Your Hand*
9. Sid Bernstein,
10. George 20, Ringo 23, Paul 21, John 23

PAGE 186
Holiday Treats

B	L	O	W		P	O	T	S		D	S	L
B	E	A	R		E	A	R	P		E	T	A
C	A	K	E		P	R	A	L	I	N	E	S
		A	Y	E			A	S	S	E	T	
A	B	A	T	E		F	A	T	H	E	R	S
G	O	T	H	S		U	P	S				
E	Y	E	S		A	D	O		W	R	E	N
				W	I	G		P	I	A	N	O
C	O	M	P	A	R	E		E	N	D	E	D
E	X	A	M	S		D	A	D				
D	I	V	I	N	I	T	Y		O	D	O	R
A	D	E		O	D	I	E		W	O	R	E
R	E	N		T	A	N	S		S	T	E	M

Answers

PAGE 187
Binairo

0	0	1	1	0	1	0	1	0	1	1
1	1	0	1	1	0	1	0	0	1	0
0	1	1	0	1	1	0	1	1	0	0
1	0	1	1	0	1	0	1	0	0	1
0	0	1	1	0	0	1	0	1	1	0
1	1	0	0	1	1	0	1	0	0	1
0	0	1	1	0	1	1	0	1	1	0
1	1	0	0	1	0	1	0	0	1	0
0	0	1	0	1	0	1	1	0	1	1
1	1	0	1	0	1	0	1	1	0	0
1	0	1	0	0	1	1	0	1	0	1

MISSING LETTER PROVERB •
PENNY WISE / POUND FOOLISH

PAGE 188
Taking a Leaf from Literature

1. **c.** *The Scarlet Pimpernel*
2. **c.** The shrew
3. **c.** *Of Mice and Men*
4. **a.** Flies, in *Lord of the Flies*
5. **a.** The Jackdaw of Rheims
6. **a.** Nathaniel Hawthorne
7. **b.** The lion in winter
8. **c.** A sperm whale
9. **b.** Cedar (*Snow Falling on Cedars*)
10. **b.** Raven

PAGE 189
Letter Logic

nulxa. All underlined words contain the letter X—when X isn't the last letter of the word.

FIVES AND FOURS •
S W O R D S P I T
T A B L E Z U L U
A B O V E S O A R
R A D A R M O O N

PAGE 190
Cage the Animals

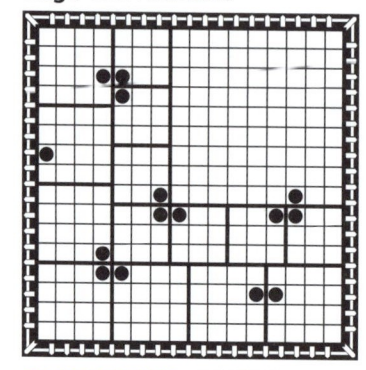

ODD CAP OUT • BASEBALL CAP 2. THE LOGO ON THIS CAP IS A MIRROR IMAGE.

PAGE 191
Eclectic Mix

V	E	R	B		J	I	L	L	S		S	A	F	E
E	P	E	E		A	D	I	E	U		O	R	A	L
T	I	D	E		M	E	E	T	S		M	I	N	K
S	C	O	T	S	M	A	N		P	L	E	A	S	E
			H	E	E	L		S	E	E	R			
A	C	C	O	R	D		S	I	N	I	S	T	E	R
S	O	A	V	E		V	A	T	S		E	A	V	E
P	A	N	E		S	A	D	I	E		T	R	E	E
I	C	O	N		E	G	A	N		A	M	E	N	D
C	H	E	S	T	N	U	T		B	R	A	S	S	Y
			S	I	T	E		M	E	N	U			
A	D	V	I	S	E		M	A	H	O	G	A	N	Y
H	O	A	X		N	A	O	M	I		H	O	Y	A
E	R	S	T		C	H	A	I	N		A	N	E	W
M	Y	T	H		E	A	S	E	D		M	E	T	S

PAGE 192
Kakuro

8	5	6	■	3	8	■	8	6
5	4	■	1	5	9	■	3	9
9	3	6	4	■	3	6	■	5
4	■	7	■	■	■	8	1	7
■	1	5	9	■	4	2	9	■
2	7	■	2	3	7	■	3	8
5	6	1	■	5	9	7	■	5
7	■	8	■	7	■	4	1	3
4	7	9	8	■	■	7	8	6	2

ONE LETTER LESS OR MORE •
PIERCED

PAGE 193
Keep Going

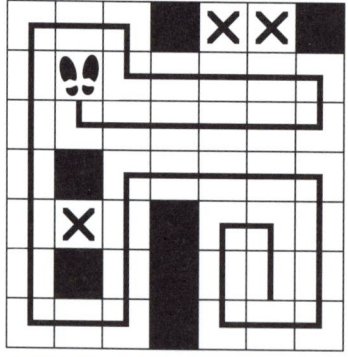

CHANGE ONE • FINE LUNCH

PAGE 194
Weights

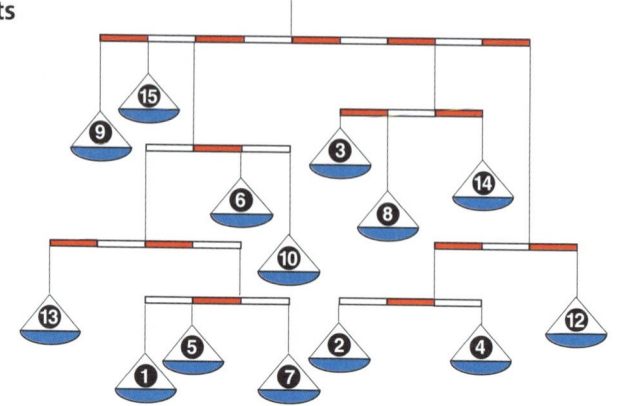

SOUND ALIKE • BEAT / BEET

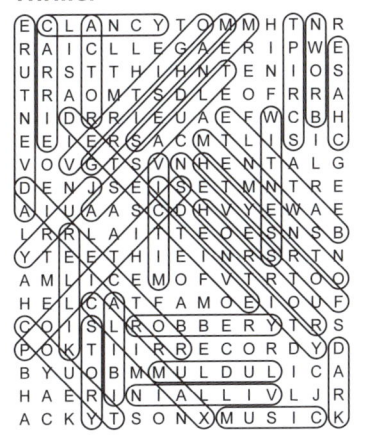

PAGE 195
Thriller

(word search grid)

PAGE 196
Verbal Misuse

1. noisome—[B] stinky. Because of its deceptive root, *noisome* is often confused with *noisy*.

2. enervated—[A] lacking energy. From the sound of it, you'd think *enervated* means "full of energy"— nope, it's the exact opposite.

3. proscribe—[C] forbid. Careful: *Prescribe* means "to dispense a drug."

4. nonplussed—[A] baffled. The *non* is the deceiver here, leading many to equate *nonplussed* with *calm*.

5. principle—[B] basic rule. A classic gaffe. Sibling *principal* is the head of a school (think "pal") or a capital sum.

6. flout—[B] scorn. Though some sources are doing away with the distinction, *flout* doesn't mean "to flaunt," i.e., "to show off."

7. discrete—[A] separate and distinct. This is a spell-check snafu. Its homonym, *discreet*, means "prudent."

8. ingenuous—[A] showing innocence or simplicity. Not—we repeat—not *ingenious*, "showing an aptitude."

9. cachet—[C] prestige. What a difference a letter makes: Lop off the *t*, and you've got "a secret stockpile" or "a short-lived computer memory."

10. allusion—[C] indirect reference. Another infamous faux pas. *Illusion* is the one referring to a sleight of hand.

11. reticent—[A] inclined to keep silent. It's in the ballpark with *reluctant*, or "unwilling," so be *reticent* if you're unsure of the difference.

12. bemused—[B] puzzled. As with *noisome*, you may *want* this to mean "entertained." But as the Rolling Stones said, "You can't always get …"

13. diffuse—[C] spread or pour out freely. You defuse a bomb or a heated situation, but a photographer might *diffuse* light.

14. eminent—[A] prominent. It's typically mistaken for *imminent*, or "about to happen."

15. apprise—[C] inform of or give notice. The president is *apprised* of a crisis; antiques are appraised (given an estimated value).

VOCABULARY RATINGS
9 & below: Wordsmith
10–12: Grammar geek
13–15: Prof. of English

PAGE 197
Classic Magazines

(crossword grid)

PAGE 198
Where the Buck Stops

(crossword grid)

PAGE 199
Number Towers

X = 67 1/2. Working down from the top of tower A, each box adds 7 1/2 to the previous number.

ANSWERS TO DO YOU KNOW?

p. 9	No
p. 10	6 legs
p. 14	Ophidiophobia
p. 18	White rice flour, tapioca flour, salt and water
p. 19	Sea Air Land
p. 22	Jupiter
p. 30	Hibernia
p. 35	Atlantic & Pacific
p. 38	Korean War
p. 42	India
p. 51	Peregine falcon
p. 58	Neither, In the physics of buoyancy, the depth doesn't matter
p. 65	John Wilkes Booth
p. 67	Calcutta
p. 73	An exaltation of larks
p. 78	Colorado
p. 82	Arachnophobia
p. 83	The Indian Ocean
p. 94	Saint Lucia
p. 97	Neptune
p. 98	Iceland
p. 105	12
p. 113	A spoiled child
p. 114	The Boston Tea Party
p. 118	The St. Lawrence Seaway
p. 131	Pumice
p. 138	A fear of falling
p. 144	Seashells
p. 146	Toronto
p. 152	Schiphol
p. 156	Ovine
p. 166	Cagliari
p. 168	Angostura bitters
p. 169	The study of insects
p. 175	40 to 50 years
p. 177	Nitric acid
p. 184	Chennai
p. 190	Chickpeas
p. 192	Dr. Samuel Guthrie

ANSWERS TO TRIVIA

p. 18	Dr. Kildare
p. 25	60 guilders worth of trade, an amount worth approximately $1,143 in 2020 dollars
p. 33	2,080 lbs.
p. 36	The Antarctic blue whale (Balaenoptera musculus ssp. Intermedia) reaching up to 98 feet in length.
p. 41	Aglet
p. 46	The Sandwich Islands
p. 60	*Vogue*
p. 62	Leslie Townes Hope
p. 66	The Thunderbirds, perform precision aerial maneuvers demonstrating the capabilities of Air Force high-performance aircraft.
p. 68	Canada, Russia, the USA, Greenland, Norway, Finland, Sweden and Iceland
p. 70	The Chrysler Building
p. 82	Excalibur
p. 86	The U.S. Virgin Islands
p. 90	Xanadu
p. 92	Vera-Ellen
p. 99	White Star Line
p. 102	Carlo Collodi
p. 115	Saratoga Springs
p. 121	A song or poem in honor of a bride and groom
p. 122	Parker and Barrow
p. 126	Throwing of a person or thing out of a window
p. 129	Starbucks
p. 134	*The Graduate*
p. 140	Katy the Kangaroo
p. 142	Very Special Old Pale
p. 144	Jim Davis
p. 153	Officer Dibble
p. 169	*Santa Maria*
p. 176	Vinci, Italy
p. 182	Youthful appearance in an old person
p. 187	Acrobatics
p. 199	Frankie Laine

CREDITS

Cover photo credit:
ziviani/Shutterstock

Puzzle Credits:

David Bodycombe: 79, 121, 158

Book Creation Services: 56-57, 136

Sam Bellotto Jr.: 77, 128, 141, 145, 198

Emily Cox & Henry Rathvon: 20, 52, 76, 108, 132, 164, 196

Gerald Elwood: 111

Peter Frank: Binairo, Cage the Animals, Concentration, Kakuro, Keep Going, Number Cluster, Pixel Fun, Sport Maze, Spot the Differences, Sudoku, Sudoku Twin, Sudoku X, Weather Chart, Word Search, Word Sudoku

Arthur Koehn: 180

Don Law: 21, 53, 112, 137

John McCarthy: 29, 32, 37, 64, 117, 120, 157, 165

Myles Mellor: 85, 125, 170, 197

Chris Peterson: 96

Karen Peterson: 8, 40, 61, 69, 93, 154

Ken Russell and Philip Carter: 105, 194, 199

John M. Samson: 45, 162, 173

Michele Sayer: 13, 24, 48, 72, 88, 104, 109, 149, 181, 191

Justin Scroggie: 135

Melvin Siebold: 39

Debra Steilen: 44, 92, 140, 185

Tim Wagner: 80, 101

Kelly Whitt: 17, 133, 178, 186

RD-owned:
Sudoku: 78, 134
Trivia Quiz: 12, 28, 36, 60, 68, 84, 100, 116, 124, 148, 160, 172, 188
Word Search 123, 179

Puzzles unless noted above: BrainSnack®